Qui Plantavit Curabit

Roosevelt.

GRANDMÈRE

We should rejoice in the accomplishments of those before us,
Be proud of the heritage that we inherit,
But be always vigilant that the future is ours alone to make.

I dedicate this book to my children Matthew and Chandler, to my wife Michele, to my sister and brothers, cousins, and to those generations before who provided the legacy we pass along. And for those generations yet to come, may the expectations of your inheritance never become a burden of life.

GRANDMÈRE

A PERSONAL HISTORY OF ELEANOR ROOSEVELT

FOREWORD BY ALLIDA M. BLACK, PH.D.

INTRODUCTION BY MIKE WALLACE

With a special contribution by Her Royal Highness
Princess Margriet of the Netherlands

DAVID B. ROOSEVELT

with

MANUELA DUNN MASCETTI

A BOOK LABORATORY BOOK

WARNER BOOKS

An AOL Time Warner Company

Produced by Book Laboratory Inc., Bolinas, CA
Designed by Moonrunner Design Ltd
Picture research by Melissa Shaw

Warner Books, Inc., 1271 Avenue of the Americas,
New York, NY 10020

Visit our website at www.twbookmark.com

 An AOL Time Warner Company

A Time Warner Company

Printed in Singapore
First Warner Printing: October 2002
10 9 8 7 6 5 4 3 2 1

Library of Congress Control Number: 200210522

ISBN 0-446-52734-3

CONTENTS

Early in September, the phone on my desk rang. The semester had just started at George Washington University and all of us at The Eleanor Roosevelt Papers were eager to get to work, to introduce yet another generation to ER's power, vision, and grace. Students (enthusiastic, sweet, and noisy) huddled around the worktable outside my office door carefully reading letters Eleanor Roosevelt sent to Harry Truman, while I rushed to get one more report in the mail. As soon as it was completed, I could go back to what I love; reading, researching, and teaching Eleanor Roosevelt. The insistent ringing was a rude intrusion into this work plan. Swamped, I brushed papers aside to answer it, trying to keep from sounding testy over the line. After all, I told myself, ER would answer it too.

A voice boomed, "Allida, this is David Roosevelt. I have just written a book on my grandmother and I want you to read it. I admit I'm nervous. I'm no scholar. But I want it to be good, to be worthy of her and honest to me." Well, in about three nanoseconds, David talked me into reading the manuscript. His commitment to and love for ER was so strong I just couldn't say no. But I was still worried. I am a political historian rather than a biographer. My Eleanor Roosevelt is a political warhorse, a woman of courage and grace and fierce tenacity. I wanted people to see her strength, sense her determination, and appreciate her contributions. In particular, I wanted people to see her as someone more than "FDR's eyes and ears." I worried that a book entitled *Grandmère* might make her seem weak. Three days later the manuscript arrived and my doubts faded.

David Roosevelt has shared his grandmother with us and given us a glimpse of what it was like to love her, lose her, and find her again. The woman he presents is as complex as her times and as loving as a grandparent can be. As a leader, ER juggled many often-conflicting responsibilities: journalist, first lady, diplomat, and humanitarian, social activist, party leader. As a woman, she tried to balance the expectations of family, friends, and colleagues against her own needs for love, security, and respect. ER led a full but difficult life, defined by conflict and disappointment while empowered by duty and vision.

Grandmère is an honest depiction of the greatest woman of the twentieth century. David's Eleanor Roosevelt was not perfect. She struggled as a parent; battled mood swings; and often doubted her own abilities. A woman of great resilience, she refused to succumb to long periods of self-pity or inaction. Rebounding from her father's alcoholism, her husband's infidelity, and the cruel epithets her political opponents dispensed, ER displayed an uncanny ability to reinvent her life, to adjust in ways that allowed her to feel safe, honorable and productive. In the process, as David shows us, she built a family defined by a tremendous sense of kinship and love, and a breadth of friendships that gave her the reservoir of strength she needed to become Eleanor Roosevelt.

This is the story David Roosevelt tells. *Grandmère* is as much about ER's relationship with the grandson she called "Little Texas" as it is about her relationship with FDR, her commitment to humanity and her work on the Universal Declaration of Human Rights. It is the tale of a woman who, despite daily painful evidence of humanity's shortcomings, refused to let it run amok. It is the story of a woman who gave her life so that we might live in a world more just, more tolerant and more understanding. And finally it is the story of her grandson, who had courage enough to say he loved her and to acknowledge that there was so much more to know about her, his Grandmère.

David Roosevelt has given all of us who read this book a gift, a glimpse of what it was like to be loved by Eleanor Roosevelt and to struggle with the legacy she left. But to me, he has given something else; he has shown me in loving prose that sweetness is also strength. For that, I will always be grateful.

Grandmère? The title of a book about the most unaffectedly American of my heroes? It struck a false chord until I found the reason for it in this engrossing account of the life and times of Eleanor Roosevelt.

Its author, her grandson David Roosevelt and I have been friends for 20 years, but I was surprised when he asked me to write this introduction. Not that his grandmother and I weren't friends; we were professional acquaintances who saw each other from time to time as I covered her along with the horde of reporters who shadowed her wherever she went. The better acquainted I became the more my admiration for Eleanor Roosevelt grew.

I was given the privilege of a few special hours with her in January of 1957, when she agreed to sit down on ABC television for a "Mike Wallace Interview." Back then it was not always easy to persuade the mighty to endure the abrasions my inquisitorial role-playing required, but she knew she could handle anything difficult I might throw her way.

And I made plain to her, ahead of time, how much I along with tens of millions of Americans, admired her gently phrased but nonetheless steely determination to oppose the politics of fear, to fight for civil liberties and civil rights, to bridge opposites by forging partnerships. She was within everyone's grasp yet remained always slightly detached, *in* the battle surely, but appealing always to our better natures.

Nonetheless, her activism angered hotheaded American conservatives so intensely that the

Ku Klux Klan placed a bounty on her head; she refused the protection of the Secret Service she was entitled to, insisting she be able to move as freely as possible, and the agents finally consented when she proved that she carried a pistol in her purse and knew how to shoot.

But, enough from me about her now. Instead, a few of her own still relevant words from our interview 45 years ago, in which she proved herself a gentle but effective political combatant, and a committed Democrat.

MIKE WALLACE: *"If we are to believe a good deal of what we read, what seem to be the main preoccupations of the American people today? Bigger and better tail fins on automobiles? Westerns on television? Sex drenched movies? Fur coats? Push buttons? Alcoholism continues to increase, our mental institutions are full. Perhaps it's too grim a picture, but nonetheless reasonably accurate. When we talked with architect Frank Lloyd Wright a few weeks back, he told us that because of all this, the United States is in grave danger of declining as a world power. Do you think that Mr. Wright is completely wrong Mrs. Roosevelt?"*

ELEANOR ROOSEVELT: "I think that estimate of the American people is completely wrong. I feel quite sure that what the American people lack is knowledge. I feel quite sure that the American people, if they have knowledge and leadership, can meet any crisis just as well as they have met it over and over again in the past. I can remember the cries of horror when my husband said we have to have 50,000 airplanes in a given period. But we had them; and the difference was that the people were told what the reason was and why. And I have complete faith in the American people's ability if they know and if they have leadership. No one can move without some leadership."

MW: *"During the Depression your husband said, "The only thing we have to fear is fear itself." Don't you think, or let me put it this way, do you think that it's that simple today? Do we have anything concrete to fear from the Russians?"*

ER: "Yes. We have to fear the fact that they have a definite objective around which they have built their whole policy. We have met crises as we came to them, but I would find it hard to answer the question of what our future objective was for the world and how we were building our policy to achieve it and that's what I think we need in order to meet the communist objective. I think that is something we have to fear. They have a distinct objective, and they have patience in planning, and they plan a long time ahead."

MW: *"Is it possible, Mrs. Roosevelt, that communism, state socialism anyway, is the wave of the future, and that capitalism is on its way out?"*

ER: "Well that is what Khrushchev says. I don't know much about capitalism, but I do know about democracy and freedom, and capitalism may change in many, many ways. I'm not really very much interested in capitalism. I'm enormously interested in freedom and retaining the right to have whatever economy we want, and to shape it as we want, and having sufficient democracy so that the people actually hold their government in their own hands."

MW: *"Mrs. Roosevelt, I'm sure that you understand the sense in which I put this question to you, but I think that you would agree that a good many people hated your husband. They even hated you."*

ER: "Oh, yes. A great many do still."

MW: *"Why? Why?"*

ER: "Well, if you take stands, in any way, and people feel that you have success in a following, why, those who disagree with you are going to feel very strongly about it."

MW: *"There's more than just disagreement involved. There are people who disagree with President Eisenhower, and yet they do not hate him. I lived in the Middle West for a good many years while your husband was President and there was a real core of more than just disagreement."*

ER: "There was a real core of hatred. The people would call him 'that man,' I remember one man who rejoiced, actually, when he died. But I suppose that that is just a feeling that certain people had that he was destroying the thing that they held dear and touched them. And naturally you react to that with hatred. And I suppose that's what brought it about. They still fight him. I mean I sometimes think that campaigns are still largely fought on my husband rather than on the actual person who is running. And as far as I was concerned, I was touching something which to some people seems a sacred thing they had to keep hold of. A major part of my criticism has been on the Negro question, of course, and I've had many others, but that is the major part

and I think that that is quite natural because to some people, that seems to be destroying something that to them is very dear."

MW: *"In your column in January of 1956, you wrote about Republican leaders, and about Richard Nixon you said: 'Richard Nixon would be the least attractive. I know that given great responsibility, men sometimes change'—which in a sense is what you are just saying—you say that, 'I know that given great responsibility, men sometimes change. But Mr. Nixon's presidency would worry me,' you said. Why do you reserve this special criticism for Mr. Nixon?"*

ER: "I think that in great crisis, you need to have deep rooted convictions, and I have a feeling from the kind of campaigns that I have watched Mr. Nixon in, in the past, that his convictions are not very strong."

MW: *"But you do admit that over the past year in particular Mr. Nixon seems to have changed, possibly to have grown with the times?"*

ER: "I have no idea whether he has grown. I would say that he is a very intelligent person and that he had a very clear idea of what he wanted and had conducted himself wisely to achieve the ends he desired."

MW: *"Well, by the same token, would you have said Harry Truman had shown great conviction prior to his being thrown into the presidency?"*

ER: "No. I would not have. Again, I did not know him very well before. I would say of Mr. Truman that he rose to the responsibilities thrust upon him in a manner which was very remarkable, really. And that his big decisions very likely are going to mean he will go down in history as one of our very good presidents."

MW: *"With really insufficient background to expect he would act that way."*

ER: "Yes, quite certainly."

MW: *"Mrs. Roosevelt, perhaps your most severe critic is Westbrook Pegler. He once wrote this about you. He said, 'This woman is a political force of enormous ambitions. I believe she is a menace, unscrupulous as to truth, vain and cynical, all with a pretense of exaggerated kindness and human feeling which deceives millions of gullible persons.'"*

ER: "Well, it seems to me a little exaggerated, let us say. No one could be quite as bad as all that. And as far as political ambition goes, well I think that rather answered itself because I have never run for office and I've never asked for an office of any kind, so I can't have much political ambition. But I can see that Mr. Pegler probably believes all these things, and I suppose one does things unconsciously that make you seem like that, and perhaps I do seem like that to him. I think it must be terrible to hate as many things as Mr. Pegler hates, and I would be unhappy I think, and therefore I think that he is unhappy, and I'm sorry for him because, after all we all grow older, and we all have to live with ourselves, and I think that must sometimes be difficult for Mr. Pegler."

"A soft answer turneth away wrath," they say. Her deft answer humbled Mr. Pegler. Now, readers, on to *Grandmère!*

x

Preface

JUST A FEW SHORT YEARS AGO I THOUGHT I KNEW and understood a good deal about my family, particularly about my grandmother's life. I was raised in a fairly sophisticated and relatively political yet warm and definitely idiosyncratic family, whose three luminaries were Theodore, Franklin, and Eleanor Roosevelt. Of course, growing up I took for granted most everything that surrounded my childhood, with the exception of my grandmother. She, perhaps more than any other person, influenced me as a teacher, as a molder of much of my life philosophies, and certainly as a role model, long ago planting seeds of wisdom that formed a legacy for me and I feel certain also for my siblings and cousins, our children and grandchildren.

For many years I have had the pleasure of speaking with high school and middle school classes about my grandparents, and perhaps the one thing that has struck me is how impersonal and scant most history classes are about Franklin and Eleanor Roosevelt. Oh, it's certainly true that the historical facts of his presidency will be a part of national and world history curriculum throughout time and that the details of her extensive accomplishments have been well chronicled. But the more intimate memories of their incredible partnership are quickly fading. As I talk with young people, even in elementary grades, I find that there is real curiosity about my grandmother in particular when their lives are put in a human context. Something about Eleanor makes her story "real," whereas his story seems to them almost beyond reality. But of greater immediate concern to me was how I might provide my children, who never had the opportunity of knowing her, and my grandchildren with a more personal and informal chronicle of her life. No one knew Eleanor in quite the way my generation did. We called her Grandmère, from the French she had spoken since she was a child. Grandmère stood at the center of my childhood, and many of my fondest memories return to that idyllic time, a time that was private and intimate and in which she was simply my grandmother.

My original intention when beginning this project was to present Grandmère's life story mostly from recollections and anecdotes provided by her family members and close friends. I knew the project would be challenging since, as I realized, my generation of Roosevelts is really quite private, mostly shying away from sharing our intimate times with Grandmère with anyone beyond our close family circle. I also discovered that many of her friends and colleagues, people whose memories I had hoped to tap, were no longer with us, a truth that served to confirm my own fears that I too was rapidly forgetting details of years gone by. This alone made my quest all the more urgent. I knew, however, that a treasure trove of memorabilia—all sorts of personal letters, oral histories, and photographs—resided in the archives at the Franklin D. Roosevelt Library at Hyde Park. Over the years friends, the government, and family members had donated these important documents, which now form a vast collection that includes many of my grandmother's personal papers. These papers and my own memories of Grandmère have provided much of the basis for this book.

My work began in earnest in February 2000, when I made the first research visit to the library, accompanied by my wife, Michele, and my colleagues Manuela and Philip Dunn of Book Laboratory. After that visit I began reviewing and copying volumes—literally thousands of pages of letters and oral histories—and undertook to see what unique photographs might be available. But as much time as I have spent browsing through all of that fascinating material, there was no way I could have been prepared for the seemingly insurmountable task of sorting through it for just the right elements. I was caught between a panicked feeling of frustration and excitement at finding so much. It was then that I knew this project was much larger than I had initially imagined and would require far more effort to accomplish.

As I began my review of the some three thousand pages of oral histories, I realized that I needed the help of someone capable of seeing the more personal nuances—an extraordinarily difficult task if you're not familiar with the interviewees and their relationships to Grandmère—and so called upon my son, Matthew. In addition to the oral histories, literally thousands of photographs had to be culled, reviewed, and initial selections made on the basis of the book's content, all before the first draft was completed. For this I enlisted the photo-editing skills of the talented Melissa Shaw, who made a preliminary selection of more than six hundred photographs (which would eventually be reduced to the two hundred or so included in this book), many of which have seldom if ever been published before.

The more I read, researched, and studied, the more I found that I really knew little of this simple yet so complex woman. The more previously published works I read, many by people who knew her intimately as a friend and even mentor, the more convinced I became that something was lacking in their otherwise insightful works, and that was the very personal side of Grandmère. I came to see her life as a web of triangular relationships. From her youngest childhood until some time after my grandfather's death, Grandmère seemed to always end up caught in the middle of two powerful individuals, individuals who then helped her to define who she was within their psychological triangle. Hers was a life of tragedy, self-doubt, and unhappiness, barriers she fought constantly; moreover, it was a life of paradox at every turn.

What I hope to accomplish here is to provide my children, future generations of my family, and you with the story of Grandmère, as told from that perspective of pride we all hold for our grandparents—mine just happen to be two of the most celebrated of modern times. I try to give as complete an overview of the many facets of her life and personality as possible, but with the full realization that this is not a definitive study. The more I have learned of her accomplishments and her life, the more I have come to respect—indeed, be influenced by—her legacy. But this legacy is not for me, my family, nor my family's future generations. It is a legacy for every man, woman, and child, whether American or world citizen.

Grandmère would say of my grandfather that he possessed an incredible strength of perseverance in the face of many challenges. I would have to believe that she, perhaps, served as a model of perseverance for him. I suspect that she provided him with inspiration more often than he inspired her, and yet together they formed a unique, if not truly extraordinary, partnership. Many marvel at the strength of Franklin Roosevelt in overcoming a debilitating physical malady and achieving great status in political history. I marvel at the resiliency of Grandmère in overcoming personal defeat and tragedy, not once but many times over, always to emerge stronger, more knowledgeable, more committed. Grandmère had every right, if not expectation, to grow doubtful and bitter toward humanity, but she chose to believe, and above all to fight for her beliefs, in the innate goodness of humanity. Her instinct to nurture those far beyond her closest family never waned.

While Franklin Roosevelt may have been considered a father to a generation of Americans, Grandmère was a mother, and grandmother, to the world. Her inspiration perseveres for my generation, for that of my children, for you, and I hope for generations to come.

HET LOO

THE NUMBER OF PEOPLE WHO HAVE PERSONAL memories of Eleanor Roosevelt is probably limited. They must be an even more select group when only Europeans are counted. I have the honour and pleasure of belonging to this group.

I was born in Canada during the Second World War. Not in The Netherlands, but in exile, in Canada. The Roosevelt White House and The House of Orange became closely connected during those years. My grandmother Queen Wilhelmina, my parents and I, as a baby, were frequent guests at Hyde Park and at the White House.

President Franklin Roosevelt died a mere three weeks before The Netherlands was liberated by the Allied Powers. As a token of gratitude for his leadership in the war efforts of the United States, my parents asked him to become my godfather. Proud as he was of his Dutch ancestry, he gladly agreed. This created the special bond between him, Eleanor and myself, which I still cherish today. I was named after him: Margriet Francisca.

As his goddaughter I was present at the dedication of the Franklin Delano Roosevelt Memorial in Washington, D.C., in 1997, for which occasion a new rose variety had been cultivated, bearing his name, as a subtle reminder that "Roosevelt" is Dutch for "Field of Roses."

In The Netherlands the memory of both Franklin and Eleanor is kept alive by the annual presentation of the "Four Freedoms Awards," reminding us of the four freedoms they believed every individual had a right to: freedom of speech, freedom of worship, freedom from want and the freedom from fear.

This was the cause Eleanor continued to defend after Franklin's death. In the words of the poet Archibald MacLeish: If democracy had saints, Mrs. Roosevelt would be one.

I hope these memories and reflections show how happy I am to introduce this book to you.

PART ONE

"Little Texas" invades Grandmère's home at Val-Kill.

Grandmère

*When we were children we used to collect pine cones
and paint them with airplane paint and then put
sparkly things on them...She would burn them in the
fireplace, and they made pretty colors when you burnt
them. It was great! And she really just loved those
things that children end up doing for you. It was the
love that she loved coming from us.*

—Nina Roosevelt

THERE ARE MOMENTS OF CHILDHOOD
that lodge in our memories and sometimes linger there tenaciously for the rest
of our lives. This or that instant, rather
than a million others, sheds light and glows warm-
ly years after the moment. I have many such vivid
memories pervaded by the presence of Grandmère.
Though photographs exist of me as a small child sitting on my grandfather's knee at the White House
or at home in Texas, my earliest and most vivid
memories are of holidays spent in unadulterated
freedom at Grandmère's Val-Kill, her beloved home
and retreat from a hectic life in upstate New York.

An intense feeling of anticipation marked
the beginning of school holidays, when I would fly
in the early days of American Airlines from my family's home in Fort Worth to New York, and then
take the train up the Hudson River Valley to
Poughkeepsie, where I was met by my father and
stepmother and, of course, Grandmère. In fact, as
happens so often with small children, the sheer
pitch of the excitement of being once more in the
thrilling atmosphere of Grandmère's home surrounded by an onslaught of cousins, aunts, uncles,
friends, and the occasional famous visitor would at

times be overwhelming. But the return to
Grandmère's Val-Kill was the highlight of many holidays. Perhaps because I lived so far away with my
mother, sister, and brother, the times spent with
Grandmère were all the more special to me. For a
small, ever-inquisitive child, the endless stream of
activities and interesting people in her home made
it the most absorbing, wonderful place imaginable.

Upon arriving at Val-Kill I would be swept
up into the busy, adventurous atmosphere that surrounded Grandmère. My older brother, Tony
(Elliott Jr.), and my sister, Chandler, had that same
sense of Val-Kill. For us it was a time to be reunited with our father, who, after the divorce from my
mother and subsequent remarriage, lived for a period at Top Cottage, just a short walk from
Grandmère's through dense woods. But while that
reunion was always a time anticipated, the real
excitement lay just down the hill at Val-Kill.

For us children, Val-Kill was paradise. There
were few rules and even fewer schedules, and we
were left free to do practically whatever we wanted
—riding horses across the open fields and through the
woods, boating in the Fall-Kill Pond, carousing with
cousins for endless hours, swimming in the pool,
playing games or drawing on rainy days in the
Playhouse. Grandmère was always attentive and
warm, and we had the constant feeling that no matter what important person had come to see her or
what her work demanded, her grandchildren always
came first. She used to call me the "little cowboy" or
"little Texas" because of my penchant for wearing
cowboy boots and shorts, my favorite attire as a small
child. And though I might have been a charming and
engaging little boy, as some said, even then I was
hardheaded and self-driven. Never one for napping in

the afternoon like the other small children, I would spend hours playing outside and making up great adventures, and then I would tear through the house at great speeds to get to her bathroom (usually the closest to wherever I might be at the time of urgent discovery!), racing through the study where Grandmère might be quietly working with Tommy, or in later years Maureen Corr, or meeting with important people. It seems I always waited until the very last minute to make that urgent mad dash. She never scolded me or grew agitated in the least by the carryings on of her grandchildren, despite the fact

Above: *Grandmère with my cousins Nina, Sally, and an elderly Fala.* Opposite: *A typical summer day around the Val-Kill pool with cousins and siblings. My sister Chandler took these photographs in 1947.*

that there were often many of us causing utter chaos. Of course, I'm certain even we could push the limits of her patience, but perhaps I have just forgotten those rare moments.

I think I must have been aware that Grandmère was an important person—surely I knew she was somehow special. But to me she was simply my grandmother, and I related to her in that warm, intimate way a small child does to someone who is consistently loving and attentive. She had an amazing facility for engaging even very small children in conversation. I remember her as always encouraging me to tell her about myself, the things I was doing, and what interested me, no matter how young I was. I could go on walks with her if I wanted to talk about something special, or she would often invite me to go with her to run errands in the village of Hyde Park. We would go to the post office or grocery shopping, and local people would always greet her with "Good morning, Mrs. R" or address her as "Mrs. Roosevelt." To my memory, only a few of her closest friends and family ever called Grandmère by her first name, Eleanor, perhaps out of deep respect. Minnewa Bell, my father's fourth wife, used to call her "Mother R," a salutation that many of her other daughters-in-law used as well.

Grandmère's Val-Kill was a very special place, not just to me but to practically everyone who visited there. I find it interesting today when I return to listen to the reactions of other visitors: "Why, it's so *simple,* so unimposing, not at all what I would have expected!" Yet others will remark on its serenity, and immediately understand how it could be so important to Grandmère. For me, it is merely a place of so many memories, so many wonderful times spent with my grandmother—nothing more, nothing less.

June, 1947

THE GREATEST THING I'VE EVER LEARNED IS HOW GOOD IT IS TO COME HOME AGAIN.
——Eleanor Roosevelt

Val-Kill

The Hudson Valley meant a great deal to Grandmère. Her attachment to the area hearkened back to childhood years spent at her own maternal grandmother's great house, Tivoli, high on the banks of the Hudson River; frequent visits to Clermont and Algonac, the estates of her extended family; and her later days at Springwood, the modest yet still imposing estate of FDR and her eventual mother-in-law, Sara. And as time would pass, it was here in the Valley that she would choose to make her own home at Val-Kill, a place that nourished her deepest need for tranquility and regeneration...a place uniquely hers. In a letter to her friend Lorena Hickok, she wrote, "I shall always be a part of it here." Val-Kill represented the universe that Grandmère loved and cherished, a sanctuary and a home filled with family and friends, where the rituals of the Roosevelt clan were celebrated and where everyone gathered in the summers and holidays.

Val-Kill today is much the same as I remember it as a child; virtually everything in this place of powerful landscape and memory remains untouched. A simple wooden gate marks the road winding its way beneath the canopy of trees—mostly old birches and fir and pine—flanking the virgin woods and green fields that once belonged to it as part of the original Springwood estate that belonged to FDR's parents, James and Sara. The National Park Service, caretakers of this now National Historic Site, have marked the entry by a slightly formal yet unobtrusive sign that identifies it as Val-Kill, home of Eleanor Roosevelt. Immediately one notices the quiet and tranquility, broken only by the sounds of a breeze in the branches and the melodic cacophony of birds. Less than a mile up the narrow road one crosses a rickety wooden bridge (more substantial today than when I was a child) marking where Fall-Kill Pond once again becomes Fall-Kill Stream. It is at this point that one enters the realm of Eleanor Roosevelt's private world, the only place she would ever refer to as home.

The Hudson Valley is full of beautiful landscapes and imposing homes, but to me Val-Kill is the epitome of the idyllic New York setting. The cluster of gray-stone buildings at the top of the expansive natural lawn, giving way to the small pond and stream surrounded by ancient trees, sit serenely in a landscape of unanticipated beauty, windows catching the last rays of a late summer sunset. The Stone Cottage with its simple Dutch architecture and the "Shop," all so plain as to lull the visitor into thinking they have arrived at the wrong destination. This layered scenery was home to Grandmère and her beloved assistant and friend Malvina Thompson, "Tommy," who maintained her own comfortable private quarters in a wing of Grandmère's house until her death. It was to Val-Kill that Grandmère escaped to replenish her energy, to rejuvenate her spirit, to work in solitude, and to simply relax.

Grandmère and her friends Nancy Cook and Marion Dickerman wanted a getaway place that could also sustain itself through a small business enterprise attached to it. Thus, the idea of Val-Kill was first born. Grandmère had never been comfortable at my grandfather's home, Springwood, feeling that it would always be Sara and FDR's domain. And so she convinced my grandfather to give her and her friends property at a far end of the Springwood estate to build a cottage retreat and small furniture factory. The original structure, the Stone Cottage, home to Nancy and Marion (and Grandmère when she could manage to escape her busy schedule), was gleefully designed by my grandfather in the Dutch tradition.

The second structure was the Shop, which housed Val-Kill Industries, a small furniture factory started by Grandmère, Nancy, and Marion. It was here, during the Depression, that local craftsmen were afforded the opportunity to turn out beautifully simplistic pieces of early American furniture, to forge pieces of pewter, and to create a variety of woven materials. Even today, Val-Kill furniture is much sought after by collectors for its simple style and masterful craftsmanship. But despite Nancy's considerable artistic talents and seemingly tireless energy, encouraged by some early recognition at furniture shows in New York City, Val-Kill Industries simply could not make itself financially viable. The strain of the demise of the little business began exacting a toll on the threesome's friendship, and after several infusions of capital by Grandmère, Val-Kill Industries was eventually liquidated in 1937.

Some historians have speculated that the final split between the almost inseparable friends was the result of Marion and Nancy's almost overwhelming possessiveness toward Grandmère. I, on the other hand, think it was probably a natural evolution of Grandmère's emergence as a personality in her own right, a transformation aided if not abetted by her two friends. Nevertheless, the final split seems to have followed Grandmère's decision to renovate the former factory into her own home, while allowing Marion and Nancy to remain at the Stone Cottage. But soon the tensions became too great, and Grandmère offered to purchase their share of Val-Kill at a most generous, perhaps inflated, price. When her offer was accepted, Grandmère finally had her own private domain. It was at this time that Val-Kill truly became her home, and hers alone.

There are not and never were trappings of grandeur at Val-Kill. The Stone Cottage remains much as it originally was, and the Shop is still the unobtrusive stucco building of rather small rooms that underwent modest renovation to become Grandmère's living quarters. Knotty-pine panels encase several of the rooms in her cottage, and the many windows beckon in the sunlight. Her second-floor bedroom faces the stream and pond, overlooks the fields beyond, and enjoys a marvelous sleeping porch where she would sleep even in winter and

Above: *Workroom in the Val-Kill factory, later Grandmère's home.* Opposite: *A corner of the living room, center of much of Grandmère's entertaining.*

where I would beg, unsuccessfully, to spend my nights. There are also a few guest rooms on this floor where parents, friends, family, and even the most important dignitaries would stay when visiting.

Finally, there was also a small "maid's room" toward the rear and—all the way at one end of the floor, far enough away so as to minimize the inevitable noise and ruckus—a larger bedroom that served for a time as additional office space but more typically as a "bunkroom" for assorted young grandchildren. But to us grandchildren the most exciting feature on the second floor was the "Christmas closet," where Grandmère would store all of the family presents she collected throughout the year.

The ground floor, laid out almost like a rabbit warren of small rooms, to me at least holds most of the special memories. Warm and cozy, it

provided an atmosphere of simplicity and relaxation for everyone who entered, from friends and family to the rich and powerful. Coming in through the front door (the back door in reality) straight down the narrow hallway one enters the dining room. The long, narrow table was the centerpiece of many "intimate" dinners, often with twenty or more squeezed in. It was not unusual to hear Grandmère say to the cook, "There will *only* be eighteen for dinner tonight." Be it family, friends, or guests, the conversation was always lively and without the least bit of protocol. When the dinners included my father and uncles, the conversation would inevitably turn to politics, which would usually include lots of good-natured arguing, joking, and at times even serious disagreements. As I recall, Grandmère would hardly ever participate in those discussions, preferring to let the brothers fight it out, often amused at their bantering. If guests worried about the liveliness of the dinner discussions, when it could at times look as if the Roosevelt children

were about to murder each other, Grandmère would reassure them good-naturedly, "Plenty of variety but basically a great deal of unity."

Directly next to the dining room is the living room, situated just below Grandmère's bedroom. Here too is a screened porch overlooking the pond. Only slightly more formal than the other rooms, the living room is where Grandmère entertained larger groups of guests. With the windows and French doors draped in simple white linen, overstuffed chairs and sofas, and a fireplace and large mantel full of photographs and memorabilia of special family interest, this is a room enlivened by the spirit of home and memory. It was in this room that cold Christmas Eves were spent with family and friends crowding around as she read the traditional Dickens *Christmas Carol,* a tradition begun by my grandfather, and it was here that the chaos of Christmas Day was played out when finally the Christmas closet was emptied!

Immediately to the left of the front door was Tommy's apartment, which also served as Grandmère's office and study. Chairs and a couch were grouped around another fireplace, often littered with books and papers in some stage of incompleteness, photographs adorning practically every inch of free wall space, and a small desk toward the rear at which Grandmère and Tommy accomplished an incredible amount of work. Following Tommy's death, this room became the real universe of Eleanor Roosevelt. It was here that she would dictate responses to the thousands of letters she received over the years, work on her magazine and newspaper columns and manuscripts, and write or type the never-ending letters and notes to her children and grandchildren. She never forgot a birthday or other

special occasion, and always tried to change her schedule to attend a wedding or graduation. It was in this study that she held private conversations with national and world leaders, men and women of power and influence who would come seeking her advice, counsel, or support on some important issue. The guest list of those entertained at Val-Kill read something like a "Who's Who" of world power: Madame Chiang Kai-shek, Queen Wilhelmina of the Netherlands, Marshal Tito, Haile Selassie, Prime Minister Jawaharlal Nehru of India, the king and queen of England, several members of Scandinavian royalty, Sir Winston Churchill, and Nikita Khrushchev. And it was in this room, this modest office, that she met with John F. Kennedy as he came seeking her all-important support for his election.

Her office is also where she would feed her voracious appetite for reading everything from the classics to some current book on world or national affairs, the periodic novel, and volumes of poetry. She would have afternoon tea—oh, how I loved the cinnamon toast and other goodies!—on the adjoining porch, and

inside this warm, well-lived-in, and beloved study she would find the solitude that rekindled her spirit. There were other rooms in the cottage, but none held the same significance for Grandmère.

Over time the Stone Cottage would become a guesthouse for some of the overflow of visitors, home to my uncle John and his family, and the epicenter of much activity. It was here that the swimming pool was eventually installed, with its small changing house filled with extra swimming apparel of all sizes and styles, mostly left behind by previous guests. The pool served

for physical therapy for my grandfather and for Grandmère's ritual daily laps, time and weather permitting. One of the more amusing anecdotes about the pool concerns the first time Prime Minister Winston

Opposite, clockwise from top left: *Grandmère with Princess Juliana; Princess Margriet in a playpen; visitors around the pool; Princess (now Queen) Beatrix in foreground, Princess Irene, and Princess Juliana. Above: FDR, Queen Elizabeth and the Duke of Kent; Grandmère with Nikita and Mrs. Khrushchev, and Andrei Gromyko in the background; President Kennedy; Grandmère and Queen Elizabeth in Washington.*

The Stone Cottage, epicenter of most summer entertaining.

Churchill visited one sweltering summer day. As recalled by Marion Dickerman:

> There was a little bathhouse among the trees below the pool, where swimmers donned their bathing suits. Churchill, wearing a wide-brimmed hat, as he always did for protection against the summer sun, and with a long cigar—as always—in his mouth, entered the bathhouse with his secretary. The latter emerged a minute later. "Mr. Churchill has his bathing dress," said the secretary to Marion, "but he would like instead to wear a pair of trunks. Do you have a pair he might wear?" Quite a collection had been collected over the years in the Cottage and Marion found a pair she thought might be of adequate girth. The secretary took them into the bathhouse. In a few minutes he was back again. "You wouldn't have a bit of cotton?" he asked. "For his ears," he quickly explained to the astonished Marion.[1]

And it was on the flagstone patio and screened porch that poolside picnics were held. Naturally, during the summer months the area surrounding the Stone Cottage and pool would be filled with the frolic and play of assorted grandchildren and friends. Esther Peterson, another close friend, would tell the story of how she had invited a group of young ladies visiting from England for a picnic at Val-Kill, just at the time of the Chicago convention prior to FDR's third-term election. All the young women, in anticipation of meeting the First Lady, had gone to great efforts to get their hair done and to purchase white gloves, as was considered appropriate when meeting a queen. They had been excited to hear Eleanor's convention speech that night on the radio, but were uncertain that she could ever return in time for their proposed visit. Nevertheless, the next day they arrived on buses, dressed in their finest dresses, hair neatly coiffed, and all wearing white gloves, only to be met by Grandmère, resplendent in her wet bathing suit. Then, to their utter astonishment, she exclaimed, "I invited you to a picnic!" whereupon she set out to find each and every girl a bathing suit, and soon everyone was thrashing around in the pool...hair a mess, white gloves discarded! And it was here, at the Stone Cottage, where world leaders and dignitaries—President and Mrs. Kennedy, Vice President Lyndon Johnson, and so many others—assembled for an informal luncheon before Grandmère was finally laid to rest in the Rose Garden at Springwood.

The compound also included the Playhouse, a rather low-slung, nondescript structure consisting of a large room in the center and two smaller offices at either end, located immediately behind Grandmère's cottage. Along the walls of the Playhouse, storage boxes held an accumulation of toys, games, and books, all for the use of the children who would gather here during days of inclement weather. Set farther

Winston Churchill by the pool in his ever-present summer Panama hat.

13

GRANDMÈRE, A PERSONAL HISTORY OF ELEANOR ROOSEVELT

An annual Wiltwyck School picnic, which always included family and friends.
Opposite: *Me on a boat in Grandmère's pond.*

away from the other buildings were the stables, where a variety of ponies and horses were stalled for use by the grandchildren. (Many people do not realize that Grandmère was an avid rider for most of her life.) It was from here that guests and family would set off on summer hayrides or wintry horse-drawn sleigh rides.

And finally there was Top Cottage, located perhaps three-quarters of a mile through the woods and up the steep hill from the main Val-Kill complex. A beautiful stone cottage designed and built by my grandfather in anticipation of his own retirement years, this hideaway was snuggled sufficiently far from the hustle and bustle of the main Val-Kill activity for him to work on his papers and memoirs in peace and quiet, assemble the collection of books and papers to be given to the Franklin D. Roosevelt Library (the nation's first presidential library), and simply relax after so many exhausting years of public service. As destiny would have it, my grandfather would not live to realize this final dream. Nevertheless, following Grandmère's return from Washington and her time in the White House, my father and his wife, actress Faye Emerson, would purchase Top Cottage and live there for several years. Most of my earliest memories of summer vacations and holidays at Val-Kill were of Top Cottage, and naturally of the visits by Dad and Faye's movie friends, including Lauren Bacall and Humphrey Bogart. Today, many years after being sold to a group of investors for development, this little known but soon to be discovered jewel in the treasure chest of Val-Kill has been repurchased and refurbished to its original simple splendor, joining the rest of Grandmère's Val-Kill home as a national historic treasure.

Any description of Val-Kill would be incomplete without details of Grandmère's penchant for entertaining. With few exceptions she believed in simple, informal get-togethers, and her absolute favorite were her beloved picnics. Not only did she create plain if not altogether ordinary menus, but for her picnics she loved to serve hot dogs, and it made no difference whatsoever the guest or their status. In fact, she is credited with introducing the irascible Nikita Khrushchev and even the king and queen of England to their first encounter with the hot dog. It is rumored that she had to give the king a brief lesson on the proper way to eat one: with the fingers, of course!

The expansive lawn at Val-Kill was a special place, with its smallish, underused tennis court, a playhouse, also called the Dollhouse, down by the water (moved there from Springwood, but seldom used by the grandchildren), and a wide assortment of canoes and leaky rowboats, most of which were prone to frequent summertime sinkings. It was the site, of course, for the endless picnics of friends and family, aunts, uncles, and cousins, and for the event most anxiously awaited, the annual outing for the boys of Wiltwyck School.

For years Grandmère had been associated as a board member and later patron of this school for underprivileged (delinquent) boys. She cared so deeply about the lives of these young people, the deprivations of their home lives and what lay in their futures, that in many ways she adopted them all. Every summer she would invite perhaps a hundred for a picnic at Val-Kill, and one of the joys of my summers would be the anticipation of that one picnic—and all those new friends! The shopping list for this event would read something like this: "400 hot dogs, 200 rolls, 200 cupcakes, 50 quarts milk, 25 quarts ice cream, 100 comic books, 100 bars candy, potato salad, mustard." Often there might be other little toys or treats for each of the boys. All of the grownups would congregate around the great outdoor fireplace while the boys (and I or my cousins) would just simply run wild with freedom, out from under the structure of their normal institutional life. Soon the food would be served, and then, sated, everyone would fall at Grandmère's feet to hear her read from Kipling's *Just So Stories,* and especially "How the Elephant Got His Trunk" and "The Butterfly That Stamped."

There is a humorous story of one of the Wiltwyck boys coming up to Grandmère and asking, "Do you remember me?" "Why of course," she responded, "you were here last year," but she really couldn't remember his name. A little hurt perhaps, he indignantly told her his name, instructing her to be certain to remember it. Returning a little while later he said, "Do you remember my name?" As Grandmère repeated it, he exclaimed, "Good, maybe now you'll never forget me!" For this little boy, as with so many of them, being recognized as an individual was of utmost importance.

While Grandmère cared deeply about the Wiltwyck School and its work to open new horizons to these youngsters, often her kindness on these simple occasions left them with a lasting

Grandmère welcoming some of the Wiltwyck School kids as they arrive for a picnic.

impression and in at least one case an insight into a future of potential. The noted African American author Claude Brown dedicated his classic and compelling autobiographical work, *Manchild in the Promised Land*, to Grandmère and the Wiltwyck School, where at age eleven he was sent by court decree for a period of over two years. In his mid-twenties he graduated from Howard University, and at thirty began the study of law. *Manchild in the Promised Land* chronicles his life growing up in Harlem, to him a wondrous place where if you were quick witted, smart, and tough enough you could live like a king...or die like a pauper. His dedication to Grandmère is a testament, I think, to the inspiration she provided during those picnics at Val-Kill and throughout her life. Perhaps one might conclude that her example helped Claude Brown recognize and achieve his own aspirations.

What times those were, the picnics with so many of her lifelong friends and colleagues—the Morgenthaus, Esther Lape, Justine Polier, former New Dealer Harry Hooker—and close family like cousin Laura Delano (well known for her eccentricities of purple hair and painted widow's peak, and for one of the world's foremost jade collections) and Belle (Mrs. Kermit) Roosevelt, as well as her many, many neighbors. Grandmère loved to surround herself with those she loved and admired, and barely a day passed that there weren't houseguests, or lunch and dinner guests. But what she loved most was to surround herself with family, especially her twenty-two grandchildren and thirteen great-grandchildren.

Grandmère with Fala and his son Tamas McFala. Scotties became my grandparents' favorite breed of dogs. Opposite: *A young Fala, with his always-endearing look.*

It is a wonder that Grandmère ever found time to simply think and contemplate, but at Val-Kill she would do just that. Part of her daily ritual included long walks, often with Fala, my grandfather's Scotty dog, or Fala's grandson Tamas McFala, who became my grandmother's faithful companion. Of Fala Grandmère wrote, "He has lived with me since my husband's death. For a while after that he used to lie in the doorway where he could watch all the doors, just as he did when my husband used to come over to this cottage. Fala is still very dignified and while he is happy here with me, I do not think he has ever accepted me as the one person whom he loved as he did my husband." She would walk the long country lanes and through the towering woods often for hours at a time. Although sometimes with a friend or grandchild, most often these were periods of solitude she sought for herself; this was when she could take stock of her life, the work yet to be done, and later, toward the end of her life, the culmination of her efforts. "My heart is in the cottage…the peace of it is divine," she wrote. Following Grandmère's death my uncle John and his family continued to live at Val-Kill in the Stone Cottage, and it remained a place for many of the family to return to from time to time. In 1970, however, this special place that had seen so much life, so many interesting people, and the changes of time, and had been so central to my grandmother's life, was sold to a group of doctors for development. Although many of the more personal objects and memorabilia were saved and stored at the Franklin D. Roosevelt Library, most all the furniture, much of it produced at the old Val-Kill Industries, and other furnishings were sold at auction. Practically none of the grandchildren were told of the impending sale. I, for one,

discovered it from a cousin's telephone call just days before. On the actual day of the auction several of us converged at Val-Kill along with a horde of antique dealers, other interested buyers, and more than a few curious bystanders who hoped perhaps to win some small token of history. It was a terribly sad time for us all, as we knew that none of us had the financial wherewithal to compete against those who had come as serious contenders for these bits of nostalgia. However, as we huddled to plan some strategy to try and save whatever we could of our family's heritage, the word slowly circulated among the assembled that several of the Roosevelt grandchildren were there, and why. The reaction, as I recall it, was one of extraordinary consideration, even among the serious antique dealers and other bidders, for our desires to keep as many relevant items as possible in the family. In the end, we cousins, usually at reasonable prices and without too much serious opposition, purchased several of the items that had the most significance for each of us. At the end of the day, I think everyone left generally satisfied, but for those of us who witnessed the spectacle it was a sad day; there was a feeling of emptiness that a small part of our lives had just been sold off to strangers.

Foiled in their initial attempts to develop housing on the Val-Kill property by a Hyde Park town-zoning ordinance, the developers proceeded to turn Grandmère's cottage and the Playhouse into low-cost apartments. Walls were built to partition parts of the cottage, the grounds were neglected and allowed to fall into disrepair, and little in the way of maintenance was performed. Several concerned local citizens, fearful that a valuable historic asset was being threatened, began an effort to save the site, and in 1976 they were joined by a young woman from Rochester, New York. Nancy Dubner began the long process of contacting people in Congress, friends and family, and practically anyone else who might be interested in her crusade to help save Eleanor Roosevelt's Val-Kill. The original bill introduced in Congress that provided for the purchase of Val-Kill and its designation as a National Historic Site was immediately and roundly defeated. Subsequently, in 1977, during the administration of President Jimmy Carter, a bill passed both houses of Congress approving the government's purchase of the land for $300,000—a price immediately rejected by the developers, who demanded over $1 million. Unable to reach any sort of compromise, even after a professional appraisal confirmed the government's valuation, the entire property was eventually condemned due to its deteriorated condition. Finally, after a jury trial upheld the purchase price offered by the government, the process of restoring Val-Kill to its condition at the time of Grandmère's death was begun. Today, thanks to the hard work of caring National Park Rangers and the dedicated volunteers of Save America's Treasures, Grandmère's beloved Val-Kill once again houses the memories of her life there, and with those memories the emotional attachments of so many others who lived there, spent holidays and vacations there, or merely visited her in the wondrous simplicity of her "home."

How could one place possibly have such an effect on Grandmère, and sometimes on those who visited it, you might wonder? Let me explain by relating a story of one of the dedicated rangers, Franceska Macsali, who has worked at both Springwood and at Val-Kill since at least the early 1980s. During her first two years she was assigned to the Big House at Springwood, where, as is true of most of the rangers, she studied the lives of both FDR and Eleanor.

I came to admire and love Eleanor Roosevelt. Here was a woman who had such an unhappy and lonely childhood and so many disasters happening later in her life...yet she never turned her back on life, never felt sorry for herself. Instead, she reached out to others who needed help—the poor, the downtrodden. How much I wished to work at Val-Kill, the site dedicated to Eleanor Roosevelt![2]

Franceska's wish came true when in 1982 she was assigned to the home as the permanent park ranger. Today, Franceska and her dedicated colleagues continue to lead the restoration of Val-Kill to ensure that when visitors arrive they too will be enveloped by the true depth of feeling that Eleanor felt for her home. Perhaps those same visitors will come away sharing Franceska's feeling:

I used to be shy, and it was difficult for me to express my dissatisfaction over things I found wrong. But now, after being aware of what Mrs. Roosevelt had done, I force myself to speak up. If I feel very strongly about an injustice or unfairness in our country, I write a letter. I had always thought it easier to remain silent,

Grandmère's house from across the pond.

but now I know that the difficult ways are the easy ones. To keep quiet has become difficult for me. Val-Kill and getting to know Eleanor Roosevelt does that to you. And once you have found your way to Val-Kill, it will be difficult not to come back.[3]

Even Grandmère found it difficult to stay away from Val-Kill. Now, whenever I visit the family compound, memories of those happy times flood back. As I take my own children to Hyde Park and Val-Kill, I hope to instill in them an idea of what those times were like for me. Of course today, due to the large number of visitors, parts of Grandmère's house must necessarily be closed to the public, but I can never forget the time that my six-year-old son, Matthew,

decided to take his own private tour of where "Dad used to play." Stopped by an ever-vigilant park ranger who was conducting a tour of the house, Matthew announced, "Oh, it's all right. This is my father's grandmother's house," and merrily proceeded on his way before anyone could intervene (and much to the astonishment of the assembled tour).

I hope that the many visitors who come here every year can feel some of the serenity, peace, and tranquility that her home retains, and perhaps imagine her sitting at her desk, a single light shining late at night, writing her correspondence or reading a letter, thinking about the world, just as I do every time I return. After all, Grandmère would have wanted them to feel right at home!

21

My Journey Begins at Val-Kill

It was at Val-Kill, in November 1962, that one of the most profound events of my life occurred. As I have said, I was aware that Grandmère was a special person to many people, even a celebrity, but even at twenty years of age I still did not fully understand the stature of this incredible person. I had experienced the deference of people when in her presence, the feeling of love and admiration, and yet to me she was still "Grandmère." But all that changed for me on November 10.

They were all there: President John F. Kennedy and the First Lady, Vice President Lyndon Johnson and Lady Bird, former presidents Harry Truman and Dwight Eisenhower. There were heads of state, ambassadors from a multitude of nations, and senators and congressmen, along with friends and family and hundreds, perhaps thousands, of just ordinary folk, people from all over. And there was one twenty-year-old, somewhat awed if not overwhelmed by the entire assemblage. I have heard it said since that the funeral of Anna Eleanor Roosevelt had accomplished what perhaps no other single occasion could—the bringing together of many of the world's most powerful and influential people, allies and antagonists alike, for at least a few hours of respectful peace and common accord. For me it had quite another effect; it marked the beginning of a journey of discovery.

Most of the actual activities leading up to and including that cold and dreary November day are difficult for me to recall clearly, as so much occurred so quickly. It was a whirlwind of emotion and confusion. The simple life of a college student suddenly turned topsy-turvy by a telephone call from my sister, Chandler, a few days before, saying, "David, Grandmère has died. We need to go to Hyde Park." I had just returned to my apartment from classes at Texas Christian University when the call came. I knew Grandmère had been sick for some time now, but never, ever, did I expect this call. I suppose I thought that she would always be there, the way grandmothers are supposed to be. She always had been before. The next thing I recall was arriving at the Waldorf Astoria Hotel in New York City, where many members of the family were convening, including my father and his fifth wife, Patricia, uncles, aunts, and some cousins, and a seemingly unending array of others, most of whom I didn't know. I *do* remember thinking, for the first of many times over the next few days, "Why? Why are all these people here?" It was not at all what I had expected her funeral to be. There were so many people, so much talk of who was coming, what arrangements had to be made, concerns of protocol.

Suddenly, as a silent bystander in this storm of matter-of-factness, the reality that *my*

grandmother was someone of much greater importance than I had ever dreamed came crashing down. I had to escape the circus-like atmosphere, so I called the only person I knew in Manhattan, a cousin, Barbara Morgan, with whom I'd become friendly as we visited Grandmère during those summers and holidays at Val-Kill. I retreated to her apartment as fast as I could, and sensing that I was feeling very alone in the midst of the maelstrom, she opened her door and reached out in common bond. We sat for hours, late into the night, just talking, trying to understand what Grandmère had meant to each of us, to our lives, and knowing that somehow things would never be quite the same.

The next day everyone made his or her way to Hyde Park, first to the Stone Cottage at Val-Kill. Crowded and stifling, the little house was jammed with people. I sat for some time chatting with the marvelously effervescent Jackie Kennedy, whom I had first met with Grandmère a few years before at the president's inauguration and again briefly at a White House reception, and who I must admit made quite an impression on this young man from

Texas. There were other dignitaries as well, and of course family and old and dear friends like Trude and Joe Lash, Edna and David Gurewitsch. The person I remember above all others was Adlai Stevenson, with whom my grandmother had developed a particularly close relationship, both personally and politically. Yes, they had all come to mourn the passing of Eleanor Roosevelt, but for me one question lingered, "Why?" For the first time in my life I was slowly beginning to realize that I was part of something I had never before comprehended...or even thought about, really. By virtue of my birth I was part of a legacy, a family with a heritage and tradition that before I had merely taken for granted. Suddenly I was filled with questions about who and what, questions I had simply never contemplated much before this heartbreaking occasion. And as

Opposite: *Three Presidents and the Vice President attend Grandmère's funeral: John F. Kennedy, Lyndon Johnson, Harry Truman, and Dwight Eisenhower. Above, left: President and Mrs. Kennedy arriving at St. James Church. Right: Jim, Elliott, and Franklin, Jr. with their spouses at the graveside service in the Rose Garden.*

The Fall-Kill Stream as it enters the pond at Val-Kill.

I remembered something Grandmère had said to me more than once, "You should always be proud of your heritage, but you must live your own life," I began wondering what this heritage, the legacy of Eleanor Roosevelt, would mean to me. My questions were not answered that day as we all gathered in the Rose Garden at Springwood to say our last good-byes to Grandmère as she was placed at rest next to my grandfather's grave. No, no answers, but her death did initiate a quest for me, one that brought me to the decision to write this book. It began merely as a personal journey to learn more about my grandmother and her life, and in so doing to perhaps try to learn more about myself. I did not, *could* not, suspect what lay ahead, nor how long it would take to get there. As I've come to find, there was, in fact, no destination, no point of completion.

As I have sought this greater depth of understanding, trying to distill all of the words I have heard and read over the years into the essence of this remarkable woman, my grandmother, and as I have contemplated the impact she had on so many, many lives throughout her seventy-eight years, the words of Adlai Stevenson have constantly brought perspective and helped me to understand her essence.

> *She was a lady—a lady for all seasons. And like her husband, our immortal leader, she left "a name to shine on the entablatures of truth"—forever...What other human being has touched and transformed the existence of so many...She walked in the slums and ghettos of the world, not on a tour of inspection...but as one who could not feel contentment when others were hungry...Like so many others, I have lost more than a beloved friend. I have lost an inspiration. She would rather light a candle than curse the darkness, and her glow has warmed the world.[4]*

My original quest had a solitary and personal purpose, but as I delved deeper I came to realize that many the world over shared a passionate interest in my grandmother's life. The questions of those I have met over the years inquiring as to what life with her was really like, what made her the person she was, what she has meant to my own life were all questions that have not, perhaps could not, be addressed by the many fine scholarly works about her, for those biographers could not have experienced or seen her through my eyes, the eyes of a grandchild.

Even now, forty years after her death, the curiosity and feelings about her remain strong. Scarcely a week passes that someone does not ask me about her, or relate a story of how she had some impact or influence on their life. And yet for the next generations, those of my children and grandchildren, the interest diminishes and the memories dim, and the personal knowledge that I share with my siblings and cousins of this incredible person, our grandmother, begins to fade. So, if by what I write I can keep the flickering flame of her life and its meaning burning for only one person, if the life of just one reader finds purpose and inspiration in the meaning of hers, then her legacy lives on as a guiding light for future generations, as it has for so many before, and there will be no need to curse the darkness.

My grandparents' gravesite in the Rose Garden at Springwood, which also includes Fala.

PART TWO

Roosevelt.

Born in Another Era

To reach a port, we must sail. Sail, not lie at anchor; sail, not drift!

—B. Hall Roosevelt, Eleanor Roosevelt's brother

ROSES HAVE ALWAYS BEEN AN IMPORTANT symbol of our family's heritage, a Dutch heritage that even today remains strong among many of my cousins and siblings, but perhaps even more so for my grandparents' generation. The symbolism of the rose traces back many centuries, to the very genesis of our name, which means "Field of Roses" in Dutch, suggesting that some distant ancestor perhaps was a farmer of roses or had some other connection to those beautiful flowers. Almost every variation of our family coat of arms, which was adopted as early as the sixteenth or seventeenth century, includes prominent depiction of the rose, usually in a cluster of three. One of the most outstanding and beautiful aspects of the Springwood estate at Hyde Park is the Rose Garden, a vision of exquisite colors and smells in the spring and throughout the summer and fall, now the site where FDR and Eleanor, and even Fala, my grandfather's beloved Scottish terrier, lie in rest.

Most recently, in recognition of this flower's symbolic importance to our family, Her Royal Highness Princess Margriet commissioned a new rose variation, called the "Roosevelt Rose," for the 1997 dedication of the Franklin D. Roosevelt Memorial in Washington, D.C. I first saw this gorgeous new rose,

Opposite: The Roosevelt Family Coat of Arms. My grandfather assigned the colors shown here. Above: Grandmère receives Prince Bernhard and Princess Juliana of The Netherlands on their arrival for their first visit to the White House on April 23, 1942.

bold in size and a vibrant yellow in color, at a reception at the Dutch Embassy two days before the dedication of the memorial, a reception honoring the princess and my family, and of course our Dutch heritage. Upon entering that most impressive embassy building, everyone was enthralled by the thousands upon thousands of roses that had been flown in from Holland for the occasion, roses of every conceivable color in every room. It was an experience that will live with me forever, as will the princess' comments at the dedication itself, in which she remarked on the warm and close relationship between the Dutch people and my family. She recalled that my grandfather had served as her own godfather, and how during and following the war members of their family had always been welcomed into our household.

I think that even today, although there is no longer that personal attachment between our families, there remains an intimacy between my family and the Dutch, witnessed perhaps by the establishment in the late 1980s of the Roosevelt Study Center in Middelburg, the capital of the Province of Zeeland, our ancestral homeland. Created in a partnership between the provincial government, the Franklin and Eleanor Roosevelt Institute, and the Theodore Roosevelt Association, the RSC today serves as the leading education and research center on American history in Europe. Its stature has grown

Her Royal Highness Princess Margriet of The Netherlands and I signing pamphlets at the Inauguration of the FDR Memorial in Washington DC.

to the extent that it was accepted as a member of the Dutch Royal Academy of Arts and Sciences, a most impressive and unique achievement. And it is at the RSC, in every even-numbered year, that the prestigious Four Freedoms Awards are presented to outstanding international leaders, clergy, academicians, and freedom fighters. Indeed, for me and my cousins and siblings, and I hope for the next generations of my family, the binding and resilient relationship with the Netherlands and our Dutch ancestry will be as

*My wife, Michele, and I with
Vice President Al Gore at the Inauguration.*

*christening robes. Franklin even incorpo-
rated the "Roosevelt" three ostrich feath-
ers...into the White House china when
he was President.*

*Some say the Roosevelts were entitled
to coats of arms. Others thought that
they were two steps ahead of the bailiffs
from an island in the Zuider Zee...[1]*

Grandmère always believed that her
extraordinary energy had been inherited from her Dutch forebears:

*My uncle, Theodore Roosevelt, was
known for his remarkable energy. In
fact, he preached the strenuous life and
one of the things I remember in my
youth is hearing something which was
almost a slogan of the day, "Speak soft-
ly but carry a big stick."*

*Where did all this energy and capacity
for work and for play come from? I decided then that back of my uncle Theodore's
family must lie some very healthy, stur-
dy ancestors and when people say to me
today that for a woman of my age I have
extraordinary vitality and energy I am
obliged to point to my ancestors and say that...I must
be grateful to them for handing down to me good
health and capacity to acquire good discipline.[2]*

deeply embedded a source of pride and strength as it
was for my grandmother.

My cousin Alice Roosevelt Longworth
(Theodore Roosevelt's daughter) in her long interviews with Michael Teague that were published in
1981 in his book *Mrs. L,* traces the lineage of the
name and of our ancestry in her inimitable style:

*The name meant "field of roses" in Dutch, so we had
roses in book plates and crested rings. Roosevelt babies
always had cascades of roses tumbling down their*

The correct pronunciation of our name has
often eluded even some of the expert historians of
the Roosevelt family, and I must admit that I remain
shocked at times to hear even the most erudite
biographers continually mispronounce the name.
This has been a point of contention for many years,

The flatlands of the Island of Tholen,
in The Netherlands, believed to be the original birthplace of my ancestors.

as evidenced by a 1903 Letter to the Editor of the *New York Sun,* in which Richard E. Mayne, Chairman of the Department of Reading and Speech Culture of the New York State Teachers Association, chastised then-President Theodore Roosevelt for his own "mispronunciation" of the name. Dr. Mayne stated that, "Perhaps our President does not think as deeply about the matter as academicians do…" To this, our late cousin Robert B. Roosevelt responded in his own letter:

To the Editor of The Sun

Sir: My attention has been called to an amusing letter by Mr. Richard E. Mayne…calling the President to account for the pronunciation of his own name…It is rather a dangerous proceeding to assume that a man does not know how to pronounce his own name, and the writer who attempts not only to criticize but to dictate may find himself in that unhappy position in which "angels fear to tread," even if he be a "chairman of reading and speech culture."

A little culture and even less reading would teach men and might teach the chairman that there is no analogy or usage of pronunciation according to spelling in the English language...As there are readers of your paper who are justifiably anxious to know the proper pronunciation of the President's name, I will explain that it is Dutch. Now, I do not insist that the Dutch language is inherently superior to English...but that language possesses at least one advantage—it has a positive pronunciation. In English when we try to distinguish the long from the short "o" we get into trouble. In Dutch they do not. The double "o" is simply a long "o." The word "Roos" means rose and is pronounced identically the same way under all circumstances and all combinations. So the first syllable of the President's name is "Rose" pure and simple.

But the following "e" like the short German "e" or like the silent French "e" when read in poetry is slightly aspirated. An English analogy is the word "the," a word that our chairman must have come across in his "reading and speech culture." It is not pronounced at all as it is spelt, not like "thee," but with the sort of "the" and a breath stopped by the tongue on the teeth. So the name is "Rose-(uh)-velt"...

Robert B. Roosevelt[3]

Public and Private

For many people in the United States and in other countries as well, Eleanor Roosevelt has been a character of almost mythic stature, one of the most admired and influential people in history, the first First Lady to give definition to that role, the inspiration to and right hand of her husband, the first woman goodwill ambassador to represent the ideals and international policies of this country abroad, and, perhaps most important, a friend to literally millions of people. Her life, both public and private, encompassed momentous times in the history of the United States and the large questions of a society coming to terms with ruptures and change. Her life and career covered that period in American history during which the United States grew from an isolated nation, not only geographically but by national policy, into the most powerful country in the world, the most advanced industrial society, and a nation of great international social conscience.

An official portrait from 1960.
Grandmère always believed that her strength and energy had been inherited from her Dutch forebears.

My grandmother understood that her life was a dense and rich tapestry that wove public history into her personal and intimate world, and whenever and wherever she could she would weave in those precious moments with her family, friends, and most intimate entourage.

Throughout my life I have been asked over and over again, "What was Eleanor Roosevelt *really* like? Who *was* she?" And as one reads the many biographies written about her, it becomes clear that this single individual touched more people during her lifetime, had more influence on the personal lives of men and women, than perhaps any other person in modern history. She was loved and revered by so many, ridiculed and despised by others, and most certainly not always respected for her unwavering beliefs in the innate goodness of humankind. It is documented, for example, that her untiring support of racial issues so angered the extremists in the South that in 1957 the Klu Klux Klan placed its highest bounty ever on her life. But no one, neither historian nor close friend, knew Eleanor as "Grandmère," and no one's lives were influenced in quite the same way as were the lives of her own grandchildren.

Even today, after all these years, there continues to be a high level of interest in Eleanor Roosevelt and her role as a life model for so many. A popular e-mail occasionally appears uncalled for on people's computer screens across the country, sometimes from a friend who has been inspired by the words, sometimes anonymously. Although erroneously attributed to Grandmère, it offers what might well have been her insight on friendship and her unique approach to life:

Grandmère in 1962.

Many people will walk in and out of your life,
But only true friends will leave footprints
in your heart.
To handle yourself, use your head;
To handle others, use your heart.
Anger is only one letter short of danger.
If someone betrays you once, it is his fault;
If he betrays you twice, it is your fault.
Great minds discuss ideas;
Average minds discuss events;

Small minds discuss people.
He who loses money, loses much;
He who loses a friend, loses much more;
He who loses faith, loses all.
Beautiful young people are accidents of nature,
But beautiful old people are works of art.
Learn from the mistakes of others.
You can't live long enough to make
them all yourself.
Friends, you and me...
You brought another friend...
And then there were 3...
We started our group...
Our circle of friends...
And like that circle...
There is no beginning or end...
Yesterday is history.
Tomorrow is mystery.
Today is a gift.

Eleanor Roosevelt continues to be a role model for women in government, for First Ladies, and for young girls who are inspired by her ideals and life's work. But her influence and inspiration are not limited to women; her impact on men has been just as profound. I find it interesting that as I speak with people of all ages in the classrooms of today, it is apparent that they know little about my grandfather but always seem to know of and ask about Eleanor. I have helped many young people write term papers and do projects about Eleanor. A few years ago three young girls from Houston wrote to me asking help on a project they were doing concerning Eleanor for a national essay competition. More recently a fifth-grader wrote seeking any information I could offer on who "your grandmother and grandfather defeated to

become president of the United States" (I explained that only FDR had become president, not Eleanor, which the young girl found hard to believe). And two years ago I had the opportunity to visit several universities in South Korea and to meet with students at each, and still the same questions, the intense interest in Eleanor. I spent hours talking with these young Korean students, trying as best I could to explain who, in my own life, Eleanor Roosevelt was. Why does this great interest endure? I can't say for certain, but perhaps, just maybe, she epitomizes perhaps the best the world has to offer and thus becomes everyone's grandmother. Yes, at times I know that my siblings, cousins, and I share our grandmother with thousands if not millions of others.

As different as we all may be, as divergent as our paths in life, the members of our family share the fact that our lives were shaped in so many ways by a single force: Anna Eleanor Roosevelt. Some of the greatest joys of my life have been the family gatherings where we would listen to and share the individual stories, remembrances, and anecdotes of Grandmère. And so it is my intent to share in this book the force that was Grandmère, neither as a historical biography nor scholarly treatise, for I claim to be neither historian nor scholar, but rather as a personal perspective of her life and work. It is my intent to chronicle her life and accomplishments as well as some of those indelible circumstances of her childhood, marriage, and continuing evolution throughout her years that came to bear on her inner self. Many assume that Grandmère's life was a product of her own making, but I believe she was driven by external circumstances over which she had little control but which together formed the psyche of this most incredible individual.

A Family's Deliverance

I have heard it said that we are all the sum product of our heritage, and that in many respects we become that which those before us have instilled. For Eleanor Roosevelt I think that may well hold true, and certainly for the generations of Roosevelts since. Although not universally, the majority of my family has been raised with a sense of duty and obligation, whether to serve our nation in some governmental or political capacity, or merely through civic responsibility and volunteerism. For some, their life paths have led them into professions in the charitable sector, while others have pursued careers in business and numerous others have served in government positions. But whatever their callings, most have contributed generously of their time to causes for the betterment of their communities and society.

In an interview with Joe Lash, Grandmère's close friend and biographer, my cousin Alice Roosevelt Longworth said that politics and social duty were for our family a way of life, even though she seemed to be the exception to the rule:

> Politics were always being talked about at Sagamore (Theodore Roosevelt's home at Oyster Bay, New York). Eleanor Roosevelt would have heard politics there. She was a do-gooder and they started a junior league group. She got that from my grandfather whose interest in charity took with Eleanor but not with me. I never did those things; they bored me.[4]

For me personally, I think it was a legacy passed from Grandmère, one learned by the example of her own inspiring life of giving, that compelled my interest and professional path in philanthropy. Indeed, one of Eleanor's earliest recollections was of being taken by her father, my great-grandfather Elliott, to the Newsboys Thanksgiving dinner in New York, an annual engagement that confirmed her family's commitment to young people whose unequal fortune, circumstance, and education had landed them inside institutions. Her paternal grandfather, Theodore Roosevelt Sr., had always been devoted to the causes of social welfare, public concern for poverty, and philanthropic enterprises—relatively novel charitable ideals for the fashionable and wealthy set of New York in the 1800s—and he involved his own children and grandchildren in his activities of taking responsibility for those of lesser means.

Grandmère inherited her grandfather's "troublesome conscience," a conscience that at times would put him at odds with those of his own class. He helped found the Museum of Natural History, the Metropolitan Museum of Art, and the Children's Aid Society; helped start the Orthopedic Hospital; and was considered one of the most significant philanthropists of his day, contributing substantial amounts to the city's many charities. That social conscience became in Grandmère's own adult years a powerful character trait and a potent force in her life work.

Merchants and patriots who count themselves among America's oldest families, the Roosevelts first settled in Manhattan in 1647, when Claes Martenszen van Rosenvelt (Nicholas son of Martin of the Rose Field), with his wife, Jannetje, arrived from Holland and landed in New Amsterdam, then the tiny Dutch settlement of eight hundred hardy citizens at the foot of Manhattan Island. It is unclear exactly why Claes and Jannetje left the Netherlands to embark upon the long and

Claes Martenszen van Rosenvelt, c. 1613,
the first of our ancestors to settle in New Amsterdam in 1647.

Hall among the coats of arms of the region's fifteen most prominent families. As President Theodore Roosevelt described them, "our very common ancestors" were people of the land, teachers, clerics, and even an "inspector of the dikes" (an obviously important position given the village's below-sea-level location).

The first documentation of our family in New Amsterdam appears in the baptismal records of the Dutch Reformed Church, which records the baptism of Claes and Jannetje's first child, a boy named Christaen, on October 23, 1650. By this time, however, Claes had already established himself as a farmer; his forty-eight-acre farm adjoining the *bouwery* of the dictatorial wooden-legged governor of New Amsterdam, Peter Stuyvesant. Although Christaen died in infancy, the van Rosevelts had five more children, four daughters and a son. In 1659 Claes died, leaving Jannetje to raise their four existing children and pregnant with the fifth, Anna. Jannetje did not long survive the birth of this child, for official records show that on December 10, 1660, the welfare of the van Rosevelt children was entrusted to the "orphanmasters," as was the custom under Dutch law.

Despite Jannetje's sad fate, New York City became a home and a place of prosperity for her children and the generations of Roosevelts who descended from them. Like her ancestors, Grandmère loved New York, having lived in the city as a child and as a young woman, returned there from her European education, and as my grandfather's bride. She continued to maintain a home in Manhattan until the end of her life. She found that New York City reflected the values and passions dearest to her heart:

treacherous trek to New Amsterdam, for Holland at the time was enjoying a "Golden Age" of prosperity and culture. Claes' family had been established farmers and respected citizens of, we believe, the small village of Oud-Vossemeer on the island of Tholen. It is here, in the south of Holland at the mouth of the Rhine River, and in the provincial capital of Zeeland, Middelburg, that reference is made to the family Rosevelt (or Rosenvelt, among other variations) and recognition given in the Town

Whoever seeks artistic and intellectual stimulation (whoever hungers for knowledge and beauty) can find it in New York, in the masterpieces of sculpture in the Museum of Modern Art, in the treasure of past civilizations at the Museum of Natural History, in the expressions from other times at the Metropolitan Museum, in the exhibits of New York's Heritage at the Museum of the City of New York; in the schools and in our universities, in the words stored in our libraries, in the medieval masterpieces at the Cloisters. Out of the hustle and bustle, often from within the very center of industry, rise the spires of many faiths. Here men, women, and children of every religion worship in peace and dignity and mutual respect and understanding.

Some place in New York is a bit of every land on earth (Mott Street, Mulberry Street, Delancey Street, Yorkville) but New York claims them all as its own. The old is mingled with the new and the new is wiser for the old. New York today is the home of peoples of all nations (a living demonstration of racial brotherhood, a permanent example of a United

Nations) the pragmatic approach to one world. It represents to men in all lands a symbol of what can be achieved by the human spirit when it is unterrified. For New York is the greatest community of human endeavor on earth. Here are people from the cotton belt and the corn belt (each with ambition), writers, engineers, artists (actors, doctors, students, bankers, lawyers), among them the potential of the present for the great of the future.

New York is a small island where the tall skyscrapers, rising from the sea, pierce the atmosphere and silhouette the blue skies which blanket our churches, our cathedrals, our synagogues. It is a city of 8 million striving for sanctuary, sustenance, inspiration, fulfillment. Here are people of every race and creed and nationality to whom New York is home, haven and hope.

This is My New York City.[5]

Claes' grandsons, the brothers Johannes and Jacobus, took the family into real estate opportunity by purchasing land in the Beekman Swamp, an enterprise that was to have lasting financial effect on their own family and the city's fortune. It was Johannes and Jacobus who are credited with starting the two branches of the family that would eventually be known as the Oyster Bay (descended from Johannes) and Hyde Park (descended from Jacobus) Roosevelts. Of course, most recent history ascribes the two sides as being the "TR side" and the "FDR side." Jacobus' son Isaac is often referred to as the first Roosevelt, since he conducted business in English rather than in the Dutch the family had spoken until the mid-1700s.

Over the ensuing centuries the Roosevelt family prospered, at times marrying distant relatives

Ivory miniatures of Isaac Roosevelt (1726-1794) by James Peale, and of his wife Maria Eliza Wolfon Roosevelt (1760-1794) by Robert Fielding. Isaac, also called "The Patriot," was second in the line of the Hyde Park Roosevelts. Opposite: A view of Manhattan in the 19th century, when my family thrived in the fast-growing city.

37

Roosevelt Point, named after our family, in the Hudson River Valley.

within the two branches, and became the solid, trustworthy burghers of that rapidly growing city that led the way in the cycle of economic boom and expansion on the American continent. In the seventeenth century the Dutch patrons, or gentry, were granted large estates of land throughout the Hudson Valley, and it was remnants of these early land grants made to members of Sara Delano's family (FDR's mother) and the Livingstons (Eleanor's side) that established the strong tradition of Roosevelts along the Hudson River. At one time the Livingston portion, which included the 1730s estate Claremont of Chancellor Robert R. Livingston, stretched for more than fourteen miles along the shores of the Hudson.

For Grandmère, the Hudson River Valley held an almost spiritual significance; it was a place where she could find herself again and take respite from the chaos of the world and the never-ending stream of activities in her public life. So much of her, and indeed of my grandfather, could be traced back to the idyllic and significant times they spent on the banks of the great river as children and then as husband and wife, president and First Lady, or simply as Eleanor and Franklin. My father explained the emotional significance that the valley held for Grandmère:

The Hudson River Valley was extremely important to her because after Mother was orphaned at the age of

An 1870 painting of the Hudson River and its highlands by George Harvey.
It reflects the beauty and serenity of the setting that both my grandparents would always call "home."

A view of Hyde Park in the winter, when it became a setting
of many winter sports for both FDR and Grandmère as children, as well as for us later as young children.

twelve, she spent all her springs, summers, and falls up at Tivoli. That became really her childhood home. She associated her youth with the Hudson River Valley and the Livingstons and all the people that lived in the Rheinbeck-Barrytown-Tivoli area. Of course, the Livingstons were cousins of hers, and her ancestors on the Livingston side had been very important in the early parts of American history in this valley.... The Hudson River Valley was extremely important to my mother's "psyche,"...

That's why she started the Val-Kill Industries with Nancy Cook and her friend Marion Dickerman. She built the Stone Cottage over at Val-Kill as a hide-

away where she could get away and she could relax. Father built that house for her; it was his design and his selection of a spot. He also built the swimming pool over there, and that became a favorite place for their children and even Father to go when they were having a picnic or something of that nature.[6]

Her paternal grandmother was Martha Bulloch, a dark-haired Southern belle who had greatly impressed the antebellum society of Savannah, Georgia, with her vivacity, good looks, flirtatious ways, and audacity in horsemanship. The courtship of Theodore and Martha (Mittie, as she was known) began in 1850 with the arrival of a young Theodore at the Bulloch Hall plantation in Roswell, Georgia for a social visit with the Bulloch family. During his visit, however, his attentions focused more and more on the fifteen-year-old blue-eyed brunette daughter of his hosts, James and Martha (Stewart) Bulloch. Although it would not be until May 1853 that Theodore and Mittie would be together again in Philadelphia, it was obvious that Theodore had left his heart in Georgia on that first visit. Within a month of their reunion he had proposed marriage, a proposal accepted without hesitation by Mittie. When she married Theodore Sr. later that same year, Martha rapidly became one of the five or six leading women of New York society whose manners and civic activities were an inspiration for other hostesses of the day. Theodore and Martha had four children: Anna, born in 1855; Theodore Jr., born in 1858 and who was to become the president of the United States; Elliott, born in 1860; and Corinne, born in 1861. Theodore Sr. and Martha became instant and prominent members of New York's Knickerbocker society and active participants in the city's thriving banking, business, and civic community.

Cousin Alice never met her grandmother, but remembered stories about her being told by her grandfather Theodore Sr. and her father, Theodore:

My grandfather Roosevelt's marriage to my Southern grandmother introduced some new blood, and the subsequent conflicts between the Dutch, New England, and "Georgia cracker" sides of our personalities have been rewarding.

...From her pictures, and from what little I learned from Auntie Bye, she was extremely beautiful, with great charm of manner when she wanted to exercise it. She also seems to have been moody, tempera-

mental, and, like most hypochondriacs, she enjoyed poor health. One heard stories of her covered with veils and dust coat venturing forth in the summer heat and with cuffs of brown paper to prevent even the slightest speck of dust besmirching her. ...I know very little about her except one of her Bulloch ancestors was the first president of the Provincial Congress of Georgia.[7]

Of all the examples provided by Grandmère's forebears in establishing her own life philosophy, perhaps the one most apparent is provided by her grandfather Theodore in a letter to his daughter Corinne: "Remember that almost everyone will be kind to you and love you if you are willing to receive their love and are unselfish. This, you know, is the virtue that I put above all others and, while it increases so much the enjoyment of those about you, it adds infinitely to your own pleasure." Theodore had a strong sense of personal obligation to society, one passed along to his children and grandchildren alike, and this sense of obligation was perhaps most pronounced throughout the life of his granddaughter Eleanor.

All four children of Mittie and Theodore were quite remarkable in their own right, the most notable of course being TR Jr. Anna, the eldest daughter, assumed from a young age a controlling role in the family, encouraging the boys' lives and ambitions, and once they were all grown up became a font of wisdom for both TR and Elliott, and later for *their* daughters Alice and Eleanor, who called her Auntie Bye. In recognition of Bye's influence in their lives and in those of other family members, both women would later agree that had Bye been a man, she would have been president, not TR. Eleanor said of both her aunts, Auntie Bye and

Auntie Corinne, that they were "two women never to be forgotten, whose influence will live as long as any of us who knew them can transmit to later generations a quality which we hope will long be preserved in our family."[8]

But it was my great-grandfather Elliott, Grandmère's father, who was often described as the most lovable of all the Roosevelts. When writing about her father almost forty years after his death, Grandmère stated that her father had been "the one great love of my life as a child; and in fact like many children I have lived a dream life with him; so his memory is still a vivid, living thing to me."[9]

The Roosevelt children were all schooled at home, as was the custom in such families of position, and when Elliott was nine Theodore took the entire family on a twelve-month grand tour of Europe, followed the next year by an even more extended journey to Egypt, then regarded as part of the Ottoman Empire, the Holy Land, and southeastern and central Europe. Such extended travels were not uncommon among the wealthy of the time, but were seen as a natural extension of the children's education. Indeed, they opened the young Roosevelt children to a world of culture, the arts, and languages, and created in my great-grandfather a fascination with foreign cultures, a fascination that was unquestionably inherited by his daughter.

I should interject here that throughout her life Grandmère traveled extensively the world over and, in her later years, whenever possible, she would include one or more of her grandchildren on these trips. These were exciting opportunities for my generation, since we not only experienced firsthand many exotic places but were often in the company of some of the world's foremost leaders.

Above: *My great grandfather, Elliott Roosevelt, with his dogs.*
Opposite: *My cousin Nina Roosevelt with Abba Schwartz when they accompanied Grandmère on her trip to Israel in March 1959.*

Everywhere she went, Grandmère was not only immediately recognized but also usually treated with great deference and respect. While she might have desired a bit less notoriety on her travels, we of course thought the attention accorded was tremendous! My sister, Chandler, remembers that Grandmère would be regularly stopped by everyday people on the street who would talk to her as if she were a friend who would understand their problems:

In 1959 my cousin Nina, my uncle John's eldest daughter, accompanied Grandmère on a trip to Israel and Iran, and she remembers it as a tremendous educational experience for a girl in her teenage years:

> ...she seemed to really enjoy sharing things with me in a teacher kind of relationship, particularly on our trip to the Middle East. She would ask questions of other people (to) which I knew very well she knew the answers, but she wanted it said for my benefit, which is a perfect teacher kind of way of doing things because you don't tell your pupil everything. Then she would share feelings about things with me...She would point things out for me to look at. I'm sure she knew how valuable reading aloud is for one's education. Of course, at the time I didn't know; I thought she was doing it just to amuse us, and she certainly did. When I got older I realized it does wonders for your attention span...For instance, on the Fourth of July she would read the Declaration of Independence. She would often send clippings that were particularly appropriate for something. If you were talking to her about something, she would then suggest a book to read. She had me read Exodus before I went to Israel...So there was definitely the teacher about her, which was fun.[11]

I remember on (a) trip and in New York City also the many people who would stop her in stores and on the street and tell her of some personal problem...She would devote her complete attention to them and ask that they please write her and that she would do what she could. She had just an amazing interest in other people, particularly in difficulties they might have. But abroad people would come up to her. I didn't have the feeling at all during the war that other people were grateful for the part our country had played in the war, but all through Europe I remember people coming up and saying, "You don't know what your husband meant to us."[10]

But back to my great-grandfather. It was in 1873, upon returning from one of the grand tours, while TR Jr. was preparing for his entrance into Harvard, that Elliott began to suffer severe headaches and dizzy spells. He had wanted to go to school at St. Paul's, an exclusive New England preparatory school, but his father, concerned over Elliott's health, sent the young man abroad and then to the South for two months in the hopes that the outdoor life would strengthen his constitution. Although homesick, Elliott's health *did* improve, and upon his return he entered St. Paul's in September of 1875. Soon, however, the pressure of school and studies affected his health, and in a letter to his father, whom he called Private, he reported recurring bouts of headaches and nosebleeds...early signs of an affliction that would forever mar his life.

> Private
>
> Yesterday during my Latin lesson without the slightest warning I had a bad rush of blood to my head, it hurt me so that I can't remember what happened. I believe I screamed out, anyway the Doctor brought me over to his house and I lay down for a couple of hours; it had by that time recovered and after laying down all afternoon I was able to go on with my afternoon studies...It had left me rather nervous and therefore homesick and unhappy. But I am all well so don't worry about me. I took some anti-nervous medicine, and I would like the receipt of more...
>
> P.S. Don't forget me please and write often.
> Love from Ellie[12]

Doctors could not seem to agree on the nature of Elliott's seizures, and because his father believed that the best cure was to lead a physically active and Spartan lifestyle, the sixteen-year-old was packed off to Fort McKavett, the well-known frontier outpost in Texas that was home to the famous all-black "Buffalo Soldiers" cavalry troop. Here he learned to shoot, ride, and camp and was generally enthralled by legends from the Mexican War days and stories of Indian skirmishes. The rugged life suited young Elliott, who would develop a love of horses and riding and later become an accomplished polo player,

sailor, and adventurer. But soon after his return to New York, Theodore Sr. fell gravely ill with what was later diagnosed as colon cancer. His youngest son displayed a supreme devotion to his father and tended to him every day until his eventual death on February 10, 1878, at the young age of forty-six.

The death of a father is a devastating tragedy for any child, but for young Elliott, so sensitive and dependent upon his father's towering strength, love, and support, this loss further ruptured his already weakened sense of direction and inner stability. Realizing that his elder brother, Teddy, would soon graduate from Harvard and return home to assume the reins as head of the family, and in part as a drastic measure to curb his own rapidly addictive drinking habit, my great-grandfather decided to undertake an expedition to India, that magic land of mystery, to hunt tigers from astride an elephant and pursue the elusive ibex and the markhor, the fabled animals living in the Himalayan region.

India during the time of the British Raj was a country full of fascinations and contradictions for a young American adventurer. Elliott puzzled mightily over some aspects of British rule of this enchanted land, and yet not so much that it hindered his ability to enjoy English pastimes in the leisurely afternoons of the Orient, playing tennis and polo, hunting, and encountering for the first time knowledge of an ancient culture so alien to his own. It was while he was away on this adventure that his brother, Theodore Jr., secured election as an assemblyman from the Brownstone District of New York City and wrote his first book, *The Naval War of 1812*. When Elliott returned from India he was expected to find a direction for his life and to

My great-grandfather Elliott, the first seated on the left, with his riding club in 1885.

begin work in one of Manhattan's business institutions, to settle down and put aside his penchant to roam the world on endless adventures. And soon a very special person would enter his life, someone both he and his entire family hoped would help him find contentment even as she might provide the mainstay for the fulfillment of his destiny.

Elliott and Anna

My grandmother remembers her mother as the most beautiful woman she ever saw. (It was said of Anna's beauty that the poet Robert Browning once asked only to gaze upon my great-grandmother as she sat for a portrait.) Anna Rebecca Hall, the eldest of four of the day's most stunning debutantes, was descended from two of New York's most eminent and aristocratic families, the Livingstons and Ludlows, whose Tivoli estate on the banks of the Hudson River had been originally deeded to them by Charles II, James II, and George I. Anna's imperious mother, Elizabeth Livingston Ludlow, married Valentine G. Hall, a member of one of the wealthiest mercantile families in the nation. My great-grandmother's childhood can only be described as gothic, austere, and solemn. While her mother could be considered cold and aloof, her father was a fanatically religious despot who ruled the family with an irascible temper and an absolute iron fist. Tyrannical as he may have been, however, he had trained his eldest daughter well, for upon her father's death when she was seventeen, Anna, and not her mother, assumed full responsibility for the family's well-being.

Above, left: *My great-grandmother Anna Rebecca Hall.* Center: *Her father Valentine G. Hall.* Right: *Her mother Elizabeth Livingston Ludlow.* Opposite: *Cameo portraits of the four beautiful Hall sisters. Anna Rebecca is on the left of the first photograph.*

Grandmère would recall that although her parents' families shared the noble privileges of their class, their moral goals were drastically different:

My father, Elliott Roosevelt, charming and good-look-ing, loved by all who came in contact with him, had a background and upbringing which were alien to my mother's pattern...I doubt that the background of their respective lives could have been more different. His family was not so much concerned with Society (spelled with a big S) as with people, and these people includ-ed the newsboys from the streets of New York and the cripples whom Dr. Schaefer, one of the most noted early orthopedic surgeons, was trying to cure.[13]

Indeed, since the death of Theodore Sr., his four children had upheld the social values, bringing cred-it to him and the family name and partly responsible for earning them all a reputation as "do-gooders," a characteristic that although foreign to Anna seemed to make Elliott all the more attractive to her.

Since my great-grandparents were members of a gracious and elegant society that resembled a small social island, and whose members were in one way or another connected to either the Roosevelts or the Halls, it was almost assured that at some point they would connect. The tall, handsome Elliott was a frequent houseguest at Springwood (the James Roosevelt estate at Hyde Park) and Algonac (the Delano estate), and it was on one of these visits that he met the beautiful nineteen-year-old Anna

The Hall family playing tennis in 1890. Socially prominent, the Hall sisters were trained in all the fashionable sports of their time. Opposite, above: Portrait of my great grandmother Anna at the time she met my great-grandfather. Below: Elliott and Anna Roosevelt in St. Moritz, Switzerland, during their honeymoon.

Rebecca. Immediately smitten, he described her as "a tall slender fair-haired little beauty—just out and a great belle." Soon thereafter, at a Memorial Day house party given by Laura Delano, sister of Mrs. James Roosevelt (FDR's mother, Sara), the couple became engaged to much outpouring of excitement and affection.

The *New York Herald* described their wedding ceremony at Calvary Church on December 1, 1892, as "one of the most brilliant social events of the season...The bride was every bit a queen and her bridesmaids were worthy of her." Being ever practical, if not impetuous, rather than diamonds as a wedding present my great-grandfather gave his new bride a small coupe automobile, something she could drive around town from social engagement to engagement. Since women driving cars was viewed as a novelty to say the least, Anna's adventuresome nature most surely endeared her even further to Elliott and his family. Following their wedding, the

young couple quickly settled into the life of New York society, a life the newspapers called "the swells." A bit reluctantly perhaps (for it was difficult giving up the life of a bon vivant), my great-grandfather secured work with the Ludlow firm, New York's premier real estate establishment, conveniently owned by his wife's relatives. His young bride likewise settled right in, ordering her fashions from Palmers in London and Worth in Paris. When she would lunch at a club, it immediately became the fashionable place for social gatherings. Indeed, their life became a whirlwind of parties and late-night cotillions, the opera, and a multitude of grand rituals on the seasonal New York social scene. And, of course, attendance at the polo matches and horse races at Meadowbrook on Long Island, Bar Harbor, and Newport were an integral part of their life. Anna's striking beauty made her an absolute trophy for any man, and Elliott's ability to entertain with tales of his varied adventures made the young couple much sought after. As one friend said of Elliott, "If personal popularity could have bestowed public honors on any man, there was nothing beyond the reach of Elliott Roosevelt."

In early 1884 Anna became pregnant with Eleanor, and frail of health she took to bed for much of the summer. Her pregnancy was cause for concern and anxiety throughout the family, for Theodore Jr.'s wife, Alice Lee, had died just two days following the birth of baby Alice. Finally, after months of close attention, Eleanor was born on October 11, 1884, without complications and to everyone's great relief. No one in the family was more moved or elated by Eleanor's birth than was her father. As she would write many years later, she had been to her father "...a miracle from heaven."[14]

Grandmère as a very young girl.
Opposite: *With her father Elliott and her brother Elliott, Jr.*

As I look back, I think probably the factor which influenced me most
in my early years was an avid desire, even before I was aware of what I was doing,
to experience all I could as deeply as I could.

Eleanor's Childhood

Certain moments of childhood lodge in one's memory, sometimes for incongruous reasons, perhaps their beauty or drama, and their continued influence upon our lives is as persistent as it is unaccountable. For Eleanor, her relationship with her mother was a sum of many such moments, remembered with a certain grief for all of her years. It established a basis, I think, for that driving desire she carried throughout life to help and please others.

Rather than a joyous occasion, Anna's pregnancy was marred by fear, anxiety, and depression.

The postpartum death of Theodore Roosevelt's wife, Alice Lee, certainly wasn't reassuring for a nervous first-time young mother like Anna. Alice Lee had contracted nephritis (Bright's disease), which had gone unnoticed during her pregnancy but ended her life on February 12, 1884. To compound the family's loss, Elliott and Theodore's mother, Martha Bulloch Roosevelt, suddenly died of typhoid fever only hours after Alice Lee. Both deaths were an abysmal blow to the family, plunging both Theodore and Elliott into deep grief. These were the distressing conditions in which Anna began her first term of pregnancy.

Eleanor's birth in October was a ray of light for the family, but perhaps not for her own mother. It is difficult to conceive why a young mother doesn't immediately bond with her baby girl from the moment she lays eyes on her; perhaps Anna was simply too young and ill prepared for the responsibilities of motherhood. What is certain is she did not assume that most basic womanly destiny until the births of her two sons, Elliott and Grace Hall, some years later.

Winston Churchill, who became a close friend to both FDR and Grandmère during the White House years, once said, "Famous men are usually the product of an unhappy childhood." So much has been written and conjectured about the effect of Grandmère's childhood on her life that there can be little question that it was difficult. Her description of herself as a child is telling: "I was usually shy and frightened because I lived an entirely lonely life…."[15]

Eleanor's childhood was polarized from the beginning between the dismissive and unforgiving world of my great-grandmother and the outgoing adventurous life of her father. Anna had been brought up in cold severity, virtue, and discipline within a family that disapproved of emotional displays, and these were the qualities she sought to impart to her baby girl. Elliott, on the other hand, adored his baby daughter and from the beginning bonded with her in intense warmth and joy. From the moment he laid eyes upon his baby girl, she became the instant focal point of his love and adoration—and he of Eleanor's.

This conflicting emotional climate was to deeply influence and affect the psyche of Grandmère for the rest of her life. A powerful psychological

triangle was formed between her, her loving father, and her dismissive mother. This strange pattern of emotional, sometimes painful magnetism between her and two other people would seem to repeat itself over and again throughout her life and in her closest relationships.

Largely left to the care of nannies, when Eleanor was with either parent she became entwined in two quite different if not polarizing sets of emotions. Anna was disappointed that her baby daughter had not inherited her own physical beauty, and often was heard to refer to Eleanor as "Granny" and to ridicule her in the little girl's presence.

Grandmère in 1888 posing for a portrait.

Cousin Alice would remember Grandmère's early life as being difficult:

Poor Eleanor!... She had a miserable childhood, which I don't think she ever got over. There was her exquisite, empty-headed mother, Anna Hall, who was one of the most beautiful women of her time. She was rather mean to Eleanor. She called her "Granny" and made her feel unwanted and unattractive. Eleanor had also two very pretty Hall aunts and a hateful grandmother. Then there was her father, my Uncle Ellie, who was the black sheep of the family.[16]

As a consequence, Eleanor became a shy and timid little girl, quiet and extremely introverted, with few friends her own age and no apparent talents. Anna was cool and distant throughout her daughter's childhood, almost to the point of neglect. In her later years Grandmère seldom spoke of her mother, except to comment on her beauty and vivaciousness. Her father, though, was quite another thing. To describe Elliott Roosevelt is difficult without perhaps providing an erroneous portrayal. His physical maladies, which began early in his teen years and only intensified later, drove him to seek relief in many ways. It is well documented that he developed alcoholism at a young age, and that his headaches and other complications were treated with an abundance of morphine and other drugs, which in that day were commonly prescribed painkilling medicines. Use of alcohol and drugs to ease his pain became dependencies in short order and remained so throughout his brief life. These dependencies, in turn, led to other less admirable traits; extended periods of absence from family, philandering, and eventually an imposed exile from his wife and family for "treatment."

Again, Alice remembered her uncle Ellie as a source of worries for TR and her aunts Bye and Corinne:

There was this attractive and intelligent young man who ruined himself with drink. He was considered far more promising than my father when young, but once he started hitting the bottle his slide downhill was spectacular. Conversation about Uncle Ellie and his problems was frequent when I was young. I could tell because it would stop when I entered the room. Apparently he had a form of epilepsy, which obviously wasn't helped by the drinking. I have vague recollections of him, usually fast-moving ones. He would take one for walks as a child and would set off at such a pace that one's feet barely touched the ground.[17]

There is an often repeated story that Elliott's "forgetfulness" and lack of concentration also extended to the way he treated his own daughter: he once abandoned little Eleanor at the door of the Knickerbocker Club for several hours while he was inside enjoying an extended bout of drinking with his cronies. Although one shudders at the thought of such an episode, and perhaps it has been inflated, it probably did occur. Eleanor, a child deprived of motherly attention, drew from her father's admiration all the tenderness she so desperately needed, and so could perhaps too easily forgive his recklessness.

Grandmère's love of her father would translate into a psychological imprint that would later be projected into several intimate relationships, most strongly in her marriage to Grandfather. The flirtatious, debonair, socially brilliant male would later return and evoke in her simultaneous and powerful feelings of love and rejection.

For Anna, it must have been trying to find herself in the grips of a marriage that brought little emotional and psychological security. She balanced her husband's excesses with her more staid and reserved nature, but even so her everyday life was curtailed and conflicted by his recklessness and addictions. But in spite of everything, throughout their entire marriage she remained an amazingly resilient, dedicated, loving wife, wanting only to see her husband recovered from his dependencies and returned to the fold of the family. However, the situation imposed tremendous strain on the familial relationship, and most especially on my great-grandmother's relationship with her daughter.

The most effective way to relate the depth of feeling Grandmère held for her father is by her

GRANDMÈRE, A PERSONAL HISTORY OF ELEANOR ROOSEVELT

own words. In 1932 Grandmère lovingly compiled a collection of letters written by her father commencing in 1873, when he was but thirteen years old. Her introduction to that work, *Hunting Big Game in the Eighties,* accurately reflects the depth and complexity of her feelings for my great-grandfather:

About 1894 a little girl of nine was studying her lessons in an old-fashioned New York City house. The house belonged to her grandmother, Mrs. Valentine G. Hall, and this little girl with her small brothers had come to live there when their mother, Mrs. Elliott Roosevelt, had died.

On this particular day there was a suppressed excitement in every movement of the child. She expected the person that she loved best in the world to come and see her...Suddenly she heard his voice and she fled and found herself in the arms of a rather young-looking, very charming man still in the early thirties. This man was my father, Elliott Roosevelt; the little girl was, as you have guessed, myself.

...My brother was just a baby when my father died and I was only ten years old. He never accomplished anything which could make him of any importance to the world at large, unless a personality which left a vivid mark on friends and associates may be counted important...He was the one great love of my life as a child, and in fact like many children I lived a dream life with him; so his memory is still a vivid, living thing to me.

...Of course, whatever I tell you of his childhood is entirely from hearsay, but there are one or two stories which have been told to me by other members of the family which I feel should be an introduction...because they indicate the way in which a character unfolds and grows...

Elliott, at the age of seven, went out to walk one day in a new overcoat and he returned without it. On being questioned, he admitted that he had seen a small and ragged urchin who looked cold, and he had removed his new coat and given it to him. I can think of many occasions in his later life when generosity of the same kind actuated him, not, perhaps, to wise giving, for unlike some people he never could learn to control his heart by his head. With him the heart always dominated.[18]

Grandmère's first nurse was French, and because her mother believed that it was essential to study languages, Grandmère spoke French before English. Indeed, she spoke the language as if she had been born to it, and throughout her life she often spoke French with friends and family members while at Val-Kill.

In 1887, when Eleanor was three, her father became disinterested in his business pursuits and resigned from the Ludlow firm, deciding that an extended trip abroad would restore his health and outlook. In May of that year, Elliott embarked for Europe on the *Britannic,* accompanied by Anna, little Eleanor and her nurse, and Anna's sister Tissie. During the crossing, an incoming ship called *Celtic* rammed their ship in the fog. The collision was severe, with the *Celtic* slanting a blow that penetrated her nose into the *Britannic* a full ten feet. Some passengers were killed and many were injured, and the whole ship was thrown into wild confusion and utter panic as people attempted to board lifeboats. Eleanor was picked up by a stranger, who lowered her into the outstretched arms of my great-grandfather standing in a lifeboat below. This terrible event became so indelibly etched in Grandmère's psyche that she never lost her fear of the sea. Eventually the *Celtic* picked up the passengers of the *Britannic,* and it sailed back to New York. Once recovered, everyone was ready to set off for Europe again—everyone, that is, but Grandmère. There was absolutely no way of convincing little Eleanor to go with them. With the terrible ordeal fresh in her mind, she simply refused, despite her father's pleas. And so my great-grandparents decided to leave her behind to spend the summer with her aunt and uncle. Not only had Eleanor been traumatized by her sea experience, but her parents had abandoned her for reasons she could not begin to comprehend at the age of three.

At the end of the summer, Grandmère's parents returned to New York, and her father settled at his uncle Gracie's banking and brokerage firm in an attempt to bring his family and his own life back into order. He began the building project of a large, patrician house at Hempstead on Long Island that he intended as their summer retreat, a happy place for Eleanor, as she would be able to play there with her cousin Alice, who was her same age. But the two girls were very different in temperament: While Eleanor was shy and introverted, Alice was bold, self-assured, and as competitive as her father.

Throughout their lives, what developed early on as differences in personality and temperament between the two would continue, and as Grandmère began to emerge as a more assured person in her own right, the chasm between them broadened, perhaps accentuated during Eleanor's eventual courtship with Franklin. Nevertheless, TR and his family provided a safe haven for Eleanor, and the older brother was a constant and steadying

Edith Kermit Roosevelt Carow,
TR's beloved wife.

influence on Elliott. Teddy had become a seasoned statesman, having served three terms in the New York State Assembly. Though he was distraught by the deaths of his wife and mother, his interest in politics remained keen, and in 1886, at the beckon of New York City Republican Party leaders, he ran for mayor. Following what he considered an appropriate period of mourning for Alice, and desperately yearning for a wife and a continuation of his family life, Theodore married a longtime family friend, the genteel Edith Carow.

55

The TR clan.

Although handed the nomination of the party, TR was under no illusions about his chances of winning the election, but noted, "at least I have a better party standing than ever before…" As anticipated, he was soundly defeated, but by a margin far greater than even he expected. Undaunted, Theodore set about to establish himself at his imposing Sagamore Hill home with his new wife and adored daughter, Alice. In short order, Theodore and Edith added to their family with the births of Theodore Jr. (1887), Kermit (1889), Ethel (1891), Archibald (1894), and Quentin (1897). TR loved spending time and playing with his children and, in sharp contrast to Eleanor's unhappy family life, this side of the family seemed cemented by a solidarity of love and strong relationships. Indeed, life at Sagamore Hill could appear to an outsider rather raucous and unruly, especially when TR was in residence.

Meanwhile, Elliott's fresh beginnings were as idyllic as they were short-lived, for he once again succumbed to the roller coaster of drinking, partying, and polo playing, causing great distress not only to his wife but to TR and the rest of the family. But the fall and winter of 1888 were the last few months in which Eleanor would endure being an only child, for in 1888 her mother became pregnant again. Elliott Jr. was born in October 1889, an event that prompted Eleanor's first letter to her father, written while she was exiled at her grandmother's house during Anna's convalescence:

Grandmère with her brothers Elliott Jr. and Gracie Hall.

Dear Father:

I hope you are well and Mother too. I hope little brother doesn't cry and if he does tell the nurse to give him a tap tap. How does he look? Some people tell me he looks like an elephant and some say he is like a bunny. I told Aunt Pussie today she would be very unhappy if she were a man because his wife would send her downtown every day she could only come home on Sunday and then she would have to go to church. Goodby now dear Father, write me soon another letter. I love you very much and Mother and Brother too, if he has blue eyes.

My great-grandparents were ecstatic with the new addition, but Eleanor never sensed any diminishing in her father's affection. In comments made in the collection of letters in *Hunting Big Game in the Eighties,* Grandmère confirmed her father's constancy of affection toward her: "He loved to give and tried always to find just the thing which would rejoice the heart of the one receiving his gift. You always felt somehow surrounded by his thought and love and that you made him grateful by accepting it."

Despite the happy birth of Elliott Jr., by 1890 Grandmère's family began to disintegrate. Elliott's alcoholism had become more pronounced, and in another attempt to hold the family together, he set off once again with Anna, Eleanor, and baby Elliott for yet another tour of Europe. Anna, who by now was taxed to the limit by the entire situation, decided to intern Eleanor in a convent near Neuilly "to learn French," which the little girl had spoken practically since birth, while she attempted to recover her strength and make sense of her broken life. This was a period of terrible unhappiness for six-year-old Eleanor, who was yet again abandoned by her mother while having no idea of her father's whereabouts. In June 1891, my great-grandmother gave birth to her third child, Hall. Elliott's excesses worsened, and finally, completely exasperated, she returned to New York with the children, leaving her husband behind. She agreed not to seek a divorce if Elliott consented to stay under the care of physicians for six months at the Chateau Suresnes outside Paris.

It is easy to sense the anguish of my great-grandmother and her three young children during this time. Her husband's actions and emotions cast a deep shadow on all of them, and in wanting to shield the children she retreated once more to her morally upright world—cold, distant, and void of emotions too strong to bear. Unfortunately, Anna's constant aloofness continued to afflict Eleanor, desperate for emotional security and psychological reassurance from the only adult left in her everyday life. Grandmère was convinced that in her mother's eyes she was a great disappointment, but she still hungered for her praise and affection. In an effort to gain the attention of her mother, who by now was prone to bouts of monumental headaches herself, Grandmère would spend hours upon hours sitting at her bedside, gently stroking her brow to relieve the pain. But no matter how hard she tried, she was painfully aware that her own mother preferred her other children, and demonstrated that preference continuously. This solemn, frightened, and insecure little girl, considered by her own mother to be "old-fashioned" and a "granny," would be told by one of her aunts that she was "the ugly duckling of the family," a moniker that stuck with her for years and served to bolster her feelings of inadequacy. "I was always disgracing my mother," Grandmère would say in later years, and she was constantly "afraid of being scolded, afraid that other people would not like me."[20]

In hopes of reconciliation, my great-grandfather returned to America in 1892, promising yet again to seek a cure and establish himself in an occupation. He secured a position with his brother-in-law, Douglas Robinson, managing the family's extensive timber and coal properties in Virginia, and for a period proved to be adept.

But again, Grandmère's beloved father had left her. Unable to understand the reasons for this new separation and desperately lonely, she could only blame her mother. All that bolstered Grandmère during this newest absence were the frequent letters from her father, in which he expressed his almost passionate love for his "Little Nell." So important were these letters to seven-year-old Eleanor that she waited every day for another word, carrying the letters around with her constantly, almost as a talisman. The letters are symbolic of the intricacies of her feelings for her father, for she had a most curious way of writing both horizontally and vertically across the page. The peculiar crisscross practice made the letters almost indecipherable. It was as though there were an avalanche of feeling waiting to erupt and yet carefully controlled and concealed, for perhaps there was never enough time with her father, and she did not want to worry him with her unhappiness in his absences nor when he was with the family.

It seemed that happiness was not in Grandmère's early destiny, for in late 1892 unexpected tragedy again rocked the Roosevelt family. Eleanor was staying at her grandmother Hall's house when the devastating news was delivered:

I can remember standing by a window when Cousin Susie...told me that my mother was dead. She was very sweet to me, and I must have known that something terrible had happened. Death meant nothing to me, and one fact wiped out everything else—my father was back and I would see him very soon.[21]

Anna Hall Roosevelt died at the age of twenty-nine of diphtheria. As indicated by Grandmère's recollections, the gulf that separated mother and daughter was obvious; all that she was capable of relating to was the fact that she and her beloved father would soon be reunited and that "someday I would make a home for him again...and someday we would have a life of our own together." In order to cope with her mother's death, Grandmère further retreated into that universe of an idyllic fantasy life to be shared with her father, even if she could not live with him. My great-grandmother's will had prescribed that her mother was to be guardian of her three children, not their father, and they were immediately installed in the elder Mrs. Hall's brownstone residence on New York City's fashionable West Side. Realizing that her grandmother was not prepared to undertake the role of mother to three young children, Grandmère assumed that role with her two little brothers.

Forlorn and completely at a loss following his wife's death, my great-grandfather fell apart. He now moved to a New York apartment, resumed his life of alcohol and leisure, and assumed an anonymous relationship with a mistress. Despite his wayward ways, he never stopped loving his children, and would involve himself in as many details of their lives as he was allowed to under their grandmother's watchful eye. For Grandmère, however, her father's affection proved to be the first and foremost influence on the shaping of her early life. As she would say in later years, she always tried to live up to the ideals that her father had set for her—to be brave, truthful, loyal, and well educated. My great-grandfather wrote to her almost daily, letters she would read, reread, and then answer. He encouraged her in her studies and education, and in learning to ride her pony well. Though physically absent, my great-grandfather maintained a strong emotional link to his daughter. Letters were then, and would continue to be throughout her life, important emotional links to the people Grandmère loved. She wrote letters to all her family constantly in order to maintain an intimacy in relationships even when she was far removed.

Years later, Grandmère would chronicle in her memoirs the state in which Elliott found himself following the death of her mother: "No hope now of ever wiping out the sorrowful years he had brought upon my mother…He had no wife, no children, no hope!"[22]

But fate's cruel hand was still not far from Eleanor. The year following her mother's death, her darling little brother Ellie died of diphtheria at barely four years of age, and once more she was cast into a deepening sense of abandonment and loneliness. Elliott explained in a touching letter to Eleanor that Ellie would be up in heaven next to their mother, but to eight-year-old Eleanor it was a bewildering loss.

My own little Nell—We bury little Ellie tomorrow up at Tivoli by Mother's side. He is happy in Heaven with her so now you must not grieve or sorrow. And you will have to be a double good Daughter to your father and good sister to your own little Brudie boy [Hall] who is left to us. I know you will my own little Heart. I cannot write more because I am not feeling very well and my heart is too full. But I wished you to know you were never out of my thoughts and prayers for one instant all the time. I put some flowers close by Ellie in your name as I knew you would like me to do. With abiding and most tender devotion and Love I am always,

Your affectionate Father[23]

By now my great-grandfather's behavior became so unpredictable and erratic that Grandmother Hall prevented him from visiting his children unless supervised by a nanny or herself. Elliott was restless and desperate, and while Eleanor was on holiday with Hall and her grandmother in Bar Harbor, his final disintegration began. On August 14, 1894, just two months short of her tenth birthday, Grandmère suffered the greatest loss of all: Elliott Roosevelt died. She refused to believe her father was gone forever. Since Grandmother Hall forbid Eleanor and Hall's attendance at the funeral, Grandmère would simply continue to live her "dream life" with her father. There was no closure provided, and none allowed. The powerful feelings Elliott elicited in his young daughter of powerful but ultimately tragic and flawed love would remain shut down in her heart and one day be awakened again in another powerful relationship.

At his untimely death at the age of thirty-four, my great-grandfather had again been living in Abingdon, Virginia, for two years. The local newspaper noted his death as follows:

DEATH OF MR. ELLIOTT ROOSEVELT
The New York papers announced the death of Mr. Elliott Roosevelt. This gentleman has been a member of this community for the past two years, and although his stay was so brief, it was long enough for him to make his impress as a whole souled, genial gentleman, courteous and kind at all times, with an ever ready cheer for the enterprising or to help the weak. His name was a byword among the needy, and his charities were always as abundant as they were unostentatious. He was public spirited and generous, this much we can truthfully say. His influence and his aid will be missed, and more frequently than is generally known among those to whom it was a boon.

Ensconced in a reality of loneliness and solemnity, Grandmère resided in her own dream world, a world in which "I was the heroine and my father the

Grandmère in front of the Hall family home in Tivoli, 1894. Her aunt Maude is in the horse cart.

hero." As strange as it may seem, her time with Grandmother Hall and her aunts and uncles was deeply healing for her. Her days, no longer punctuated by long holidays abroad and family dramas, acquired peace and structure. Her studies, erratic until then, assumed a new meaning. She went to school every day, read poetry and prose, played the piano, rode her pony, and spent long afternoons in the magnificent nature surrounding the family's estate at Tivoli. During this time Eleanor immersed herself in literature, reading many books in their original French, including Victor Hugo, Dumas, the *Chanson de Roland,* and other classic European and American works.

Her grandmother provided her with security, and for the first time Eleanor became the center of attention and gained the approval and devotion of the adults around her. She was still introverted, painfully shy, and gawkily tall, yet she displayed a constant desire to care for and please those around her in order to be noticed and loved, a trait forever etched in her character. Her life was not intentionally cloistered, although Grandmother Hall was a strict disciplinarian and guardian, but it was far from that experienced by other girls her age and status. She had few friends and only occasional playmates. She frequently visited her father's relatives in Oyster Bay, her uncle Ted and aunt Edith. TR was an affectionate and loving uncle to the daughter of his "poor Ellie," and Grandmère genuinely loved this bear of a man, who would literally sweep her into his arms in a huge hug upon her arrival. Edith, although concerned about Eleanor's plainness and social awkwardness, was prophetic, seeing in Eleanor something that others had failed to recognize. "Poor little soul, she is very plain," she told Auntie Bye. "Her mouth and teeth have no future, but...the ugly duckling may turn out to be a swan."

Grandmère's fondness for her Oyster Bay relatives, and particularly her uncle Ted, lasted throughout her life. In many ways he became the father figure she had so desperately sought, and she another daughter in his already bulging family. Indeed, her reverence for her uncle would in time cause her to be torn between that devotion and her own husband's eventual political designs.

During the next few years Eleanor became a devotee of classical ballet, primarily because her grandmother thought this would be a marvelous way for her to acquire elegant posture, grace, and decorum. But Eleanor was also keen to become a professional singer, as she loved singing and practiced

With her pony also in Tivoli, where she began to find some harmony after the harrowing years of early childhood.

assiduously. It was in these adolescent years that she became intensely interested in her studies, and although still shy and at times painfully lonely, she learned that discipline and application were conducive to positive feelings of self-worth.

Allenswood

Although her grandmother's house now represented a refuge for Grandmère, she still lived a cloistered existence. Whenever she visited her Oyster Bay Roosevelt family she felt socially awkward, shy, and unsophisticated in dress compared with her more lively cousins; she felt an outsider in the world and society to which she had been born.

Once again Cousin Alice would recall that Grandmère's feelings of inadequacy were caused by her unhappy childhood and had little to do with reality:

> *Many aspects of Eleanor's childhood were indeed very unhappy but she had a tendency, especially later in life, to make out that she was unattractive and rejected as a child, which just wasn't true. She claimed that nobody liked her. Well, we all liked her. She made a big thing about having long legs and wearing short dresses. Well, as far as I was concerned I envied her long legs and didn't notice her short skirts, if indeed they were short. She was always making herself out to be an ugly duckling but she was really rather attractive.... I think that Eleanor today would have been considered a beauty, not in the classical sense but as an attractive, rather unusual person in her own right.*[24]

Grandmère with her youngest brother Gracie Hall, New York City, 1898.

Grandmère's poor self-image was a cause for sadness and concern to her family. When she turned fifteen her aunts finally decided to help her regain her luminosity and spirit. Auntie Bye had been educated at an English boarding school run by the formidable Mademoiselle Marie Souvestre, a remarkable teacher who had done wonders for Bye, imparting her with confidence, a solid education, knowledge of languages, and the experience of living and traveling in Europe. In fact, once when Anna and Elliott were touring France they visited Marie Souvestre in Paris, and my great-grandmother was greatly impressed by her. On her deathbed Anna conveyed her wishes that Mademoiselle Souvestre might also educate her daughter. At first reluctant about the idea, Grandmother Hall eventually acceded to the persuasion of the aunts. She too became convinced that time at a school abroad would be the best gift for the young teenage girl.

Allenswood was located in Wimbledon Park, on the western outskirts of London. It was a small school offering the daughters of Europe's aristocracy and America's patrician class a wide-ranging education with emphasis on social responsibility and personal independence. Marie Souvestre was the daughter of the esteemed French philosopher and novelist Emile Souvestre, and was a luminary presence in the liberal intellectual circles and community of radical thinkers that included John Morley, Joseph Chamberlain, Leslie Stephen, and Jane Maria Grant (Lady Strachey). Mademoiselle Souvestre founded two schools, Les Ruches in Paris, which she had been forced to close when the Germans invaded during the Franco-Prussian War, and Allenswood. The schools were distinguished because they offered a more sophisticated educational program than most finishing schools in fin de siècle Europe, and Mademoiselle Souvestre took the education of young women seriously at a time when most girls were denied access to colleges and universities. Both Les Ruches and later Allenswood were considered feminist and progressive and were responsible for the education of several generations of notable and remarkable women.

Grandmère sailed to England accompanied by her aunt Tissie and Tissie's husband, Stanley Mortimer, who had lived in England for many years. Her aunt and uncle would become traveling companions for Eleanor during her holidays from school, and she also visited them in London, where her aunt introduced her to new people and experience. From the beginning, Grandmère and Marie Souvestre were drawn to each other like magnets. Entirely bilingual, Grandmère was well prepared for the French-speaking school, and from the first day she sat opposite

Mademoiselle Souvestre,
Grandmère's mentor and most beloved teacher.

Mlle. Souvestre and chatted away in perfect French. Quickly becoming one of the teacher's favorite students, she was immediately included in Mlle. Souvestre's more intimate student circle. Sitting close to her at dinner and engaging in lively, thought-provoking conversation, Grandmère would often be invited into the teacher's study in the evenings to read and discuss literature or philosophy, recite poems, or improvise theatrical pieces. Eleanor delighted and flourished in the attention and privilege bestowed upon her and bonded with the teacher in the most influential relationship in her life, second only to the rapport she had shared with her own father. Uniquely different in a Victorian world that believed education would drive women to madness and sterility, Mlle. Souvestre demanded that her students take themselves and their studies seriously, encouraging them to apply their own understanding,

Grandmère in a student group portrait at Allenswood, England, in 1900.

ideals, and convictions to problems and demanding that they work hard and thoroughly. She was dismissive of shoddy work habits and laziness, punishing such frivolous behavior harshly during her lessons. Under her guidance and tutoring, the girls at Allenswood learned to work hard, consider deeply, research their facts accurately and astutely, develop their intelligence, and converse with ability on any and every topic from the arts to philosophy to languages, music, and history. It was truly a unique liberal arts education, one not universally afforded young women of the day.

During her three years at Allenswood, Grandmère thrived and blossomed into a young woman, one whose presence and opinions were greatly admired and sought after by the other students.

In her first year she quickly emerged as a class leader, creating a circle of friends she would keep up with for the rest of her life. Marie Souvestre encouraged her to dress well, and, as the girls exercised and played field sports every day for at least two hours despite the sometimes bleak and wet English weather, Grandmère lost her physical awkwardness and gained a gracefulness of movement not before evident.

It was at Allenswood, under the loving care and gentle guidance of Mlle. Souvestre, that the ugly duckling began her transformation into a swan, as predicted by her aunt Edith. It was under the tutelage of this remarkable woman that Grandmère was instilled with the deep sense of public duty and social idealism that would be the exacting marks for

Grandmère, second from left in the second row, with her schoolmates at Allenswood.

the remainder of her life. Allenswood provided her with an emotional and psychological stability of the "home" she had missed for so many years, and Mlle. Souvestre helped her discover that the character of her person lay beneath the façade of her looks. For the next three years Grandmère was transformed, if not reborn. Not all of her insecurities, nor the affect of her earlier life, would or could be obscured entirely, but the essence of her personality had begun to take shape.

In her second year at Allenswood, Grandmère was invited to accompany Mlle. Souvestre in her travels across Europe, and together they visited Italy, France, and Germany. Left in charge of all the details of packing, purchasing tickets, and making arrangements, Grandmère found

this responsibility thrilling and learned much in their journeys, considering these times "one of the most momentous things that happened in my education." She was allowed to wander through the streets of Florence and Paris on her own, and for the first time in her life she experienced the freedom that comes from being trusted and valued, two feelings she had been unable to share with her mother and grandmother.

Leaving Allenswood at the end of her third year was heart wrenching for eighteen-year-old Eleanor. She was being called home by her family "to come out" in society, but she felt quite sure that she would soon return to the school to teach. She exchanged many affectionate letters with Mlle. Souvestre, chronicling her sadness and nostalgia as

---

well as details of her new life in America. In the archives at Hyde Park I discovered a letter that Mlle. Souvestre wrote to Grandmère, a letter that vividly explains the profound feelings of love and care this teacher had for young Eleanor:

> Allenswood
> Wimbledon Par
> London   5 October 1902
>
> Dear Child
>
> I have just given to your aunt Mrs. Robinson the picture you requested. If by chance she should forget to give it to you, ask her for it, for she will surely have it among her belongings.
>
> Yesterday, quantities of letters from you arrived at Allenswood. There were none for me among the ones I distributed, but I hope I shall be luckier next week...
>
> Dear child, my mind is so divided in respect to you. I should like to know that you are happy, and yet how I fear to hear that you have been unable to defend yourself against all the temptations which surround you; evenings out, pleasure, flirtations. How all this will estrange you from all that I knew you to be!...
>
> Ah! how we miss you here, my dear child. There are many new girls and, as is their habit, the English girls do not know how to welcome them, and leave them in the corner. You would have known how to make them feel rapidly at ease, and happy in circumstances so different from their usual lives...
>
> You never told me how your money problems were resolved. Have you the control of a definite sum given you as long as you are a minor, or does someone simply pay your expenses, without your having to worry about balancing your expenses against a definite sum given you?
>
> Till soon, my good child. Winter is coming, the flowers are dying in the garden, the horizon is hidden behind a heavy, motionless curtain of gray mists, the sad days are beginning in this country where they are sadder than anywhere else. I wish you what we lack: light and sun.
>
> Tenderly yours,
> M. Souvestre[25]

Her heart was never far from her beloved teacher and the happy times at Allenswood that had so validated who she was. Throughout the remainder of my grandmother's life, Mlle. Souvestre's portrait would always be prominently displayed, and a final photograph of Grandmère's study at the time of her death in 1962 will find that portrait on her desk, an ever-present reminder of lessons learned and those to be learned. As she would say in a *Look* magazine article written in 1951 entitled *The Seven People Who Shaped My Life*, "For three years I basked in her gracious presence, and I think those three years did much to form my character and give me...confidence..." In another 1932 article in *Women's Home Companion* Grandmère would add, "To her [Mlle. Souvestre] I owe more than I can repay for she gave me an intellectual curiosity and a standard [for] living which never left me."

It is my belief that had it not been for the impact of Mlle. Souvestre's influence at this specific time in her life, Grandmère would have been trapped in the dark unhappiness of the world in which she had dwelled prior to Allenswood. So, while much credit has been accorded this remarkable headmistress, in my view it has been too little, for she was the defining factor of Grandmère's life direction.

PART THREE

Franklin

Oh darling, I miss you so, and I long for the happy hours which we have together. I am so happy, so very happy in your love, dearest, and all the world has changed for me. If only I can bring to you all that you have brought to me, all my dearest wishes will be fulfilled.

—Eleanor to Franklin

GRANDMÈRE'S RETURN FROM ENGLAND and her Allenswood experience in 1902 must have given her a difficult if not utterly shocking jolt. She had left behind the warmth of lifelong friendships that had developed with her classmates and Mlle. Souvestre, only to face the prospect of being a society debutante, something she truly feared, and of thereby reentering the confining atmosphere of her grandmother's life. No longer the awkward little girl who had arrived at Allenswood three years before, Eleanor at eighteen was the niece of the president of the United States. Theodore had assumed the presidency following the assassination of President McKinley, making Eleanor a debutante from one of the most prestigious patrician families in the country. A recognized and respected leader among her newfound friends at Allenswood, she returned to the States a blossoming young lady with a developing self-respect and an ability to think for herself. She wanted more than anything to remain at Mlle. Souvestre's school for a fourth year, and harbored dreams of perhaps continuing there as a teacher. But these hopes and dreams were not to be. Of her time at Allenswood, Grandmère would say, "I have spent three years here which certainly have been the happiest of my life," and that it marked the beginning of the "second period of my life."[1]

Coming home to Tivoli, however, was not as sweet as she had hoped. Her uncle Vallie, eldest son of her grandparents, Valentine and Mary Hall, was in worsening stages of alcoholism and behaved more and more bizarrely. He was known to sit at a second-floor window taking potshots with a shotgun at neighbors and complete strangers who might arrive on the premises of the estate, while her aunt Pussie Hall was experiencing emotional problems caused by her many dalliances with young suitors. Almost immediately Grandmère was handed the responsibility for her brother Hall's education and upbringing. In that first summer, when all other debutantes were in gay and carefree moods, Eleanor was once again thrust into emotional responsibilities beyond those of a normal eighteen-year-old. In September, she and her grandmother accompanied Hall to the Groton School, which had become the traditional preparatory school for the Roosevelt clan males, most of whom enrolled at age twelve. During his stay there, Eleanor would visit her brother one weekend every term, joining all the other parents visiting their children. Above all, she didn't want Hall to experience abandonment or to feel as if he had no one in the world to care for him.

Her times away from Tivoli were spent making the family rounds, visiting her many Oyster Bay relatives. The nation was experiencing so many changes at that time—socially, economically, and technologically—and at the forefront of the upbeat mood was Eleanor's favorite relative, her always effervescent and ebullient uncle Ted. Teddy Roosevelt was enjoying the presidency to the fullest; his optimism and enthusiasm had captured the country, and America was enchanted with its youngest president and his entire family, as was his niece. Eleanor still felt the great chasm caused by the loss of her father, and Teddy's role as her surrogate father was the one true sparkle in her life.

TR was very fond of her (Eleanor). My father had "tribal affection." He loved all his nieces and nephews. ER...was Elliott's daughter and he was very devoted to Uncle Ellie.

The family was over effusive in a Queen Victorian manner. That may have been a Southern trait. My father naturally felt a great sympathy for Uncle Ellie's two children who had to live with their grandmother who was a gloomy tartar.[2]

Although at the time it was not apparent to Eleanor, I think TR became the role model she had missed in her own father, instilling in her the deeply ingrained characteristics of social obligation and caring so prevalent in generations of Roosevelts.

If life became too tumultuous at Tivoli, Eleanor could retire to the relatively safe haven of her grandmother's house in New York City, but she longed to have a place where she could begin to make sense of her life back in the States:

I was 19. I had returned from school in Europe to the ordeal of trying to be a "belle" in New York City society where I had lost touch with all my girl friends, and where I never had known any young men. My grandmother was in the throes of dealing with a son who was becoming a confirmed alcoholic, and moved with him to our country house at Tivoli, New York. For one winter I lived with a young aunt who was a New York "belle" for many years, Edith (Pussie) Hall, but finally my grandmother decided to sell our New York City house, and my second winter in New York I spent with a very kindly Godmother who was my mother's double first cousin, Mrs. Henry Parish, Jr.

She and her husband were more than kind to me, they had no children of their own and were set in their ways, and I was accustomed to a very unconventional, haphazard way of living. Their household was strictly run and required of me promptness and an accounting of all of my time. There could be no impromptu comings and goings, no young people in and out, no extra demands on the servants. My kindly Godmother would occasionally give for me a lunch or a dinner and now and then in the little room downstairs off the entrance hall, I could have a special guest for tea, but all this had to be arranged and planned for, and seemed to me often, more trouble than it was worth. By spring I went to see my father's sister, Mrs. William Sheffield Cowles, in Farmington, Connecticut. All of the younger generation called her Auntie Bye. If we wanted advice we went to her, just as we went to our very charming Aunt Corinne (Mrs. Douglas Robinson) when we wanted warmth and entertainment. I asked to talk with Auntie Bye alone and very diffidently I explained that I found my present way of life none too easy, and that I would like to take an apartment of my own in New York City!

This was fifty-three years ago, and the idea that a young girl could live alone in New York City was rather a startling suggestion.

"My dear, you will never please everyone in this world. If you think this is the right thing to do, go ahead and do it. Always remember whatever you do, be sure that you would not mind telling someone you love, and who loves you, the truth about what you are doing." Here was advice that Auntie Bye had herself lived by, and as I did not take the apartment because shortly after that I became engaged to my distant cousin, Franklin Delano Roosevelt, that piece of advice stayed with me all my life.[3]

Grandmère, a young debutante when she returned to New York from Allenswood, with her friend Muriel D. Robbins and cousin Helen R. Roosevelt.

Social Duty

Eleanor began to spend time with those less fortunate than her. Perhaps this was a way of taking solace from the predicament of her living situation. Perhaps it was also out of concern for the social welfare of others, a concern deeply instilled by Mlle. Souvestre. Coming home from Europe, Eleanor quickly came to realize that not all were sharing in the country's enthusiasm and providence. New York City itself had blossomed in Eleanor's absence. It was no longer the quiet, sophisticated city of her early years, but one marked by booming growth and all of

the attendant problems. Now known as "Greater New York," the city had a population of close to 4 million, and an ever-growing presence of slums on its East Side, where some two-thirds of its people were jammed into ninety thousand tenements. Many of Eleanor's most fulfilling hours during this period were spent volunteering in these neighborhoods.

A few patrician daughters, all older than Eleanor, had also been moved to action by the terrible conditions of the tenements, which lacked sanitation and suffered from terrible working conditions, overcrowding, deep misery, and increasing poverty. These young women had started a few private

Grandmère in 1903, young and beautiful.

welfare programs to help "forgotten" citizens, see-ing as how the traditional philanthropists and social do-gooders were not dealing with these problems. An emerging class of women marked this period with the true beginning of the women's rights movement and a reformation of the traditional role of women. It was these women, sometimes those of the upper social strata, who were addressing the inequities of life in America. Eleanor and some of her friends from before her time at Allenswood

decided to join in and helped to found the Junior League for the Promotion of Settlement Movements, making it the "smart" thing to do in New York. She became a calisthenics and dance teacher for the children of the tenements, who soon joined her happy classes and developed a strong bond with their young teacher. She was immensely proud of this work, even if some members of her family did not understand her enthusiasm and worried that she might get an "immigrant's disease" or that something might happen to her while in the tenements. She insisted on taking public transport to her classes and always refused rides from friends when they were offered, preferring to walk alone even at night through the tenements. What she saw were the ravaging effects of alcoholism, poverty, and lack of hope and opportunity, lessons that would prove valuable to her insight as First Lady many years later.

In 1903 Eleanor joined the Consumers' League and witnessed firsthand the poor working conditions of women in factories and garment shops, gaining knowledge of how many millions of Americans toiled in the name of progress. Marie Souvestre had prompted Grandmère's initiation into the atrocious conditions of the working classes during visits they made to the settlement houses in London, and now Grandmère became actively involved in a major lifetime vocation. It was in the tenement houses on Rivington Street, and later in other places, that Eleanor's eyes were opened to the horrors of the poor and downtrodden. She was sickened by the terrible living conditions endured by the families with whom she worked and the children she taught. She would later recollect, "I was appalled...I saw little children of four or five sitting at [work] tables until they dropped with fatigue..."[4] Her work also reconnected her to her Roosevelt ideals of a charitable life and brought back happy memories of when she was a child and accompanied her father to the Newsboys' Thanksgiving dinners. Her good works were perhaps a refuge for Eleanor from the subtle pressure all debutantes feel to find a good husband and to become a successful matron of society. During these times, Grandmère balanced social duty with the expectations placed upon her by the society she lived in. Eleanor, however

greatly she might have felt the pressure, did not have to go far to look for the love of her life.

One day that summer, she was traveling by train from New York City to Tivoli. Walking through the train, the young, handsome Franklin noticed his tall, slim distant cousin, whom she hadn't seen for four years. After striking up a conversation, he invited her back to his mother's compartment to say hello to "Cousin Sallie." Though it wasn't love at first sight, there was on this occasion certainly an immediate attraction between the two.

As the fall of her nineteenth birthday approached, Eleanor began the social duties of a debutante, attending parties, dances, and cotillions. Much has been said of her social awkwardness, but her cousin Alice denied any such rumors, hinting that Eleanor may have imagined herself clumsy, whereas she was in fact quite adroit: "She was always making herself out to be an ugly duckling but she was in fact rather attractive. Tall, rather coltish-looking, with masses of pale, gold hair rippling to below her waist, and really lovely blue eyes." Later she dressed in beautiful, fashionable clothes as Mlle. Souvestre had suggested and that her aunt ordered from boutiques in Paris. More important, she was intellectually vivacious and enjoyed witty and intelligent conversation, staying at parties until the wee hours of the morning if the company was stimulating and original. New York Society, as it was then called, marked its return to the city in November with attendance at the great horse show in Madison Square Garden. The *New York Herald* reported Eleanor's presence in a box full of Roosevelts that belonged to her distant cousin James Roosevelt Roosevelt, half-brother of Franklin Delano Roosevelt, who was one of James' few select guests at the horse show.

My grandparents with 13 grandchildren at the White House, January 20, 1945.
I'm the little boy sitting on FDR's knee on the left. My sister Chandler is the first young girl on the right,
kneeling in the first row, and my brother Tony is sitting to her left.

A Most Fateful Meeting

When our children's children study the history of the twentieth century, they will see Franklin Delano Roosevelt as one of the most influential and decisive of all world leaders, a man possessed of a driving and immensely inspiring force who articulated the dreams of freedom for millions during his presidency. FDR is remembered by the nation as the man who declared, "The only thing we have to fear is fear itself." He waged war against the economic depression that gripped the country at the time of his election; pioneered the politics of inclusion; built a broad and long-lasting coalition uniting different regions, classes, and races; and was pivotal in the battle against fascism and the obliteration of

Roosevelt family portrait with my grandparents, their four sons,
Sara Delano Roosevelt, and grandchildren.

FDR holding my brother Tony, Grandmère holding my sister
Chandler, and my parents Ruth and Elliott, on occasion of one of
my grandparents' visits to our ranch in Texas.

individual freedom. He identified with the hopes and fears of forgotten Americans.

Although I was too young to have really known my grandfather, my memories being those of a three-year-old, others of my generation had that opportunity. Photographs of FDR with his grandchildren and recollections of elder siblings and cousins make it clear that he loved having us around him. One well-known photograph, taken in the White House at his fourth inaugural, shows him with thirteen of us, a cousin and me sitting on each knee. In time there would be a total of twenty-two grandchildren, plus five adopted. Those who have the most vivid memories of FDR, or "Papa," were the two eldest—Eleanor (Sistie) and Curtis (Buzzy) Dall—all my aunt Anna's children. My own siblings, half-brother William, sister Chandler, and brother Tony (Elliott Jr.), also have reminiscences of visits to Springwood and the White House. And there were several occasions when both FDR and

Grandmère would visit my father and mother's ranch, the Dutch Branch Ranch, just outside Fort Worth. Such visits usually occurred when FDR would make train trips through the South and to other parts of Texas, which he did fairly often. Indeed, as I think about the various holidays and other occasions when aunts and uncles, grandchildren, and various other "extended family" would gather at the White House, they must have been raucous and chaotic times, seldom experienced before at that venerable house, with the possible exception of TR's own occupancy. And Grandmère, of course, always made such occasions as homelike as possible, planning activities for the children and the always-simple family meals that she preferred over more formal trappings. But whatever the circumstance, FDR always seemed to have time for his grandchildren; he exuded warmth and love and, as with his own children, exercised little discipline.

My great-grandfather James traced his lineage back to Jacobus, who is credited with establishing the Hyde Park branch of the family. It is interesting to note that for a time the tradition of this branch followed a pattern of naming first sons by "generation skipping." After Jacobus there was Isaac "The Patriot," followed by James, followed by Dr. Isaac, followed by James (FDR's father). However, the last James broke with tradition by naming his own first son James, despite an intense dislike of the use of "Junior" to distinguish between father and son. So, to make that distinction for *his* son, he merely added the middle name "Roosevelt," thus making FDR's half-brother James Roosevelt Roosevelt (better known as "Rosy").

FDR's father, James, inherited a rather dark and gloomy estate called Rosedale from his father, Dr. Isaac, who lived a cloistered life at Rosedale, virtually shut off from his neighbors. (It was the popular conjecture at the time that the estate served as a way station for slaves making the treacherous trip from the South to Canada.) Shortly following Dr. Isaac's death in 1863, the original manor house was destroyed by fire, giving James the perfect excuse to sell the property and escape the dreary surroundings of his childhood. He proceeded to purchase a modest 110 acres just two miles upriver, where he established his own estate of Springwood. Eventually Springwood would grow to include more than a thousand acres, making it one of the larger estates of the day.

James was very much a man of his own following, independent minded and restless in his early career. He refused to follow the family tradition of attending Harvard, graduating instead from Union College in upstate Schenectady. He did manage, however, to graduate from Harvard Law School, though he followed his penchant for risky business ventures rather than the practice of law. One of his great dreams was to join the Atlantic and Pacific Oceans by canal across Nicaragua, an unsuccessful

Opposite: *Three portraits of my great-grandfather, James Roosevelt, FDR's father.*
This page, left: *James Roosevelt's first wife, Rebecca Howland Roosevelt.*
Right: *When Rebecca died, James Roosevelt married Sara Delano, photographed here in 1869.*

enterprise yet not altogether without vision, as his dream was attained by his distant cousin Theodore's Panama Canal project. Finally, in 1888 James joined the Delaware & Hudson Railroad, becoming a highly respected railroad financier.

James married Rebecca Howland shortly after entering into business. FDR's elder half-brother, "Rosy," was born in 1854. Then, after twenty-three years of marriage, Rebecca suffered a fatal heart attack at the age of forty-five. Devastated by this loss, James seemed to founder. He withdrew from much of his business activity and secluded himself at Springwood, becoming a true patrician farmer. In 1880, however, James met the much younger daughter of a close Hyde Park friend, Sara Delano, herself a member of a seafaring merchant family of considerable renown.

Sara and James first met at the house of Eleanor's grandmother, Mittie Bulloch Roosevelt. He was a fifty-two-year-old widower who had

adopted the lifestyle of an English squire, riding around his estate in formal English country attire. Sara had grown up on the family estate of Algonac, and was an active member of the New York and Hudson Valley social set. She was a close friend of Auntie Bye's, and a frequent visitor at Theodore Roosevelt's homes in New York.

Warren Delano, Sara's father (who had rejected all of her previous suitors as being unworthy of his daughter), had become a business associate and friend of James. So impressed was he by the achievements of James that when the widower came asking for Sara's hand in marriage, he happily blessed the union despite the significant age difference, a favorite topic of gossip on the social circuit. Sara was a sophisticated young woman, well educated and widely traveled, and had the classic beauty to match her impeccable patrician background, which dated back to William the Conqueror. The first Delano, called de la Noye, settled in Plymouth

in 1621. Sara was born at Algonac, a magnificent property twenty miles south of Springwood on the Hudson, and it seemed from the beginning that she was destined to marry a neighboring Roosevelt. Upon doing so, she easily settled into the life of mistress of the Springwood manor.

On January 30, 1882, Franklin was born. Even though the pregnancy had been easy, both mother and child nearly died from a near-fatal over-dose of painkillers administered by a careless doctor during labor. James proudly reported, "At a quarter to nine my Sallie had a splendid large baby boy. He weighs 10 lbs. Without clothes."[5]

James had lived in Europe for a time, and there he had witnessed the extreme deprivation of working-class life, the ravages and squalor of poverty, the overworked and malnourished children, the condition of women, and the horrors deepened by the lack of a social welfare system. These experiences left an indelible impression, and throughout

his life he encouraged and campaigned to reach out to the poor and helpless. He imparted these ideals to his son, Franklin, from the beginning, impressing upon him the need to work toward the elimination of the conditions afflicting the socially deprived. These were ideals that Franklin met again in Eleanor Roosevelt.

While Eleanor's life had been fraught with instability and loneliness, her fifth cousin Franklin had had a happy, secure, and harmonious childhood. Springwood, set in six hundred acres of dense woods and rolling hills on the banks of the great Hudson River, was a paradise that young Franklin could freely roam and explore. His father taught him to ride, fish, skate, shoot, sail, hunt, and golf—in short, to become a physically confident and self-reliant boy. Both parents doted on their son, who grew up speaking in the clipped English accent his father had adopted, and was more comfortable in the company of adults than that of children, whom

he seldom encountered. Under the stern yet doting eyes of his parents, Franklin was raised to assume the role of a typical Hudson Valley country squire, or, as Sara would say in later years, in hopes that he would grow to be a "fine, upright man like his father and [my] own father, a beloved member of his family and a useful and respected citizen of his community just as they were, living quietly and happily along the Hudson as they had."[6]

Top left: *Springwood, Sara's country estate, seen from the South.* Right: *Sara and baby FDR.* Above left: *The front of Springwood before it was enlarged to accommodate ER and FDR's growing family.* Right: *FDR and his father James Roosevelt on horses, with Sara holding their dog, on the south lawn of Springwood in 1891.*
Opposite, left: *Sara Delano with her sisters Laura, Kerrie, Annie, and Dora in New York City, on November 5, 1882.* Center: *Sara in Rome in 1881. She was quite a beauty!* Right: *A very young FDR, Sara's pride and joy, sitting on a fur rug.*

FDR on his father's shoulders in June 1883.

FDR with his aunt Laura Delano in July 1884.

That Franklin would grow up under the influence of his mother was undeniable, for when his father died in 1900, he stipulated in his will, "I wish him [Franklin] to be under the influence of his mother." Like Eleanor's brother Hall and many other Roosevelt boys, Franklin attended Groton School in Groton, Massachusetts, entering at age twelve. Like Eleanor at Allenswood, young Franklin's eyes were opened to a life beyond the ambitions of his mother while under the exacting tutelage of the school's headmaster, Endicott Peabody. As Mlle. Souvestre

had influenced Eleanor's future course, so Reverend Peabody would prove to be one of the most influential people in Franklin's life. A Cheltenham- and Cambridge-educated Anglican minister, Dr. Peabody recreated at Groton the environment of an English public school that prepared the sons of America's well-to-do for a life of leadership. Franklin did not excel academically, but he thrived at the school and came to consider himself a model Grotonian, studying Latin, Greek, history, and literature for six years; adopting the school's ideals and manners; and living the Spartan, ethical life Groton promoted. Although Sara never dreamed of a life of politics for her son, Dr. Peabody's philosophy was one of public service. As he would often say, "If some Groton boys do not enter political life and do something for our land it won't be because they have not been urged [by their Groton experience]."[7]

Although the specific nature of service Franklin would pursue was undetermined, he was deeply influenced at Groton and as an undergraduate at Harvard, which he entered in 1900, by his tremendous admiration for the successes and popularity of his cousin Theodore. But it was during his tenure at Harvard, where Theodore was a greatly admired alumnus whose political actions and personal adventures countered the traditional Harvard student's "indifference" toward social consciousness, that Franklin's tilt toward public service and politics began to form. This emergence can best be demonstrated by a passage from an essay titled "The Roosevelt Family in New York before the Revolution," written during Franklin's sophomore year:

> Some famous Dutch families in New York have today nothing left but their name—they are few in numbers, they lack progressiveness and a true democratic spirit. One reason—perhaps the chief—of the virility of the Roosevelts is this very democratic spirit. They have never felt that because they were born in a good position they could put their hands in their pockets and succeed. They have felt, rather, that being born in a good position, there was no excuse for them if they did not do their duty by the community, and it is because this idea was instilled into them from their birth that they have in nearly every case proved good citizens.[8]

Above: *FDR with members of his second football team at Groton, October 1899.* Below: *My great-grandparents, Sara and James Roosevelt.*

FDR at Harvard in 1901 with members of the Freshmen Glee Club.

Franklin's pattern at Harvard was much the same as it had been at Groton; while he didn't excel as a scholar, he was nonetheless dedicated to his studies and involved in multiple extracurricular activities. However, when he applied to become a member of the prestigious Porcellian, the club to which both his father and TR had belonged, and was turned down, he felt the disappointment to be the worst of his life. He recovered from the Porcellian defeat by becoming more politically aware and by enthusiastically joining and participating in the activities of two other clubs: Hasty Pudding and Alpha Delta Phi. He also became a proud member of the Harvard *Crimson*, the influential school newspaper. Rising eventually to the exalted position of Editor, Franklin considered his time with the *Crimson* to be the best training he'd had for his future as a politician. It taught him to be a man of his own convictions and, further, instilled in him a sense of self-determination that throughout his political life would become a defining characteristic.

A couple in love. Here my grandparents
were photographed at the Delano country estate Algonac on May 7, 1905.

Distant Acquaintances, Future Partners

The blossoming of love between a young woman and a young man who had known each other all their lives as distant cousins was as thrilling as it was unexpected. My grandparents met for the first time when Grandmère was but four years old, and saw each other again on several occasions during visits either by Eleanor to the Hudson Valley or by Franklin to Long Island, and of course in the City at the various social venues enjoyed by the young elite of their day.

In the busy days of her social debut, Grandmère was invited to many parties and events where she met eligible young men, but she made again a strong impression on FDR at a dinner following the Madison Square Garden Horse Show on that November 17, 1902, an occasion he noted in his diary. Although she enjoyed the company of adults and thrived in intelligent conversation, the frivolities

83

Left: *Eleanor and Franklin at the wedding of cousin Helen R. Roosevelt to Theo Douglas Robinson, June 18, 1904, in Hyde Park.* Right: *Eleanor and Franklin sitting for a portrait with their friends.*

associated with the whirl of her debut proved agonizing for Grandmère. Constantly in fear of what other girls would think of her, and shy about her height and looks, she seemed to have trouble securing escorts to the many dances to which she was invited, and was most often escorted by a friend of the family or a family member. Every girl attending the dance had a dance card tied to her wrist, where each beau was supposed to write his name among a long line of prospects. A full dance card was indication of a girl's popularity, and Grandmère was highly conscious that she descended from a long line of beauties who had had no trouble filling up their cards. But to someone totally disinterested in this demeaning custom, the entire thing could be mortifying. As the social season wore on and she became known among her peers, however, her fears diminished, and she experienced

for perhaps the first time since Allenswood that sense of acceptance and respect for her inner self, not for superficial qualities.

Over the next several months Eleanor and Franklin would see each other at various social events and the coincidental house parties, and would spend New Year's together at the White House with Theodore Roosevelt and his family. On January 30, 1903, FDR's half-brother, Rosy, threw a party to celebrate Franklin's twenty-first birthday. Franklin invited Eleanor as his secret star guest, secret because he was hesitant to reveal any of his feelings to Sara, who was still highly possessive of her son. As their early, casual relationship blossomed into a full-fledged courtship over the ensuing months, Grandfather would often show up at the settlement houses where Grandmère was teaching, and he would often accompany her on tours of these establishments. It was on one such visit that he witnessed firsthand horrendous living conditions and was astonished that "human beings lived that way."

As different as Eleanor and Franklin might have appeared—he an outgoing, debonair, and vivacious young socialite, and she a reserved and thoughtfully serious young lady—they shared the bond of their educations, their aristocratic upbringings, and even a kindred way of thinking. Grandmère had been an outsider most of her life, he had experienced his share of disappointments both at Groton and Harvard, and was himself developing something of an inferiority complex. But these early trials only deepened their empathies; in truth, their strong inner personalities and views on life were the single most tinseled thread between them.

It was late in 1903 that Franklin invited Eleanor to attend a Harvard-Yale football game in Cambridge. As arranged, she left following the game to visit her brother Hall, who was still a student at Groton. To her astonishment (she found it impossible to believe that this, or any, handsome man could truly be interested in her), Franklin followed her to Groton the very next day and promptly extended his proposal of marriage. So taken aback was Grandmère that an immediate answer was not forthcoming. She returned to New York and confided this most frightening yet marvelous proposal to, of all people, her grandmother. Several days later she wrote to him, quoting from a poem she had tried to remember the prior Sunday, "Unless you can swear, 'For life, for death! Oh, fear to call it loving!'" His answer was an obvious and deeply felt "Yes, I swear," and Eleanor accepted his proposal to marry.

Franklin and Grandmère emerge from an invigorating swim in the sea.

85

Caught in the arms of young love, they began an extensive exchange of letters and poems, and met as often as they possibly could. Both saved each and every correspondence, until years later when Grandmère destroyed all of FDR's letters to her, saying they were "too personal." In fact, these letters, which then provided her with much love and warmth, would become a source of great pain.

Friends and family alike met Eleanor's sense of astonishment at her good fortune, and not all regarded the chain of events with happiness. Although there is no verification of this, I have heard it said that perhaps the one person most surprised by the rapid development of Grandfather and Grandmère's relationship was none other than Cousin Alice. Never a great admirer of her first cousin, Alice apparently *did* find her distant cousin Franklin most attractive and perhaps worthy of her own attentions. Her feelings may well have been exacerbated by her father's fondness for and kindness toward his niece. More important, Franklin's own mother, Sara, could not believe the news of the engagement of the young couple, finding Eleanor a far cry from the woman she envisioned for her son. It is natural, perhaps, that mothers have their own ideas pertaining to their sons' future life, and certainly Sara had formed hers. She had fully expected that the young FDR would follow in his father's footsteps, becoming master of Springwood and a country gentleman worthy of his lineage. It would be acceptable if his career included some period in a respectable business, the legal profession qualifying as such. And naturally she had every expectation that her son would "marry well" and up to his life station, preferably one of the beauties of the New York social circles.

Sara, hoping to waylay the couple's plans, insisted that there be no public announcement of the engagement for eighteen months, and immediately began planning a five-week Caribbean cruise for her son. For several weeks following the informal and unannounced engagement, Franklin and Eleanor tried to spend as much time together as possible, usually in the company of friends and family but at times slipping away to catch a moment alone. Finally, on February 6, 1904, Franklin, his Harvard roommate, Lathrop Brown, and Sara departed on their cruise of the Caribbean. Miserable at the thought of such a long separation yet undeterred, Eleanor wrote to Franklin almost daily, and both yearned for their planned reunion in Washington, where Grandmère would be visiting Auntie Bye. During these visits, Grandmère gradually acquired yet another layer of social polish as she navigated and began to understand the currents of Washington's political and social circles. Until then, she had been largely unaware of the meaning of politics and the correlations between the poverty she saw in the New York tenements and the legislations supported by her uncle. With the help of Auntie Bye she began to understand more clearly how politics were played and what a difference they could make to the lives of thousands, and these were invaluable lessons to the life she was, unknowingly, about to embrace.

Sara Delano Roosevelt, however, was still battling the reality of Eleanor and Franklin's intense devotion to one another and their growing love, and like all possessive mothers, she was not yet prepared to concede defeat. She attempted to persuade Theodore's ambassador to England, Joseph Choate, to engage her son as his private secretary back in

Sara adopted Eleanor as a daughter and sought to give her constant advice. Here they're seen chatting on the steps of Sara's Campobello holiday home.

London. This ploy too failed, as FDR refused to even consider the opportunity, and Sara reluctantly gave up. Writing to him after her return to Springwood from the Caribbean trip and Washington:

Darling Franklin,

...I am feeling pretty blue. You are gone, the journey is over & I feel as if the time were not likely to come again when I shall take a trip with my dear boy, as we are not going abroad, but I must try to be unselfish & of course dear child I do rejoice in your happiness, & shall not put any stones or straws in the way of it. I shall go to town a week from Friday just to be with you when I can...Oh how still

the house is but it is home and full of memories dear to me. Do write. I am already longing to hear.

Your loving Mother[9]

Eleanor was well aware of Sara's concern about the situation, and sympathetic to her feelings of loss. "I knew your mother would hate to have you leave her dear," she wrote, "but don't let her feel that the last trip with you is over. We three must take them in the future together that is all and though I know three will never be the same to her still someday I hope that she will love me and I would be very glad if I thought she was even the least bit reconciled to me now...." Although resentful and jealous, Sara was graceful in defeat, realizing that perhaps the best way to preserve her relationship with her son was through Eleanor's deep sense of duty and loyalty and even greater eagerness to be accepted and loved by her soon-to-be mother-in-law. Hoping that she could win over Sara's affections, Grandmère spent as much time as possible with her, as well as with other members of the family, and yet Sara continued to insist on the secrecy of the engagement. Eleanor became accomplished at maintaining the charade that she and Franklin were no more than friendly cousins, although to some of her friends and cousins it became clear that Franklin was in love with her even if she seemed indifferent toward him. Perhaps a result of her newfound ability to love, which in turn allowed her to be more open and effervescent, Eleanor soon discovered that more and more men became attentive to her, finding her an interesting conversationalist and companion.

Finally, in the autumn of 1904, Franklin made the decision to enter Columbia University Law School rather than continue his law studies at

My grandmother on her wedding day.

Harvard. Although this was a decision prompted by his feelings for Eleanor and his desire to be near her, Sara found great pleasure in the fact that her beloved son would also be closer to her. During that first year at Columbia, his law studies commanded little of FDR's attention, and even the activities surrounding TR's presidential campaign seemed to hold little interest to the couple; they were fully involved with their feelings for each other. On October 7 Franklin went shopping for an engagement ring, and after much deliberation selected one from Tiffany's. On Grandmère's twentieth birthday he presented the ring to her. Still under the spell of her promise to Sara to keep their relationship a secret, Eleanor found it hard not to wear the token of their engagement until December, when the news was finally announced. Both sides of the family were ecstatic with joy, congratulating Franklin on his ability to attract such an extraordinary woman. A few of Grandmère's unsuccessful suitors were not quite so pleased, first among them being Nicholas Biddle, who confessed to his friend Franklin in his congratulatory note that he had "thrown away three unsatisfactory starts" at winning Eleanor for himself. Even her cousin Alice sent a warm greeting, "Oh, *dearest* Eleanor—it is simply too nice to be true...you old fox not to tell me before." The love and affection that her uncle Theodore held for Eleanor was obvious when he wrote to congratulate Franklin:

> ...*We are greatly rejoiced over the good news. I am as fond of Eleanor as if she were my own daughter; and I like you, and believe in you. No other success in life—not the Presidency, or anything else—begins to compare with the joy and happiness that come in and from the love of a true man and a true*

woman.... You and Eleanor are true and brave, and I believe you love each other unselfishly; and the golden years open before you.

Although the plans were to hold the wedding in New York at the adjoining Seventy-sixth Street brownstones of her cousin Susie (Mrs. Ludlow's daughter) and Mrs. Ludlow, Theodore (whom Grandmère had asked to stand in for her father to give her hand in marriage) tried to entice the couple to hold the wedding at the White House. Despite the generous offer, they decided to keep their original plans. Finally, after enduring the long and secretive months of waiting, Eleanor and Franklin were married on March 17, 1905, her mother's birthday. Immediately following the announcement that the couple were husband and wife, the happy high-pitched voice of the president of the United States could clearly be heard proclaiming, "Well, Franklin, there's nothing like keeping the name in the family!" Of course, having the president in attendance of the bride caused great fanfare, and soon during the reception the newlyweds found themselves quite abandoned, with all the attention being joyously garnered by TR. As soon as the president left to give a speech elsewhere in Manhattan, so many of the other guests began departing that the young couple decided they too would leave, retreating to Springwood. Graciously, Sara had turned the place over to them to spend some time at her sister's in Tuxedo, New York.

FDR and ER in San Remo,
Italy, during their honeymoon in 1905.

A Very Close Partnership

Success in marriage depends on being able, when you get over being in love, to really love...you never know anyone until you marry them.

—Eleanor Roosevelt

BELIEVE THAT GRANDMÈRE HOPED TO FIND in her marriage the sanctuary she had sought all her life, moorings that would provide her with the security and connection to the sympathetic nucleus of a supportive family. The catalogue of tragedies and deaths in her own family created in Eleanor a deep yearning to belong to and to be contained safely within the intimate confines of her life with Franklin. Her past must have risen like a ghost to bring on the fear of further loss and to make her need of her husband all the more poignant.

Following their wedding ceremony, Eleanor and Franklin had but a few short days at Hyde Park before returning to New York, where they made their home in an apartment at the old Webster Hotel. He resumed his studies at Columbia, and she became engrossed in the details of starting a home.

As bleak as a hotel apartment might sound, this unusual arrangement was quite welcomed by Grandmère, as it would give her and Franklin time to adjust to their life together. She also hoped the experience would help conceal how ill-prepared she felt she was to assume the role of housewife and homemaker. Their plans for a honeymoon holiday had to be delayed until FDR finished his exams, but in the interim Eleanor busied herself making the arrangements for their much-anticipated three-month honeymoon abroad. In those early days, the young bride eagerly hoped to forge a solid relationship with Sara, who from the beginning became a constant presence in Eleanor's daily routine. Once Franklin successfully completed his term at Columbia Law School, family and friends threw a rousing society bon-voyage party, after which the newlyweds finally departed on the *Oceanic* for their honeymoon…alone.

The late Victorian era had a remarkable ability to sweep "delicate" subjects under the carpet, especially sexuality, the most delicate subject of all. In Grandmother Hall's household the subject was completely evaded—a closed door—and that aspect of married life was simply not discussed. Thirty-five years later, Grandmère confessed the puzzlement of her early married life in saying, "There were certain subjects never discussed by ladies of different ages, and the result was frequently very bewildered young people when they found themselves faced with some of life's normal situations!" She would later confide to my aunt Anna that like all women of that era she was taught that sex was an ordeal to be borne—a wifely obligation and duty. According to my aunt, the sexual nature of a marital relationship had always seemed to Grandmère an extremely

difficult part of married life. She had been told before marriage that this was something one simply had to endure.

For Eleanor, who naturally shied away from expressing distressing emotions, this ill-preparedness must have proven difficult, especially as she was confronted by Franklin's obvious pleasure in the attentions showered upon him by admiring young ladies. His playful flirtations could only have heightened Eleanor's feelings of anxiety, and perhaps she even experienced fear at the unnerving

My grandfather took this photograph of Grandmère on a gondola in Venice on the very last day of their European sojourn.

91

power with which sexual attention could change people. Although certainly without malice or intent, the stage may well have been set during this period for the evolution of their future relationship.

During the couple's absence from New York, Sara too had been busy. Although Eleanor had looked forward to house hunting on their return, Sara had taken it upon herself to rent the Draper House (a mere three blocks from her own home) for them, and had staffed the house with three servants settled into the routine of his last two years of law school, finally completing the bar exam in 1907, while Eleanor, under the erstwhile guidance and observation of her mother-in-law, became the proper social matron, attending luncheons and teas and serving on the boards of "acceptable" and "proper" charitable organizations. Her keen interest in working in the settlement houses and among the poor had not diminished, but Sara and her friends convinced her that being around "those people" could have terrible consequences—she could bring home unspeakable diseases—and promptly dissuaded her from pursuing her social concerns.

Sara's view of the less privileged was different from the principled perspective Grandmère had inherited from her grandfather, father, and from TR. My aunt Anna explained that "[Grandmère's] brand of concern goes back to her childhood—if you read the credo of the TR family it was different from Granny's [Sara's] family; which was truly noblesse oblige and charity. That wasn't so with the TR clan. They got in with the newsboys."

Perhaps Sara wanted only to mold the young bride to fit within the inner circle of privileged society by bringing her into her own circle, as she would have her own daughter. Aunt Anna

cast light on the differences between Sara and TR's brands of society:

The TR clan were real extroverts. They loved to recite poetry (and write it). They made up limericks, etc. and were very outgoing whereas with Granny there was great affection but there was also a reserve mixed in with it. Halls were very much the same. The Delanos stayed very much with their own class while TR picked up a friend anywhere and expected his family to make that friend feel at home.[1]

A Douglas Chandor portrait of Sara. Opposite: *This photograph of Sara's house in New York City, to which my grandparents' first residence was attached, comes from my aunt Anna's photo album.*

The young couple's social life pivoted around the old and staid order, skirting the newer, gayer social crowd, but it was nevertheless eventful. Eleanor acquired a new set of friends, contemporaries of Sara, with whom she discussed art, music, and literature. She encouraged Franklin to enjoy his male contemporaries, return for visits to Harvard and old haunts at Cambridge, play polo, and take part in the hunts. Far from wealthy, they nevertheless benefited from income provided by their trust funds.

Although Franklin's new job as a clerk in the law firm of Carter, Ledyard and Milburn paid no salary the first year, they were able to live comfortably, without financial burdens or concern.

Eleanor later remembered this as a time of change, recognizing that old psychological patterns of insecurity and self-effacement began to erupt in the early months of her marriage. Eleanor confronted a life dominated by Sara with powerfully mixed feelings. An extraordinary intimacy existed between mother and son; by marrying Franklin, Eleanor had threatened to loosen, perhaps even sever, a bond that had existed since nursery days. Franklin had invited a stranger, another woman, into the most private recesses of his life, places where Sara had dwelt alone up to now. From the beginning Eleanor was caught in a tug-of-war between conciliation and restraint of feelings; quickly she found herself in an emotionally charged triangular situation. My aunt Anna was able to cast an interesting perspective on the triangle when biographer Joseph Lash asked her why she thought Grandmère had submitted, subordinating her own personality to Sara's:

...it went back deep into her childhood and her hunger for love and security. She thought at first she would find that love and security between Father and Granny. Her self-effacement and submission was a natural thing—here was a family that always had love and security and she was going into it and was part of that family. Once Granny accepted the fact of FDR's marriage, she gave FDR and ER more than love. She was a widow and this son was her only child. She took literally the statement that she was going to have both a son and a daughter now...In those days people didn't analyze themselves as they might do today. For Granny this was simply a matter of self-

My grandparents with baby Anna in Springwood in 1906.

preservation. She had an only child and she thought she might acquire a daughter as well, but to get her, she had to give them everything—at the level of material things—so she made arrangements for servants and a house, etc. for her little daughter-in-law. The implication was that she did these things not because she wanted to take ER over, but to fasten her closely to her.[2]

Love is never simple, and for Grandmère it was complicated from the beginning. On the one hand, her growing need for Franklin and her commitment to the marriage proved to be positive and strengthening. Having found the one person she had sought for so

long to love—and the one to be loved by—Eleanor finally had her own home. Such as it was, she had found a sense of contentment. However, feelings that had been buried early in her childhood began to resurface in her relationship with my grandfather. In some of the letters to FDR she signed herself "Little Nell," the name her father had used for her. Again, my aunt Anna was most eloquent about this aspect of my grandparents' relationship:

That false picture she had of her father she invested FDR with. He had similar qualities—debonair, charming—but FDR was her contemporary. He was a purely human being with all the faults of a human being and all the faults of his super-security and

FDR and ER sailing with their baby daughter and friends in Campobello.

super-love that he had had from his father and mother. Against the idealized picture she had of her father, FDR was bound to disappoint her. And because of his super-security FDR took her very much for granted and that she couldn't take.[3]

These early dynamics took years to develop into the many strands that would make up the extraordinary partnership my grandparents shared. Initially their marriage was a source of happiness and fulfillment to them both. Not long after their return from Europe, one of Grandmère's greatest premarriage fears was proven unfounded...she was pregnant! The excitement of the good news was soon overshadowed by the difficulties of her first pregnancy, and although she kept up a good face, she was plagued with considerable discomfort during the whole term. In February 1906 Eleanor was confined to bed, and she remained there until the announcement on the afternoon of May 3 of the birth of a beautiful little girl, Anna Eleanor, a strong baby weighing in at ten pounds one ounce. Although Sara had hoped for a boy, which may have been a common desire in families of that day and age to ensure continuation of the name and heritage, Eleanor was ecstatic at her daughter's arrival. It was, perhaps, a small source of triumph over her mother-in-law's dominance.

*Grandmère with Anna and baby James,
in the fall of 1908, at Springwood.*

With her first baby boy, James.

Motherhood

For the next ten years Eleanor settled into the role of mother, as planned by Sara, who continued to be in evidence in practically every aspect of her life, from the choice of servants and nannies to the planning of meals for the household. Grandmère's insecurities became more pronounced at this time. She walked a thin line between wanting to be guided by and to have the support of her strong mother-in-law and resenting the loss of power this entailed. She was seemingly unable to establish rules and boundaries, even with her own children. As they would later confirm, whenever Eleanor denied one of their requests, no matter how insignificant, they could always turn to their grandmother, who would often countermand their mother's denial. Sara's constant presence only intensified Eleanor's feelings of inadequacy, breaking down the qualities of solidity and security she had sought in marriage and family.

By 1909, Franklin, Jr., the first, was born, and here we see him with Anna and James.

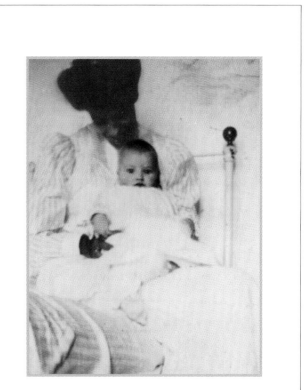

Grandmère with baby Franklin, Jr. just before he died.

Eleanor's silent endurance was made steadfast by her acute need to be loved and accepted by both Sara and Franklin, and although resentful of the constant intrusions, she continued to depend upon Sara.

These ten years were characterized by pregnancies and the rearing of a young family, a decade when she was "either getting over having a baby or getting ready to have one." James was born in 1907. Their second son, the first Franklin Jr., followed in 1909, but was born with a weakness of heart; he died at eight months after a bout of influenza and pneumonia. His death was devastating to Eleanor, and she assumed much of the blame for it. During these months of grief she became pregnant again. The deep sorrow she felt at the death of her baby boy had reawakened the melancholy of her relationship with her own father, and so she named the new baby—my father—after him. Eleanor would later say that Dad reminded her most of her father, and was thus perhaps her favorite of all her children.

My father's birth consoled Grandmère's grief after the death of Franklin Jr. Here we see him as a baby with James and Anna in 1911.

The children were educated by "proper English nannies"—as was the Roosevelt custom—who made all decisions about their upbringing. As she would later state, "If I had it to do over again, I know now that what we should have done was to have no servants those first few years.... Had I done this, my subsequent troubles would have been avoided and my children would have had far happier childhoods."

Sara's authority over Eleanor's family

Three photographs taken by FDR.
Left: *Grandmère with James.* Center: *With Anna on a swing.* Right: *With my father Elliott.*

reached a climax when she and Franklin, with no consultation with Eleanor, decided that the young family would move into a house immediately next door to one Sara was building on East Sixty-fifth Street, a house with connecting doors on each of the three levels. Even with Grandmère's capacity for absorbing shock, this was something she could not endure silently. Once again, even the furnishings and decorations of the house were planned and executed by Sara, right down to the choice of Eleanor's dressing table. Eleanor was livid, and shortly after moving in made her unhappiness an issue with FDR. His reaction was feigned bewilderment at her dissatisfaction, a skilled avoidance of all confrontation arising from the two women of his life. My aunt Anna commented that the tensions erupting in this powerful triangle were due to the diametrically opposite childhood experiences my grandparents had had:

I'm sure Father fell down here. You couldn't find, in emotional matters, two such different people as Mother and Father. Father had too much security, too much love. His mother, father, and aunts all doted on him. There was complete security. No really traumatic experience. He was fourteen when he first went to school. His letters show that he realized he was dealing with two doting parents, whom he treated with humor, whereas Mother never had a goddamn soul she could depend on, whose star in heaven she was.

You know that story about Mother breaking down at her dressing table in a fit of weeping. Father quickly got out of the room. I'm sure he could not understand this—Mother's feeling that nothing was her own: her house, her children, etc.—maybe he could with outsiders, but not when his wife was involved.[4]

The thing that will always live with me
is the fact that I think she grew more than any other human being that I've known.

—James Roosevelt

Also, Franklin's relationship with Sara was dramatically different than Eleanor's relationship with her mother-in-law. It is again my aunt Anna who, as their eldest child, articulates best the differences:

I saw him being cheeky as hell to Granny. He loved to shock her. Mother stresses much too much how they (Franklin and Sara) used to fight; sure they fought...but on other occasions he would love to outrage Granny, tease her. He could never do that with Mother. She was much too serious. Mother was inhibiting to him. She would never go along.[5]

This difficult period, I believe, marked the turning point, the beginning of Grandmère's emergence from Sara's domination and her assumption of the role of head of the house (FDR chose to distance himself from all matters relating to the household and child-rearing). According to my father, it was the constant chafing against Sara's will that helped to strengthen Grandmère's own determination:

> *My grandmother played a big part in the development of my mother...My grandmother was a very strong, powerful woman...Later, she was forced into the background and her domination started to dwindle with my mother as my mother grew stronger and my mother learned that she had the ability to do things on her own and that she could ignore my grandmother...The net result was that it was my grandmother's iron will working on Mother that helped to have Mother grow—because Mother had to bump into it all the time, as did Father. Father grew in the same way.*
>
> *So you see, you don't always get your development from the all-seeing, wonderful person who guides you...you also get guided by the people who are a terrible, terrible thorn in your side. And you think, "Oh my God, how can I put up with them?" They come through, finally, as helping to develop your character.*[6]

Even though Franklin left the responsibility of the education of his children in the hands of Sara, Eleanor, and a troupe of nannies, he would happily romp with his "chicks" around Springwood and ride, sleigh, and join in a multitude of other weekend activities. Above all, he loved the times at the family's summer retreat at Campobello Island, a Canadian isle off the coast of Maine, where he shared with the children his love for the sea and sailing.

My grandfather found his career as a legal clerk in the admiralty division with the Carter, Ledyard and Milburn law firm of minimal interest and challenge, and so in 1910 he decided to make his inaugural run for the New York State Assembly. However, at the twelfth hour, the incumbent decided to run for reelection, forcing FDR to challenge for the seat in the heavily Republican Twenty-sixth Senate District. Though party leaders considered his chances for success nil at best, my grandfather waged an enthusiastic campaign and was rewarded with a remarkable landslide victory. Interestingly, as she would later explain, Grandmère was never consulted on his decision to enter politics, but with his victory she realized that their lives would be forever changed.

Top: *My grandfather loved to romp around with his chicks. Here my father is on FDR's knees.* Bottom: *Grandfather campaigning in Dutchess County in 1910.* Opposite, clockwise from top left: *Grandmère with my father Elliott in 1913. My grandparents with Anna, James, Elliott, and a young friend, are joined by Harry Parish, a family friend, for a sailing trip at Campobello. My grandmother and my father in 1917.*

The Beginning of a Public Life

The changes that Grandmère had anticipated in her life began soon after FDR's triumph. From the moment they arrived in Albany, she found the atmosphere surrounding the political environment of the State Capitol invigorating, if not reenergizing. She had entered an altogether new period in her life, although certainly not one for which she had prepared herself. Intellectually stimulated, she found her new acquaintances interesting and the world of politics engrossing. She loved spending evenings with FDR and his colleagues discussing issues of the day. But more, and for perhaps the first time in their marriage, she reveled in the closeness of the periods she would spend with my grandfather and his willing openness and inclusion of her in discussions of political matters. No longer hesitant to voice her opinions, many of which were at odds with his, she blossomed into a new maturity, a heightened awareness of her role as the wife of a rising political star. Without doubt, these early days in Albany, and her integration into her husband's political world, formed the embryo of the emergence of their remarkable lifelong partnership. In that little town, so open to and encouraging of discourse and debate, Grandmère found a strength and a mission that was not only supportive of her husband's new career but was nourishing for a part of her persona that had been dormant since her days at Allenswood.

Although initially disapproving of her son's decision to enter the world of politics, Sara most certainly reveled in his success and the attention drawn to him. While a frequent visitor to the young family in Albany, usually on occasions of political

FDR in the State Senate Chamber in Albany in 1911.

significance or when she felt Eleanor was in need of her "assistance," fortunately Sara did not decide to move there herself.

Eleanor took inspiration from the political acumen of the Oyster Bay Roosevelt women, particularly Auntie Bye, and found that the more she engaged others, the more sought after she was for her own opinions. My aunt Anna remembered this as being perhaps the time when Grandmère realized that she too had personal ambition. Her aunts Maude and Pussie regarded her as belonging to their generation, and perhaps expected her to carry the torch lit in her younger years by the TR clan. But Grandmère didn't think of herself as glamorous like her aunts and cousins, which is why, until now, she had remained eclipsed from participating more fully in public life. At some point, however, she must

Louis Howe became a crucial ally in my grandfather's political career.
From left to right: Louis, Tom Lynch (a campaign supporter), FDR, and a very timid-looking ER.

have realized that she had a strong desire to be successful as an individual. I have to think that Grandmère was delighted to find that she was being accepted as a person in her own right, not just as the wife of FDR. She was not utterly transformed, but certainly the transformation was beginning.

Throughout this period, life in general was settling nicely for Eleanor and Franklin. FDR was thoroughly ensconced in his political routine, and Grandmère had settled the family into a routine that she, not her mother-in-law, determined, a routine that allowed her more time with her children and husband.

It was during this period that Franklin and Eleanor met Louis Howe, a man who in Grandmère's view was neither refined nor particularly stimulating, but who would forever change the

course of their lives. Pokey and disheveled, urbane in speech and manner, and seldom without a cigarette dangling from his mouth, this wily newspaper reporter would quickly entwine himself in their futures. Louis early on recognized the potential of this young politician and immediately began nurturing a friendship. Hungry for power himself but realistic enough to recognize his political limitations, he attached his star to that of Franklin Roosevelt. He was uncannily shrewd and a master of developing public opinion and support, and his devotion to both Franklin and Eleanor would make him one of the most influential and driving forces behind their collective successes. In the course of the years, Louis Howe would achieve a level of political power, influence, and importance even he could not have imagined.

My grandparents and their political supporters on their 1920 campaign trip.

Barely a year into his first term as senator, Franklin Roosevelt (or at least his name) was being bandied about political circles as a potential gubernatorial candidate even though many considered him a political "prude," "progressive," and too much in the mold of Theodore Roosevelt. His famous relative, in the meantime, was attracting both Democrats and Republicans in an effort to unseat then-President Taft; having defected the Republican Party, he was now heading the Bull Moose Party. FDR, faced with a split within his own party between the conservative wing and the more progressive Wilsonian faction, decided to cast his lot with the latter. Although the initial prospects for his own reelection seemed dim, the chaos reigning within the Republican ranks assured his success at the polls once more. On

Election Day, Woodrow Wilson emerged as the resounding victor for the presidency, but unfortunately this meant that cousin Teddy was soundly defeated. While ecstatic at their own political success on the local level and at the Democrats' success at the national level, a personal sadness also pervaded Eleanor and Franklin. Their beloved Teddy, the one political inspiration upon whom FDR had attributed so much of his own political underpinnings and philosophy, had been defeated. My grandparents realized that this could signal the beginning of the end of the political career of one of the nation's most brilliant and exciting leaders, a man who had forever transformed the meaning of American politics, and a mentor to them both.

In a different vehicle, but on the same campaign trip in 1920.

Splitting and Coming Together

Much has been written and surmised about the split between the two branches of my family, and many suppositions put forth about the causes. From what I can tell, it was the 1920 election that sowed the seeds of discord. Since entering politics, FDR had quite successfully and unabashedly drawn upon the reverence for and popularity of his distant cousin. This was a way to narrow the gap of political philosophy between his Democrat supporters and Republicans, particularly important since most all of his campaigns had been in either marginally Democratic districts or those ensconced in Republican ideology. It cannot be said, however, that his paralleling of philosophies with those of TR

was disingenuous. FDR not only held TR in the highest esteem both personally and politically, he even credited Theodore with influencing the core values of his own political beliefs. And for Eleanor, of course, Theodore Roosevelt was both her uncle *and* surrogate father; she adored him above all other family members. She was, after all, born and raised in that "Oyster Bay Republican" political philosophy.

However, many members of the Oyster Bay Roosevelt branch felt that if any Roosevelt should be garnering national recognition during this election it should be TR Jr., not the upstart FDR. According to cousin Alice, her side of the family did not support FDR's adventure in politics because of an attitude of a priori presumptuousness:

We all wondered how Franklin would vote in the

105

1904 election—for his party or for his cousin. And he chose his cousin. We never returned the favor and none of our family ever voted for Franklin as far as I knew. We called him a maverick. We behaved terribly. There we were the Roosevelts hubris up to the eyebrows, beyond the eyebrows, and then who should come sailing down the river but Nemesis in the person of Franklin. We were out. Run over.[7]

FDR's exploitation of Teddy's popularity and achievements caused great resentment, so much so, in fact, that the National Republican Committee quickly recruited TR Jr. to dog FDR's public appearances, denouncing him as a maverick without "the brand of our family." FDR would respond to these attacks by TR Jr. by saying that "in 1912 Senator Harding called Theodore Roosevelt first a Benedict Arnold and then an Aaron Burr. This is one thing at least some members of the Roosevelt family will not forget." Senator Harding had at the time considered TR's bolting from the Republican Party an unforgivable act of political treason. Grandmère was shocked by the attacks on her husband by certain members of her closest family, and was devastated by the personal nature of the denouncements. Her relationship with Alice was never again the same, and it is said that she and TR Jr. never spoke again. The rupture between the two sides of the family remained for many years, often with family members having neither real understanding of the circumstances nor recollection of the causes. Although several of us had close friendships with members of the opposite side of the clan, and a certain pride and respect for the achievements of our ancestors, it was not until the late 1980s that the healing process began at a joint reunion of the

FDR with President Woodrow Wilson listening to Secretary Daniels speaking at Flag Day celebrations. From left to right: William Jennings, President Woodrow Wilson, Henry Breckinridge, and Secretary Joseph Daniels. Opposite: Grandmère on a reviewing stand during my grandfather's campaign.

Hyde Park and Oyster Bay Roosevelts at Springwood. I am delighted to say that these reunions continue on a fairly regular basis today, usually every other year, at various locales connected with the family: Springwood, Sagamore Hill, Campobello, the Theodore Roosevelt National Park in North Dakota, and elsewhere. And as my generation and the next become well acquainted, there shall be greater understanding of the legacy of our ancestors and fewer divides between us. In many ways, I think it is a rediscovering of our own roots, and of the importance of not just the three most prominent family members in our nation's history but of so many others as well.

On to Washington

Soon after Wilson's impressive victory and Franklin's own reelection to the New York Senate, his early support of the new president was rewarded. Early in 1913 Josephus Daniels, the Secretary of the Navy, asked Franklin if he would be interested in a position in the administration as Assistant Secretary of the Navy. FDR was ecstatic; how could he *not* be interested? First, it appealed to his singularly great passion, a love of the ocean and ships. And of course it thrust him onto the Washington political scene in a position of authority, visibility, and responsibility. This fit right within the patterned prescription that FDR had defined for his political career, and closely paralleled the path of TR's own success. On March 17, 1913, on the eighth anniversary of their marriage, FDR took the oath of office to this position, and everyone congratulated him on this fundamental step in a

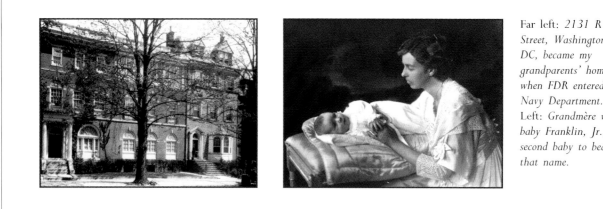

Far left: *2131 R Street, Washington, DC, became my grandparents' home when FDR entered the Navy Department.* Left: *Grandmère with baby Franklin, Jr., the second baby to bear that name.*

rapidly rising career in Washington. Whereas his new boss, Secretary Daniels, was a hopeless landlubber with little understanding of the Navy, its importance, or its hierarchy, Roosevelt immediately built upon his knowledge and keen interests to form a base of respect and admiration within the service, and more often than not found himself at odds with his superior. Realizing that he needed the help of someone loyal to his ambitions and well versed in "making things happen," FDR once more relied on his most loyal aide, Louis Howe, who immediately joined him in Washington.

For Grandmère, the move from New York was unnerving. Fulfilling her obligations as a Washington political wife was a much greater task than it had ever been in quiet Albany, but Grandmère went about it with enthusiasm and high energy. Men and women alike admired her easy manner and friendly approach, her inexhaustible energy, and the wisdom she offered in her opinions. The social obligations of the Assistant Secretary were heavy, but buoyed by her successes in Albany she was confident that she could rise to whatever occasion presented itself.

While in Washington, the young family rented Auntie Bye's house, very nearly across the street from the Executive Office Building, the location of FDR's office, and began settling in. The lives of the children now revolved almost totally around their father, even though he still refused to assume any responsibility for their discipline. He would refuse, for example, to scold the children when on occasion they would drop paper sacks filled with water on the heads of arriving guests to the house, excusing their acts as "childish but harmless pranks." My father, Elliott, once described my grandfather's method of discipline.

The children learned early in life that when Mother tried to discipline them they could always go and get around that discipline with Granny.... Father was the one who used to take us...into his office...off the cloakroom in the house, when Mother would send one of the small boys in and say, "Franklin, there is this terrible thing that this one has done." And it was

Far left: *Grandmère with Franklin, Jr., and my father Elliott on the steps of Springwood in 1916.*
Left: *Grandmère and the children in descending order of height!*

either instructions to spank him or to give him a good lecture. Father was known to sit you down and say, "Well, now I think it's time that you let out a yell, and then she'll think I've hit you, and that will be enough because I don't think what you did was serious enough to be spanked." Or it was something that she sent you in for that you had to be talked to, as happened when you were slightly older—sixteen, seventeen, eighteen years old and had cars and were driving. Father would say, "All right, we'll just talk here for a while, and when you go out, look very grave."... So he was not a disciplinarian—Mother was—but Mother was overruled ninety percent of the time by Granny.[8]

Soon, however, the extensive travel required of their father and his increasingly busy schedule as Washington's ascending political star began to take a toll on FDR's relationship with his children: He was simply never around to feed their insatiable appetite for his attentions.

During the Washington years Eleanor gave

birth to her last two children: the second Franklin Jr., born in 1914, and John Aspinwall, born in 1916. Although the children did not lack for attention and care, Grandmère would later realize that her child-rearing abilities were less than ideal, probably a result of her own unusual childhood experiences coupled with Sara's intrusions in all matters of the children's lives. She would in time acknowledge that as a young parent she had been overly protective, too stern a disciplinarian, and in many ways puritanical to the extreme. When the children were younger Grandmère tried to be a dutiful mother, but perhaps lacked the confidence to make the bond really close. But a sense of intimacy was something she developed later, once she had achieved so much more in her life, with all of her children and especially with her grandchildren. My aunt Anna felt that her own relationship with her mother only began properly when she turned eighteen, and they started to have warmer, franker conversations:

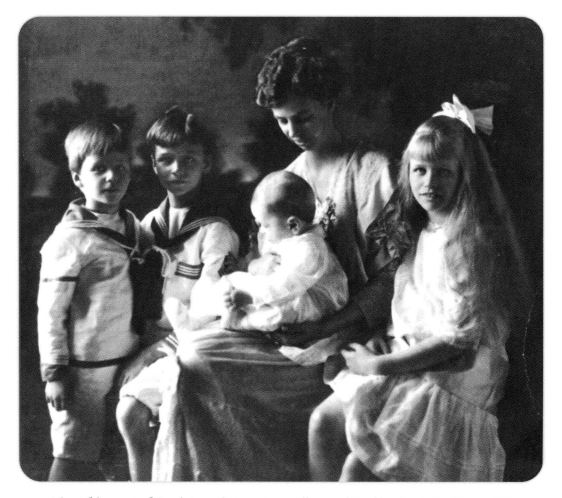

A beautiful portrait of Grandmère with Anna, James, Elliott, and Franklin, Jr., in Washington, DC.
Opposite: Lucy Mercer, my grandmother's social secretary, with whom my grandfather had a lasting affair.

I would say she felt a tremendous duty to her children and it was part of that duty to read to them, hear their prayers and sing a hymn to them before they went to bed, but their really intimate lives were run by nurses and governesses and she had no real insight into the needs of a child for primary closeness to a parent.[9]

This was also an important period in Eleanor Roosevelt's education as a public persona, and though she gained skills, she would regard it as a period of great personal sacrifice. The demands of a political career are indeed stressful on any family, and often the conflict between private and public lives cracks relationships, opening an emotional chasm between partners. Grandmère made an effort to preserve her young family from the effects of the merry-go-round of dinners and social engagements. Whenever possible and during the children's school holidays she would take refuge either at Springwood with Sara or at Campobello, where the solitude provided her with the serenity she missed in the capital. The work constraints of her husband and his own official social schedule and travels often kept him away from Eleanor and the children for weeks. The period from 1913 to 1917, the devastating years of World War I, was extremely intense for Franklin, whose obligations and duties became more critical than ever before.

By late 1913 Grandmère's Washington schedule had become so hectic that it required her to hire a social secretary. She chose Lucy Page Mercer, a twenty-two-year-old who was well based in social circles, for she came from a socially prominent and well-to-do patrician family from Baltimore whose members included several Washington insiders. Lucy quickly became an integral part of the household, where she was adored by the children and approved and accepted by Sara. Interestingly, Lucy was possessed of a beauty and femininity that Eleanor thought lacking in herself.

During the spring and summer of 1917 Eleanor and Franklin's schedule kept them mostly apart. In July, while Franklin sailed to Europe to inspect the U.S. fleet, Grandmère gave generously of her time to the Red Cross, among others, for the war effort. Her work for the Red Cross was considered inappropriate for a woman of her social standing. It was dirty, dangerous work that often put her personally in peril and most certainly exposed her to the loud criticism of her peers. Her uncle Theodore was perhaps the only member of her family who supported her work and so admired her tireless efforts and leadership that he contributed one third of his 1906 Nobel Peace Prize money to support Grandmère's work for the Red Cross. She met with the wounded sailors and their families, victims who awakened in her the same feelings as had the children of New York City's tenements all those years ago, and she extended heartfelt compassion and kind words in the face of their devastation. Grandmère and her five children spent August and September with Granny at Springwood.

Grandmère was at Sara's estate when she received a telegram on September 12 asking her to meet her husband's returning ship with an ambulance and a doctor. Like most men on the ship, many of whom had died at sea from the viral infection, FDR was deathly ill with double pneumonia and influenza. Unless he received immediate treatment, it was possible her entire household would soon be in the same condition as Franklin. That first night of his arrival home, as she unpacked his suitcases and sorted through his mail, she found a neat and hefty bundle containing scores of Lucy Mercer's love letters. One can only imagine what a devastating and unexpected shock this was for Grandmère, who had dedicated the last thirteen years of her life to Franklin's life and career, accommodating everything no matter how hard or difficult it was for her. She confronted him with her find, offering him freedom despite the fact that divorce was regarded as a social and most certainly a political disgrace. Sara was aghast at the prospect that her son might choose that other much younger woman over his devoted wife and five children, and her immediate reaction was to threaten to completely sever all financial support of FDR. When offering him the chance for divorce, Grandmère suggested that he should "think things over carefully" before giving his answer. To choose divorce would have devastating results for his career as a politician, with no guarantee that he would win Lucy in the end, for she was a Catholic and likely would not marry a divorced man. According to my aunt Anna, she doubted that his sole reason for not getting a divorce was his political career. However, in her view, Grandmère punished herself for years with that belief. The doubt in her mind and heart was that he didn't truly love her.

He had a choice to make, and choose he did—Eleanor—promising to end all "romantic involvement" with Lucy Mercer. My father attempted to explain his mother's feelings of devastation at the discovery of the affair:

Mother spent the first seven years of her marriage constantly pregnant, and my father went through World War I being busier and busier and busier.... And my mother was such an insecure person during those first few years that I think it became a tremendous blow to her to realize what was going on. I don't think she had any inkling that such a thing was possible between two people who had said their vows, and so it was horribly upsetting to her.[10]

For Eleanor this was the beginning of a long path of extricating herself from the total if not all-consuming devotion she felt for Franklin. So devastated was she, that her agreement was to be his partner and to support his career, but that was the full extent of her commitment. She recognized, I think, their compatible destinies, but effectively ended the more intimate romantic bonds that she had worked so hard to establish between them. My father described the partnership that existed from then on between his parents:

This partnership was to last all the way through their life; it became a very close and very intimate partnership of great affection—never in a physical sense, but in a tremendously mental sense. And while I think both of them were inclined toward other people from time to time, they both realized that they were never going to get out of harness from then on.[11]

On one level this unexpected turn of events could be viewed as yet another tragedy in Grandmère's life, but perhaps Franklin's debonair, flirtatious manner predestined the failure of the intimate partnership, to be nurtured in faithfulness and honesty, Eleanor so desperately sought. This was an episode of which she seldom spoke, to anyone, except some twenty-five years later when she confided in her close friend and official biographer, Joe Lash, that "The bottom dropped out of my own particular world. I faced myself, my surroundings, my world honestly for the first time." Such a devastating and long-lasting effect did this have on Grandmère that at some point, perhaps several years later, she destroyed all of the love letters and correspondence she'd received from FDR—correspondence that had been so important to her and which she had so meticulously saved for so many years. She suffered the betrayal in solitude, vowing her support but at the same time reclaiming that part of herself that she had given so unselfishly when declaring their wedding vows.

She emerged many months later as if from a period of long hibernation during which she had found a new strength and determination. She had liberated herself from the emotional imbalance of their one-sided relationship and had been released from her ever-present fear of losing him. She had broken the bonds of dependence on Franklin, and on Sara. Aunt Anna remembered this as a period of resurgence for Grandmère:

> Then came the period in Mother's life when she began to discover her true abilities, organizationally, communicationally, her grasp of problems. Since she could not get from Father the kind of total love and devotion she needed, she sought people whom she could depend on to love her... Once she grew to accept that Father was not going to be what she thought he should be—or at least unconsciously had hoped he would be—it was then that she really started to build her own independence of thinking on many, many issues... She thought through her position on such issues as women's rights, labor, welfare, so that when Father went back into public life she had such definite opinions of her own, she could pester the hell out of him... Yet through all those years and in the last year and a half I was very close, I saw that the two had preserved a mutual respect and their own type of affection and a tremendous feeling of duty toward each other.[12]

Although their relationship was forever altered, she now shared a more powerful and certainly unique bond with him, one that was responsible on many occasions for happiness, shared glory, and greatness.

My grandparents shared a unique partnership few understood yet many admired. Here they're sitting on the porch of Springwood.

As this new relationship evolved, Grandmère and Grandfather developed a rare and unusual personal and political companionship; it was a close partnership that many would come to envy, but few could ever fathom. But it was the uniqueness of what they built together in the years following that created one of the most enduring collaborations of modern times.

A stunning Chandor portrait of FDR.

The Close of the Washington Years

By 1918 World War I was coming to a close. It was still a busy and exacting time for the Assistant Secretary of the Navy, yet Franklin Roosevelt was becoming restless and somewhat disenchanted if not discouraged with his immediate prospects. In 1919 he talked Secretary Daniels into allowing him to travel to Europe to direct the disengagement of the naval forces from their wartime stance, and perhaps as an olive branch offering he took Eleanor with him on the trip. Her first return to Europe since their honeymoon fourteen years earlier was an exciting and welcome opportunity, marred only by the news received on their crossing aboard the USS *George Washington* of the death of Theodore Roosevelt. The last few years had been filled with disappointments for TR. He had worked diligently to moderate his former Republican Party colleagues, but had also engaged in a strong opposition of Wilson's Administration policies. So antagonistic had the relations between the sitting and the former Presidents become that at TR's death Wilson could only offer the statement that Theodore Roosevelt had made "no constructive policy to his record." Grandmère, on the other hand, was more accurate, as history would prove, when she wrote in her diary, "Another great figure off the stage." She and FDR were both saddened by this tragic loss for the country, and she for the loss of a father figure.

During these years Eleanor did not directly enter into political affairs, still considering the political arena her husband's domain. Nevertheless, she was beginning to venture forth by developing her own views on public and political events, often privately expressing them among her friends and colleagues.

As the Washington years drew to a close, Grandmère would look back at both the triumphs and travails by observing in the final entry of her diary for 1919, "I do not think I have ever felt so strangely as in the past year...perhaps it is that I have never noticed little things before but all my self-confidence is gone and I am on the edge though I was never better physically I feel sure." As bitter as the times had been, Grandmère was emerging a matured woman, although she certainly did not recognize the

transformation in herself. She had become thoughtfully sophisticated in her political analysis, unequivocal in her opinions, and capable of achieving her own destiny. She was finally realizing that self-fulfillment could not be achieved through someone else's beliefs and accomplishments. "Somewhere along the line of development we discover what we really are, and then we make our real decision for which we are responsible. Make that decision primarily for yourself because you can never really live anyone else's life...The influence you exert is through your own life and what you become yourself." And it was now that she assumed total control over the lives of her five children, wresting away the influence that Sara and the nannies had previously usurped with her tacit approval. Times in the Roosevelt family were forever changing.

Seeing as how 1920 was an election year, FDR was busy traveling about New York preparing for either a U.S. Senate race or the state's governorship. When he left to attend the Democratic convention in San Francisco, neither he nor Eleanor knew which race he would make, but it was assumed they would be returning to New York, a move for which Eleanor was anxiously preparing. Certainly the results of the convention were as shockingly unexpected for Grandmère as they were for everyone else. James M. Cox, a relative unknown in national politics, was nominated as the presidential candidate, with Franklin D. Roosevelt the overwhelming choice for vice president! The chance for FDR to launch himself onto the national political stage was as disagreeable for Eleanor as it was agreeable for him, but she was again accepting of her role, even realizing that the prospects of success for her husband and his running mate were practically impossible. She adapted to these new circumstances with a sense of detachment and objectivity, as though participating from the outside.

From Campobello, Eleanor followed the progress of the new vice presidential candidate. Then, in September, Franklin quite unexpectedly asked her to join him and Louis Howe on the campaign trail. The 1920 election was the first national election in which women voted, and at that striking hour the wife of a vice presidential candidate could have great impact on the crowds. The relationship between my grandparents at this time was troubled; as they both sought to live their own separate lives under one roof the only common thread between them appears to have been politics. Grandmère joined Franklin and Louis to tour the country week after exhausting week, always remaining gracious and highly energetic but definitely in the background. Usually she was the only woman in the crowd, and all she could do was listen to the political speeches, unable to offer her own opinions. To make matters worse, Franklin had little time to pay her any attention. She spent increasingly long and lonely hours in her own quarters on the campaign train, being completely left out of FDR's loop. It was Louis Howe who noticed her absences and who took it upon himself to include her as the campaign unfolded. He appreciated her excellent political instincts and sense of humor, and, recognizing her value as an advisor on important points of political strategy and issues, would often seek her opinions. It was during these weeks that the friendship and close conspiracy between Grandmère and Louis was forged as together they reviewed press coverage of FDR, helped with speeches, and found ways of collaborating. Not only was she flattered by his attention and obvious respect, but she also began to recognize Louis's own keen intelligence and political savvy. The friendship between them was sealed when one day, having discovered that she had never seen the Niagara Falls, Louis invited Grandmère to leave the campaign for a few hours and to play tourists together, returning where they had left off. It was perhaps on that day that Grandmère felt trusting that Louis was becoming as devoted to her as he was to my grandfather. Louis's role acquired an unexpected facet for both Franklin and Eleanor: He not only supported FDR but had started to help bridge whatever gaps of communication existed between them; he also provided her with a closer involvement in Franklin's work. Finally, after all the years of Louis Howe's "hanging around," so obviously riding the coattails of her husband's political star, Grandmère began developing a true respect and fondness for this unkempt, rough little man; they were becoming soul mates of a sort.

My aunt Anna remembered that Louis had been a pivotal force in helping Grandmère recognize her own potential and express her own ambitions:

Louis Howe as far as I know was the first person who brought out her ability and talent so there was much gratitude toward him in her heart for what he had done for both of them.[13]

On the Monday before the election, Franklin and Eleanor returned to Dutchess County, where he gave his last speech in Poughkeepsie. On the day of the election, Franklin held an open house for friends and neighbors at Springwood to anxiously await the results. Hopes that the million new women voters would all cast their vote for Mr. Cox were quickly dashed. As the first telegraph

*My grandparents with Franklin, Jr.
and baby John in Campobello in 1918.*

referred to himself as "Franklin D. Roosevelt, Ex.-V.P., Canned. (Erroneously reported dead)." In fact, although the loser, he had firmly established himself as a national political figure, had developed his own cadre of followers and assistants, and as the FDR historian Frank Freidel has said, the campaign "was not so much a lost crusade as a dress rehearsal" for what lay ahead.

Eleanor's close friends had been delighted at the news and saw her as Franklin's "running mate" in Washington, for they knew that as the wife of America's vice president, Eleanor could contribute much that would benefit the country at large. Eleanor was happy that Franklin had achieved a role into which he could channel his passion for politics, but she was at a point in her life when she wished more for herself than to just be his wife. In an early interview given to the *Eagle News* during Franklin's homecoming ceremonies at Poughkeepsie, she declared an active interest in the League of Nations:

> *I am particularly interested in the League of Nations issue and I am firmly in favor of it, though I think we should adopt it with the reservation that Congress shall vote on whether or not we shall enter a war. But the League of Nations is, I believe, the only way that we can prevent war. We fought for it, and we should adopt it. If we don't adopt it, it will be useless. The U.S. must be part of the alliance.*[14]

Her views, so distinctly stated, paid tribute to a woman who thought for herself and was no longer shy about sharing her viewpoints on topics that interested her. Slowly but surely, a new Eleanor was emerging from a long incubation, from the chrysalis she had inhabited most of her life, and people were beginning to take an active interest.

bringing election news was read, Franklin learned that voters had chosen the Republican candidate by an overwhelming majority. His reaction, although surely disappointed, was good-natured; he jokingly

A Return to New York

That fall the family returned to New York, and Grandfather joined a new law firm, which became Emmett, Marvin, and Roosevelt. He also became vice president at the New York offices of Van Lear Black's Fidelity and Deposit Company in Maryland, was a Harvard overseer, and headed the Navy Club and the New York Boy Scouts Council, keeping a schedule that was as busy as it would have been had he been elected. Suffering from his first political defeat and forced to return to the world of private business that he found so constraining, FDR had no intentions of abandoning his political ambitions; they were merely delayed temporarily.

Grandmère had likewise decided not to remain idle, and she enrolled at a business school where she learned typing and shorthand. She became active in the League of Women Voters, engaged dynamically with women legislators who promoted better working conditions for women, and campaigned for children's rights and other issues that were of intense significance to her. In joining the LWV board, she educated herself in the legislative process, selected bills on which she wanted to be briefed more fully, and became close and lifelong friends with Esther Everett Lape, an important figure in the suffrage movement. For those many occasions that she now spent in Manhattan, she shared an apartment with Esther on East Eleventh Street that would soon become a "place of her own" away from her family duties and a refuge, from Springwood as well as from Franklin and Sara.

Esther's friendship had a thoroughly positive effect on Eleanor; it helped her to learn how to approach public issues and how to debate and speak forthrightly, and it inspired her to do always serious, sustained work for the causes to which she was sympathetic. This was a crucial time in Grandmère's life. For the first time since her Allenswood days she was forming lasting friendships, and immersed herself in political and labor activities and groups. It was also at this time that she began her political writing that would continue for the rest of her life, and much to her own surprise perhaps she was recognized as a political player in Democratic politics in her own right and with little to do with who her husband was. Before now, I think, she had seen herself merely as an extension of my grandfather's political ambitions, but it was during this period that she realized that she too was possessed of the political intellect and leadership needed to embrace a path of her own.

So important was the period in Grandmère's political education that when we began asking her political questions, even as teenagers, she was always keen to teach us and helped us to see politics from her acute perspective, but she never forced her views upon us. My cousin Franklin D. Roosevelt III

remembers that his political awakening was guided by Grandmère in the subtlest way:

In my own case, what changed our relationship...from a rather distant, one-of-the-pack type of relationship to a more personal one was my own coming of age politically and becoming aware of certain things in the world (race relations, problems of race and poverty, international relations, and political issues in general...). As I began to open myself up to these things, first of all, I realized who my grandmother was in a very different way than I had understood before. So the occasions I had to get together with her I treated in a different way and I took advantage of them in a different way. And I think she responded also to that, noticing that I was interested in a lot of the same things she was interested in.

...once I developed these interests she was very supportive and would invite me to lunch in New York when she was having interesting people over.... But there was never any feeling that I was being pushed by her in these directions at all. If anything, [it was] the other way; I was just pulled by her and very much influenced by her example and her life, her accomplishments in those areas, and her obviously genuine way of responding to these kinds of problems in the world.[15]

My brother, Tony, also remembers Grandmère offering him her own unique perspective on being politically active:

I think perhaps I made the statement that I felt it was better to vote for the best individual. And she said, "Oh, no. You just can't do that. Don't you understand the importance if you're going to make a meaningful contribution of becoming involved in one political party or the other, and then working within the framework of that party? Ultimately that's the only way that you can be politically effective, and while you may not agree with the man who is running for the office with that party label at this moment, the only way that you can be effective in changing anything is to back him, vote for him. But get involved in the party process and change things that way. You can't change things simply by casting a vote for an individual whom you might agree with. That's just not effective."[16]

The women who worked with Eleanor at the League saw the unveiling of an initially shy but earnest woman into someone who spoke and thought with great clarity, could be counted on for support, always offered strength to all her causes, advised wisely, and did her own work. The close bond between these professional women was something that Eleanor had craved for many years and in which she now reveled—she had found kindred spirits, a group of friends that valued her for who she was, inspired her, and mirrored back a positive image of herself. These were the women whose friendship played a big part in what she would later call "the intensive education of Eleanor Roosevelt." With her newfound independence, Eleanor was becoming an advocate and activist, "thinking things out for myself."

Eleanor Roosevelt was always sympathetic and supportive of women's causes, but didn't define herself as a feminist at the time: she enjoyed working and discussing issues with men, and even though she was developing her own interests, she remained a loyal supporter of Franklin's work. Her growing strength was an unexpected gift for him; what he now had in Eleanor was a most astute and formidable partner.

Trial by Fire

For the first time since his run for election Franklin had decided he would spend most of the 1921 summer relaxing and enjoying his family at Campobello. Grandmère, the children, and the houseguests (which included Louis Howe and his wife) went ahead to the summer cottage, while Franklin attended a wedding. He made his way to the island retreat on a friend's sailboat, and hitting bad weather he was forced to be at the wheel for many hours on end. He arrived at Campobello drawn and exhausted by the ordeal, and yet was so energetic over the next few days that his houseguests left for New York due to the overactive holiday schedule!

On August 10 the family was out sailing when they spotted a forest fire and went ashore to flail at the flames with pine boughs. Once they brought the fire under control, they took a dip in Lake Glen Severn to clean off the soot that had covered them in their firefighting efforts. Feeling tired and dull, Franklin took another dip in the icy waters of Passamaquoddy Bay and after returning home sat around in his wet swimming suit complaining of chills all evening. The next day he felt worse and ran a high temperature. Worried, Eleanor sent for a Dr. Bennett, whose diagnosis was that FDR suffered a mere cold.

On August 12, however, just two days after the swimming episode, paralysis had set in from the chest down. Eleanor turned into a devoted and loving

My grandparents in their later years, as many of us grandchildren will always remember them.

nurse for Franklin, bathing him, massaging his legs, and attending to his every need. His temperature returned to normal over the next two weeks, but the paralysis seemed permanent. Through contacts of Louis Howe, Dr. Robert W. Lovett, a specialist in orthopedics, was contacted, and he immediately left New York for Campobello. His diagnosis was that Franklin had been infected with infantile paralysis—polio—and that there was little chance of him recovering the use of his legs. Eleanor, though deep in shock, acted swiftly and skillfully and continued to nurse Franklin and even became his secretary and scribe, helping with his work and correspondence. FDR refused to be tempered by this horrible turn of events. Although inside he felt a sense of defeat and depression, he remained determined—as he would for years to come—to prove Dr. Lovett's dire prognosis wrong.

Finally, returning to New York, Franklin started treatment at the Presbyterian Hospital, believing that he would soon be able to start work again. But in the following weeks Franklin and Eleanor both came to grips with the painful reality that his recovery would be excruciatingly slow, and would need to be borne out of a supreme resilience and strict observance to a daily regime that would only yield results in very long time frames. This was Franklin's "trial by fire," a surrender to his infirmities and a rising to strength and adherence to his Spartan principles. Sara feverishly tried to persuade her son to abandon all political ambitions and settle down to a quiet life in the Hudson River Valley, a dream she had nurtured all her life. FDR, however, was determined not only to overcome this physical affliction but to lead a normal life and return to his true calling in politics. Eleanor, much to Sara's

disappointment, concurred completely with FDR's desires, believing that his involvement would be the best tonic for his recovery, mentally and physically. Sara, once more fearing that whatever influence she had left over Franklin and the family was at risk, actively engaged Eleanor's own children, and especially Anna, against their mother. Eleanor was unrelenting, and although the rebellion of her children and the constant attempts by Sara placed additional burdens upon an already trying situation, she persevered. Seemingly, Grandmère's sole source of support came from Louis Howe, who seemed to understand better than anyone what she had already tolerated and what she was now sacrificing for her husband. Finally and for all time, Sara's domination of Grandmère was at an end. "Franklin's illness made me stand on my own two feet in regard to my husband's life, my own life, and my children's training," Grandmère would later say, and, according to Joe Lash, "She and Franklin both emerged from the ordeal tempered, tested, and strengthened."

Grandmère's life became even more complex; she was nurturing an invalid, mothering five children, and still attending to most of her political and volunteer activities. She met these challenges with great courage and presence, becoming the very dependable friend and companion Franklin sought in his greatest hour of need. Had it not been for Eleanor and her stalwart attention to his physical and psychological requirements, Franklin might have remained a directionless invalid. Her strength made him strong. Her heart gave him courage.

They both emerged from this most terrible ordeal triumphant, and their bond as equal partners was now deeper than ever. Indeed, their futures were indelibly scripted and intertwined. What seems apparent is that Eleanor had survived her very own trial by fire and was now ready to become intensely active in public and political activity. She had prescribed for herself the role of "stand-in" for her husband whenever he was unavailable. She determined that his name and person would be at the political forefront, and she became an ever-present representative of his views within both the hierarchy and rank and file of the Democratic Party. Given that she had been politically engaged before, she no longer suppressed her political opinions, often engaging FDR in discussions of issues and perhaps influencing his own stands. Once more, it was the persistence of Louis Howe that gave her the encouragement necessary. Just what effect did this period of their lives have? I have no doubt whatsoever that both Eleanor and Franklin were spiritually transformed; he shedding the guise of the young, sheltered, self-serving aristocrat to don the mantle of a sensitive and thoughtful standard-bearer of the less fortunate, and she discarding the tentative for the more self-reliant and determined crusader against injustice.

It was at the 1924 Democratic National Convention that FDR decided it was time to display nationally that he had triumphed over his disability. And it was at this juncture that he determined that by his own example he would begin his long personal crusade to dispel the prevalent notion that a physical disability is a sign of personal weakness. He decided that once again he would place New York Governor Al Smith's name in nomination for president, and he would do so by taking the long walk from his seat on the convention floor to the podium, assisted only by his eldest son, James, and his walking canes. His upbeat mood and this display of courage cemented the love and respect of every delegate in the hall, and although the convention itself was marred by infighting and hopeless deadlock (and eventual disaster in the general election), FDR emerged as the obvious "winner."

Following this triumphant return to the national political spotlight but not yet ready for a campaign of his own, FDR returned to Wall Street and his position with the Fidelity and Deposit Company. Through the ensuing years of the Coolidge administration he worked hard at business, eventually starting a law practice with an aggressive young attorney, Basil O'Connor. For the first time he became excited about business, and the firm of Roosevelt & O'Connor thrived, becoming involved in many of the business and financial enterprises that were significant forces in the economy at that time, many very speculative. But no matter how involved he would seem to be in business, his ambition and love of politics was never far from center stage in his mind. Handling the political front for him was the indomitable Louis Howe, with an equally indomitable Eleanor serving as his ever-present and most effective surrogate. Together they kept FDR at the Democratic forefront and well ensconced as a party leader.

PART FOUR

It's Up to the Women

You cannot take anything personally.
You cannot bear grudges.
You must finish the day's work when the day's work
is done.
You cannot be discouraged too easily.
You have to take defeat over and over again, and pick
up and go on.
Be sure of your facts.
Argue the other side with a friend until you have
found the answer to every point which might be
brought against you.
Women who are leaders must stand out. More and
more they are going to do it, and more and more they
should do it.

—Eleanor Roosevelt

GRANDMÈRE'S CHOICE OF A LIFE devoted to a political husband who now relied on her as his stand-in was perhaps the strongest construction in the intimate interlacing of her relationship with Franklin. From now on she would be catapulted into the public forum of politics. Even though she was doubtful of her ability at the beginning, she may have allayed those fears by telling herself that it was her duty to keep his name before the public, to provide a vital link to the party's officials and public personalities, and to be effective in all Democratic organizations in which she became involved.

In part the capacity to overcome emotional and physical traumas was an intrinsic Roosevelt characteristic. Cousin Alice, in her interviews with Joe Lash, noted that Grandmère had a great capacity for self-discipline, and that her father, Elliott,

had shown the same quality at least in his youth, in transforming himself from physical frailty into a specimen of the strenuous life. My grandfather, of course, also had it, as he too transformed himself through the trials inflicted by his physical paralysis.

For Grandmère, self-discipline was something she had learned in childhood from her family; it kept her on a steady course toward greater and greater responsibility throughout her life:

To my grandmother social life was very important and in her code women must do their share in making life pleasant in the society in which she moved. If you felt sad, you certainly did not air your sadness in public. You were decorous even in showing any kind of emotion but your obligations to meet social commitments were somewhat like an actor in a play—the show goes on—and with my grandmother what you said you would do in a social way, you did. Therefore it was incumbent on you to see that you felt well. There was no sympathy for a headache, just a sense of irritation that whatever brought on a headache must be avoided since you had this obligation. This kind of code is very good discipline and...is always useful in later life.[1]

Grandmère's self-discipline together with her yearning to be needed were the motivational forces that allowed her to overcome her insecurities and finally position herself into the foreground. My aunt Anna said that my grandparents and Louis Howe, once he had been accepted almost as another member of the family, worked as a team, plotting and strategizing as to what steps should be taken next in order to advance FDR's political rise.

Mother by then had accepted Louis so it is very hard to know who launched the idea that he was to stay

*active. I always felt it was a team. Mother still look-
ing for guidance (from Louis and FDR) it gave her
the feeling that she could be useful. That was terribly important particularly for someone like Mother.
Probably it was more Louis leading, but someone most
anxious to be led.*[2]

Politics now became the substitute for the sexual
and romantic relationship that had ended over the
Lucy Mercer affair. FDR and Grandmère, locked in
a triangle with Louis, were able to once more feel
the vibrancy of their partnership, building together
a life of public duty. Undoubtedly this was a time
when Grandmère began to feel useful and valued,
needed and loved for the qualities that she was able
to bring to their renewed bond.

Once her fears had been overcome, her
work became a source of deep fulfillment and her
own life's mission. She too savored the thrill and
the ambition to succeed in what was then very
much a man's world, contributing fully in her feminine, politically astute, and socially conscientious
way. Not only had she emerged as a new leader in
the struggle for women's and children's rights; she
had also earned her stripes as FDR's full-fledged
partner and advisor.

The stamina that helped my grandparents
survive the tragedy of polio was a wellspring of triumphant energy that was now channeled toward his
ultimate goal—the presidency. There was never any
question; if Franklin was going to play, he was playing to win. However reluctantly Grandmère may
have felt about his ambitions, she supported him
with utter devotion. At the same time, she carved
a unique, far from subordinate, role for herself, a
role that allowed her freedom of movement,

expression, and involvement at the White House
seldom seen before. Although she was not the first
First Lady to take up a significant cause (Ellen
Wilson had been concerned with the housing issue
and Lou Hoover had bravely championed the issue
of race) Grandmère's fervor and the sheer multitude of causes she took on made her far more visible and thus vulnerable to scrutiny. She used her
position to directly affect so many issues in the
Administration and soon became a far cry from previous First Ladies, who had generally retreated to
the background of their husbands' lives.

Prompted by both Louis Howe and
Franklin, Grandmère became active inside the
Democratic Party structure. In moving to that more
active side of politics, she was stepping into very
new territory: Even if she insisted she was only act-
ing on behalf of Franklin, the reality was that she
was becoming an accomplished politician on her
own. She was also breaking from Roosevelt tradition, further underscoring her "outsider" perspective
as far as her family was concerned. Her aunts
Corinne and Bye were staunch Republicans, as were
cousins Alice, Corinne, and Ethel. The other
Roosevelt women had to reluctantly reconcile
Eleanor's new activist posture with their own
strong sense of family. This stepping out meant that
however feebly she may have felt about it at certain
moments, Eleanor's new mission was becoming
powerfully crystallized as well as firmly lodged at
the core of her being.

If our family name conjures images of dash-
ing, charming men of high society; wealth; and politically powerful presidents, their feminine counter-
parts were by no means less impressive. Anyone dip-
ping into the Roosevelt chronicles finds extraordinary

women sustaining the clan through generations. Reading their letters, memoirs, and interviews, it becomes instantly apparent that running through the blue-blooded veins of many is a gene of genius, independence, extraordinarily strong willpower, and above all else an intense individuality. Of all of these extraordinary women, as unlikely as it may have seemed then, Grandmère would be the one to come closest to fulfilling the family destiny. Operating from within the Roosevelt world at the beginning, she then stepped out to manifest its values and strong commitment to public service with unusual achievements and inordinate amounts of energy.

Changing Times

America in the twenties was in social turmoil: both the "Great War" and the women's vote had changed social perceptions. The surge in the number of automobiles and an abundance of household appliances altered mobility and the way people spent their leisure time. Women wore shorter clothes and hairstyles. The divorce rate increased; there was an air of frivolity and freedom. These were "changing times," times when the so-called aristocratic set, like Eleanor and her friends, would change not only themselves but an entire nation's views on a multitude of social issues and mores.

At the women's division of the Democratic State Committee, Grandmère met Chairwoman Harriet May Mills and her assistant, Nancy Cook, who in years ahead would become one of the most galvanizing organizers of the women's movement. Nancy was a gifted potter, jewelry maker, and cabinetmaker, but above all she was intellectual, a tal-

Grandmère with her two close friends, Nancy Cook and Marion Dickerman, at Campobello in 1926.

ented organizer, and enthusiastic; traits that attracted Grandmère's attention. After just one speech, Eleanor so impressed Harriet and Nancy that she was asked to chair the division's finance committee. Nancy Cook in turn introduced her to Marion Dickerman. Unlike Nancy, who was bright, sparkly, vivacious, and outgoing, Marion was soft-spoken, reserved, and, according to some, "so serious as to be glum." She had been active in the suffrage movement, and was the first Republican woman to wage a campaign for the New York State Assembly, challenging none other than the sitting speaker, also a Republican. Although Marion lost, her efforts, principles, and indomitable spirit so impressed Eleanor that she, Marion, and Nancy soon became almost inseparable friends.

FDR felt that the Democratic Party had little influence in upstate New York and so urged Grandmère to contribute as much politically as she could in Dutchess County. Soon their partnership emerged, with Franklin as the strategist and Eleanor as the chief of the troops at his command. Louis Howe coached her on public speaking and helped her lose her shyness and fear of such events. Grandmère learned to drive and then took herself everywhere, a habit that continued even after she became First Lady and refused to be chauffeured while living in Washington. (I must add that Grandmère was a notoriously poor driver who was involved in more than one fender bender, or worse. Drives with her were always an adventure!) As she took on increasing responsibilities, she synthesized what being a Democrat meant for her:

If you believe that a nation is really better off which achieves for a comparative few, who are capable of attaining it, high culture, ease, opportunity, and that these few from their enlightenment should give what they consider best to those less favored, then you naturally belong to the Republican Party. But if you believe that people must struggle slowly to the light for themselves, then it seems to me that you are logically a Democrat.[3]

Braving the extremely cold waters of Passamaquoddy Bay, Grandmère and her friends fill the boat to near capsizing.

In 1922 Grandmère joined the Women's Trade Union League, a powerful union that was formed in 1903 to "aid women workers in their efforts to organize…and to secure better conditions." She began working for the League with her usual dedication and high energy, from the beginning having a powerfully positive impact on the women. Evening classes were organized, and Eleanor came one night a week to the League's headquarters to read to the young women and to understand all she could of their conditions.

That Christmas, much to Sara's horror, she asked her children to help organize a party for the children of the WTUL members. For the Roosevelt children this was the first contact with children of the slums and trade unions, and this event, the first of many, brought back for Grandmère the fond memories of similar times she had shared with her father when she was a young girl. It was her way,

I think, of solidifying with her own children a Roosevelt family tradition.

Grandmère also firmly believed that the Democratic Party possessed a positive approach to the prevention of another war, because she felt that Democrats were "more conscious of our world responsibility and more anxious to see some steps taken toward international cooperation than were the Republicans." As a result, she sought to keep Wilson's vision of the League of Nations at the forefront of the nation's interest. She became an energetic activist in the American Foundation, whose main purpose was to work with those who shaped national opinion to promote U.S. entry into the World Court, also familiarly known as the International Court of Justice at The Hague. Grandmère believed that would be the first step in the process of taking responsibility for international peace, something she felt was not just a political duty but also a reflection of a spiritual and moral vision for the world:

> The basis of world peace is the teaching that runs through almost all the great religions of the world, "Love thy neighbor as thyself." Christ, some of the other great Jewish teachers, Buddha, all preached it. Their followers forgot it. What is the trouble between capital and labor, what is the trouble in many of our communities, but rather a universal forgetting that this teaching is one of our first obligations. When we center on our own home, our own family, our own business, we are neglecting this fundamental obligation of every human being and until it is acknowledged and fulfilled we cannot have world peace.[4]

By 1924 Grandmère had defined for herself and was articulating for the women of the nation why it was important that women be involved in politics. She encouraged women to use the power that legislation had given them. "They have the vote, they have the power, but they don't seem to know what to do with it," she would often say. Her message to women was, "Get in the game and stay in it. Throwing mud from the outside won't help. Building up from the inside will." A woman needed to learn the machinations of politics, then she would know how "to checkmate as well as her masculine opponent. Or it may be that with time she will learn to make an ally of her opponent, which is even better politics." Many people, not just women, were beginning to feel that Eleanor was emerging as a leader in her own right, perhaps becoming one of the most inspiring women of her generation. She became a feminist more by example rather than by the more vocal, activist route of many of her colleagues, always working with both men and women alike to improve the standards of society. She understood the benefits of interdependence and cooperation as a tool for achieving equality.

In 1933 Grandmère wrote a book entitled *It's Up to the Women,* in which she philosophized on the role of women in family life, business, and politics. Her voice by then rang crystal clear, and the book became a landmark volume in a First Lady's attempt to engage all women in the political process. Years later, when I read it, I was struck not so much by her beliefs regarding the importance of women and their responsibilities in every aspect of life but rather by the fact that her views, so simplistically stated in the book, were almost prophetic.

Eleanor Roosevelt stated things that would certainly be considered controversial by many modern women. And yet today she stands as one of the preeminent examples of the women's liberation movement. In the book she said, "...it seems to me that the women have got to learn to work together even before they work with men, and they have got to be realistic in facing the social problems that have to be resolved." Prophetic? It seems to me that this singular, very simple statement encapsulates the essence of the postwar women's movement, a working together that is culminating in changes throughout all aspects of our lives and in every corner of the world. She went on to say, however, that "I have often thought that it sounded well to talk about women being on equal footing with men, and sometimes when I have listened to the arguments of the National Woman's Party and they have complained that they could not compete in the labor market because restrictions were laid upon [women], I have been almost inclined to agree with them that such restrictions were unjust, until I came to realize that when all is said and done, women *are* different from men. They are equal in many ways, but they cannot refuse to acknowledge their differences." Controversial? Perhaps, but what is remarkable is that her 1933 statements mirror much of what remains at the core of women's progress since then and that which is still being achieved in the world today.

Nevertheless, as slow as her personal evolution may have been, she became one of the strongest advocates of the women's movement in this country, and doubtlessly one of the most effective world protagonists in the social issues of women's equality. It seems to me that her effectiveness came from the example she set both as a woman who had gained respect for her own thoughtful and reasoned views and from the role she fulfilled in the course of the nation's history. Her peers and colleagues, as

Missy LeHand, FDR's devoted secretary for many years, is photographed here in Washington.

well as her detractors, respected her. As was once said, "You don't have to like what Eleanor Roosevelt says, but you *do* have to listen to her." Some thought she was brash and abrasive, but for millions of others she was their voice, saying things they could not or would not say on their own.

In the early twenties, while Eleanor gravitated toward politics, my grandfather continued to seek long-lasting improvements in his health. He had recovered some of his strength and had found that warm waters and balmy skies improved his condition greatly. He spent four months of every winter on a boat fishing and swimming off Florida's sandy beaches while Grandmère remained in New York fulfilling the role of both mother and father to the children, who in 1924 ranged in age from eight (John) to eighteen (Anna). James and Elliott were at Groton, but Anna, Franklin Jr., and John were at home. Eleanor arranged for each of the children, who were either at boarding school or Springwood, to spend part of their winter holidays with their father, and employed Missy LeHand, a wonderfully competent factotum as both secretary and right hand, to take care of Franklin while she was in New York.

Sara disapproved of Franklin and Eleanor's living arrangements, especially since Louis Howe had himself moved into their Sixty-fifth Street house, and she worried about rumors and scandals. But both Louis and Missy had become their essential helpers and were devoted in their support of the Roosevelts. In 1925 Franklin purchased in Warm Springs, Georgia, a rundown resort built around "a miracle of warm water" gushing from a fissure in the rock that "never varied in temperature and quantity." Much of Grandfather's time and financial resources were poured into Warm Springs, and eventually it prospered under his leadership. Even today the Warm Springs facility exists, providing therapeutic services to scores of disabled men, women, and children.

Grandmère felt a void of true intimacy and closeness with Franklin, but she was inclined to be silent and shrank from expressing her feelings to him, choosing instead to become as capable as she could in the forum of politics in order to help his career, even if her family responsibilities were by this time immense. To the staff of her households she became known as the most practical of people. These unusual arrangements, however, enabled her to develop her own style of life and work, and this was something she was not willing to give up. Although very devoted to Grandfather's political future, Grandmère was now equally devoted to her own course and determined to maintain it. Her work was highly rewarding, she was making new and lasting friendships, felt appreciated, and finally able to trust that her work too was important. The relationship with Grandfather had given her a degree of freedom few women in her position enjoyed, and he trusted her implicitly to be his ally and partner in his life as well as career.

While Franklin recuperated his physical strengths in Georgia, Grandmère tried to be as present for her children as she was able, making frequent trips to Groton and writing letters to each child that she forwarded to Franklin so they could discuss issues in their education. My uncle James entered Harvard in 1926, following family tradition, but my father expressed a desire to go to Princeton instead. Aunt Anna became engaged to Curtis Dall, a stockbroker ten years her senior, and she was married at twenty in 1926. Sara offered Anna and Curtis a splendid apartment in Manhattan as a wedding gift without consulting either Grandmère or FDR, a situation that angered Grandmère, as she believed that such a luxurious apartment would commit the newlyweds to a lifestyle they could not afford. Anna and her husband moved into the apartment nevertheless, and in 1927 Anna Eleanor Dall ("Sistie"), Eleanor and Franklin's first grandchild, was born.

*Val-Kill as it appeared just prior to the beginning of
construction. The secluded land was part of the larger 1,000-acre family estate.*

A Place of Her Own

Much to her dismay, Grandmère's problems with Sara persisted. Poor Sara could never quite reconcile herself with Eleanor living her own life while Franklin mixed the search for a physical recovery with business and politics, and so she attempted at every opportunity to implant herself in their lives in hopes of reestablishing her lost dominance in their daily affairs. Eleanor's answer to these intrusions was to distance herself from Sara as much as possible, and in 1924 she persuaded Franklin to allow her, Nancy Cook, and Marion Dickerman to build a modest but comfortable stone cottage beside the Fal-Kill brook. Aunt Anna understood that Grandmère needed her independence:

Father realized that Mother was reaching out and needed friends independently of the Big House and Granny and that she needed her own life and he wanted to encourage her as much as he could. The evidence of that is that he drew up the original plans for the Val-Kill Cottage.[5]

Left: *An example of the beautiful furniture produced at the Val-Kill Industries factory.* Right: *ER with Nancy Cook, designer of most of the furniture produced by the factory. Val-Kill furniture remains today much sought-after by antique dealers.*

Grandfather wrote Elliot Brown, whom he had chosen to supervise the building project, "My Missus and some of her female political friends want to build a shack on a stream in the back woods and want, instead of a beautiful marble bath, to have the stream dug out so as to form an old fashioned swimming hole." On New Year's Day, 1925, the three women had their first meal at Val-Kill Cottage, sitting on nail kegs and using a crate as a table. Val-Kill was from the beginning a refuge and sanctuary for Grandmère, who considered it the first home she could truly call her own. The children and Grandfather loved Springwood, but Grandmère never felt at home there. Not only did she have to ask Sara's permission to invite friends and the women she worked with for informal lunches and dinners, but there were no traces of her own personality within the walls of that stately house. At Val-Kill she was free to see whomever she wanted whenever she wanted; to hold meetings where important issues about her work were discussed as well as to simply relax in a place she

Picnics were a favorite form of entertaining for Grandmère, and here she is with students from the Todhunter School.

Grandmère, Nancy and Marion at a campout, probably at Val-Kill before completion of the Stone Cottage.

could call her own. And it was here that she, Nancy, and Marion began their factory, Val-Kill Industries.

A few months later Marion, who was a teacher and vice-principal of Todhunter, a private school for girls in New York, was offered the opportunity to buy the school. Eleanor, whose ambitions were never fully satisfied by Val-Kill Industries, proposed that they partner in its purchase and that she herself become one of the teachers. Progressive teaching of young women was something close to Grandmère's heart, for her own awakening had been provoked by the most wonderful teacher of all, Mlle. Souvestre, whose example she had always tried to emulate. She hoped to stimulate young women to a perception of life that went beyond their social circumstances and that

opened their personal boundaries. Teaching at Todhunter provided some of the happiest moments in her life, and the pupils quickly fell in love with her and were greatly inspired by her.

By now, with Todhunter, Val-Kill Industries, and political and business obligations keeping her busy, Grandmère had little time or interest in maintaining any of the vestiges of a "society" life. New close friendships reinforced Grandmère's confidence and encouraged her to take risks and dream of new worlds. Isabella Greenway, Esther Lape, Elizabeth Reed, and Caroline O'Day gave her unstinting friendship. Life partners Marion and Nancy helped her to find sanctuary from her busy schedule. Their devotion raised eyebrows, but gossip did not undercut their friendship. Some friends permitted themselves to wonder about the true nature of the relationship between Grandmère, Marion, and Nancy, but I think my uncle James addressed that question in his own book, *My Parents:*

> *It's true they were very close. In fact they shared Val-Kill. They shared it to the extent that the linen was embroidered with the initials EMN (Eleanor, Marion, Nancy).... I think the situation satisfied a need for companionship each of them had.*[6]

The list of activists with whom Grandmère was involved grew increasingly large and included the most prominent women in this breakthrough period of social change. The more involved she became, the more impressive and effective she proved, to the point that she was recruited for so many boards and official roles with so many organizations that it is hard to imagine from whence her time and energy (a continuing source of astonishment throughout her lifetime) emanated. Through it all, Louis Howe pushed her ever harder to achieve, to be a voice for progressive and often controversial stands. Louis recognized in her a tremendous potential force, and he viewed her involvement as instrumental for keeping FDR firmly entrenched in both local and national politics. Grandmère's demeanor broke the stereotypical view of women politicians, and *New York Times* writer S. J. Woolf noted that "She is the strongest argument that could be presented that by entering politics a woman is bound to lose her womanliness and charm." By the time Franklin ran for governor of New York, Eleanor was far better positioned than he, knew more political leaders and activists, and was more versed in all the important issues of the day. Her influence on women's issues—education, labor, health, and welfare—was

one of Franklin's strongest assets and helped him to form his most progressive social policies for the entirety of his career.

Eleanor's efforts on behalf of the Democratic Party continued, and by 1927 the Democratic women were strongly organized throughout the state. Alfred E. Smith, governor of New York during these years, considered Eleanor a strong ally, partly as a representative of her husband but more importantly in her own right as a leader among women. He wanted to be nominated by the Democratic Party for the 1928 presidential election, and he counted on both Franklin and Eleanor for support in his bid. With Smith's encouragement and endorsement, FDR was considered a natural candidate for the U.S. Senate race as well. However, the preference for Franklin to seek the governorship was echoed throughout the party, and his family, including Eleanor, encouraged him to take the challenge. When Franklin chose to dedicate himself completely to the role of leader for the Democrats, he realized he would have less time for family and for efforts toward his full physical recovery. Eleanor, although highly ambivalent about what his run would mean for her and the children, encouraged him when many people questioned his physical ability to withstand such an arduous campaign.

As Election Day approached, Smith's defeat seemed almost certain, but then the wave of enthusiasm for Roosevelt picked up, culminating in his victory. Although Grandmère was happy for Franklin, she knew that as the wife of the new governor of New York she would have to resign from party committees and perhaps from any form of political involvement at all.

The 1929 Gubernatorial Inauguration Parade with FDR,
FDR, Jr. (far left), former Governor and Mrs. Al Smith (left of FDR), and James.

The Return to Albany

Grandmère immediately began making the necessary arrangements to accommodate the large Roosevelt family and entourage in the executive mansion in Albany. This move meant a complete change of life for her, and once more she wondered what she would do. Even though less directly involved, she was determined to make a success of the Val-Kill Industries. She also continued teaching at Todhunter, and was determined to be a proper mother to her sons, who were now all at Groton, except for James, who was at Harvard. Added to these were new responsibilities as First Lady of New York and mistress of the gubernatorial mansion. But if she failed to fully see what contribution she had to make to Franklin's new role, her friends quickly pointed out that her influence was just as important as his and that she had a new and useful role to fulfill in this position of power.

Eleanor had already shaped Franklin's view of women's impact on the nation's politics and tempered his political outlook and governance. Now she influenced and helped to shape the character of his administration. Together they hoped to bring a unique mark to the political process while living up to the exemplary example set by Teddy Roosevelt when he had occupied that same mansion as governor thirty years before.

Once again that great house quickly took on the informal character of a typical Roosevelt household. Its guest rooms were always full, and large groups of colleagues and friends sat down for lunch and supper. Houseguests commingled with political leaders, and, as ever, Eleanor was a gracious, elegant, and warm hostess who included everyone—workers, secretaries, journalists, friends, and distinguished guests—for tea, which was served in the family room from 4:30 to 6:00 P.M every afternoon she was at Albany. On Sunday evenings she would take the train to New York City to teach classes at Todhunter from Monday to Wednesday, when she would return to the mansion for her "at homes." She was remarkably efficient and ran her household smoothly and happily, to the great wonder of her many friends, who thought her powers prodigious. Her calendar was always packed full of activities, and many of her political interests were adapted to better suit her new position. She no longer made political speeches or served on the boards of civic organizations that lobbied for legislation in Albany, and she kept discreetly away from outward involvement in anything that could be seen as influencing her husband's work. By May, however, Franklin encouraged her to attend Democratic meetings to talk to women about the importance of being of service in politics and to champion women's lobbies for protective legislation for children and women workers.

Part of the governor's job was to inspect state institutions, something that would be physically

FDR and ER surrounded by family members, on Christmas Day 1930 in the Governor's Mansion, Albany.

trying for Franklin, so he usually sent Eleanor to meet the local officials and carry out the inspections. He was a severe and commanding taskmaster, demanding that she pay scrupulous attention to detail during her tours of the institutions and that she report back to him on every aspect, from the food served to lies hidden behind officials' facial expressions. Eleanor soon learned to be Franklin's eyes and ears, often arriving unannounced for these institutional visits. By the time she left Albany she was able to function as if she inhabited Franklin's body, observing life just as he would and reporting back in a way that would help him understand every situation.

Although Grandmère took pride in Val-Kill Industries and in her teaching and lecturing at

Molly Dewson, a powerful force in New York politics, became a close advisor and confidant to Grandmère as FDR began his race for second term as governor.

ER and FDR at Warm Springs, where FDR sought a cure for his paralysis.

Todhunter, there was a growing public interest in her as First Lady of Albany and in the ways in which she used the Governor's Mansion as a springboard for good works, to answer pleas from their constituents, and to link their lives with those of the people. Franklin supported her by assuring his state officials that he and Eleanor were a team, and they in turn began to ask for her support for their new ideas and programs. In 1930 Franklin was elected for a second term in a landslide victory of a margin of 725,000 votes, something unheard of for a Democrat in the state of New York.

His success as governor promoted him to the forefront of the Democratic Party, which saw his patrician flair, political vision, and good governance as promising indeed. Officials began maneuvering him toward the prize he wanted most of all, the presidency. Eleanor never wanted to become a president's wife, for she knew only too well how restrictive the role of First Lady would be, and she viewed this position as embodying less power rather than more influence for herself. But once again she found herself swept up in Franklin's life ambitions, regarding the future with a sense of deprivation and anxiety. Her continued work at Todhunter, with labor and women's issues would be threatened by becoming a First Lady. Franklin's plans put in jeopardy her sense of identity and belonging; as he gained centrality in the shaping of national politics, she felt keenly that everything she had would collapse in his path of victory. There was nothing she wanted less than to ride on the coattails of his success. Part of her problem was that she could not say no to him, for she believed as his partner and as a Democrat that he would energize the country, which was drowning in the difficulties of an impending depression.

And so, once more Grandmère put aside her fears and concerns to actively support him. Women's involvement in the party's politics had raised the vote by as much as 20 percent, and the Democratic women of the state believed that this kind of political awareness could be taken to the entire nation. By the spring of 1931, Louis Howe had opened the Friends of Roosevelt offices in Manhattan, and Eleanor, lest she be seen as being too involved, suggested that Molly Dewson, civic secretary of the Women's City Club and a potent political force in women's politics, serve as her deputy, effectively working as if she were Eleanor. Like Grandmère, Molly was a power in local and state political circles, serving as civic secretary at the Women's City Club. Grandmère helped in every way she could, making suggestions to the women's division of her husband's campaign and helping his biographers.

She also traveled extensively, and although she never directly spoke of the campaign, she encouraged women to think for themselves in political choices and alerted them to the vision of the Democratic Party. She was adamant that she drive everywhere by herself, which made both Franklin

and Louis nervous, and her husband insisted that Earl Miller, a New York state trooper and former amateur welterweight champion, become her bodyguard. Earl's roughneck qualities endeared him to Eleanor, and he became as close an ally to her as Louis. Earl Miller soon became yet another member of the extended household, even eating his meals with the family. Speculation over the years about the relationship between Earl and Grandmère was to be frankly discussed by my uncle James in the book *Mother & Daughter*:

I believe there may have been one real romance in mother's life outside of marriage. Mother may have had an affair with Earl Miller...I believe it is important to realize that...Victorian as mother may have been, she was a woman, too, who suffered from her self-imposed separation from father.[7]

Uncle James recalled Earl as "an extremely handsome and physical man." When he became Grandmère's bodyguard "his fellow officers originally teased him about being assigned to 'that old crab,' but she took an interest in him, her warmth won him over, and when others saw how he felt about her they stopped kidding him about his "awful assignment":

Mother was self-conscious about Miller's youth, but he did not seem bothered by the difference in years. He encouraged her to take pride in herself, to be herself, to be unafraid of facing the world. He did a lot of good for her. She seemed to draw strength from him when he was by her side, and she came to rely on him. When she had problems, she sought his help...He became part of the family, too, and gave her a great deal of what her husband and we, her sons, failed to give her. Above all, he made her feel that she was a woman.

*Earl Miller took this photograph of my grandfather, great-grandmother Sara,
Grandmère, and other family members at the pool in Val-Kill.*

If father noticed, he did not seem to mind. Curiously, he did promote a romance between Miller and Missy (grandfather's factotum), but that did not last. Miller, who'd had an unhappy first marriage, later married a cousin of his first wife, and that ended the gossip about mother and him. But this was not a happy marriage either. He was divorced in 1934.

All the while, Miller had continued to see mother and frequently was at Val-Kill. He saw other women too, and she encouraged his romances. He married a third time in 1941, though he continued

to see mother regularly. This marriage was a failure, too, I believe. Maybe because of mother. Their relationship deepened after father's death and ended only with mother's death. From my observations, I personally believe they were more than friends...[8]

During that period, Grandmère worried about the children and the fact that Franklin seldom saw them. When he did he was far too busy with the campaign to be able to contribute effectively to their emotional needs. Anna was having problems

*Grandmère with Earl Miller, her bodyguard, close friend, and companion,
and with whom it has been said she had an affair.*

with her husband, my father Elliott moved restlessly from one job to another, and the youngest brothers were driving too fast and too recklessly. Perhaps their father's position increased their bravado, making them think that they were above scrutiny, but the fact that they were robbed of their time with him, of his wisdom and companionship, certainly had an effect on all the children. Grandmère found herself in the uncomfortable role of sole disciplinarian, wishing she had more positive support from Franklin and Sara in these matters.

As the states fell in line and Franklin's presidential campaign strengthened, Eleanor contemplated her entry into the gilded captivity she associated with becoming First Lady. Friends were baffled by her calm detachment from the excitement, as few of them could read her inner dilemma. On the long night of the nomination, Franklin sat in his shirtsleeves chain-smoking while she knitted a turtleneck sweater for asthma-racked Louis Howe. Finally the phone call arrived for which Franklin had been waiting: he was anointed the Democratic candidate to the White

Clockwise from top left: *FDR on campaign trail in 1930, my father in the background; being sworn in for his second term as Governor of New York; giving a "whistle stop" speech; and with Grandmère on the trail.*

House. The morning after, he flew to Chicago to show that he intended to be an energetic leader to the country, and if Eleanor contemplated the weeks ahead with apprehension and dread, she nevertheless pitched into the campaign with her usual vigor and dedication.

Eleanor quickly became enveloped in the many details of the presidential campaign, from the printing of fliers that were packaged editorially to appeal to women voters to the smoothing of relations between everyone on the team. The Depression's grim signs were everywhere in America. It was her firm belief that if—and only if—people understood the reasons for the collapse of the nation's economic structure it would be possible for them to implement the changes needed to emerge from the Depression. In all her speeches she asked her listeners to prepare themselves to accept

Grandmère with Malvina "Tommy" Thompson, loyal and constant secretary and companion.

ER in a rare moment of leisure at the Governor's mansion.

the economic changes, changes that would require everyone to work together to transform the collapsed economy.

In the mounting hysteria of Franklin's impending victory, Eleanor remained strangely detached and composed. She knew that the role of First Lady would restrict her freedom and that she would have to give up many of the activities and involvements that she found so rewarding. From the beginning, Eleanor thought that the best thing for First Lady would be to retreat and to once again confine her activities to those that would not touch on her husband's politics. She hoped that Grandfather would use her skills in the White House and she offered to help answer and organize his mail, to handle his calendar, and to travel around the country on his behalf. He said no to all, refusing every offer she made. She was plunged in such deep

depression that she wrote to my aunt Anna, "I turn my face to the wall." Finally, Louis Howe and Lorena Hickock helped her to find a way out of the dark mood that had gripped her from the election. As she listened and considered the men surrounding the presidency, she feared that FDR's power and enormous charisma would prevent anyone, even Louis Howe, from telling him the truth, and that these men would be so influenced by him as to always say yes. The idea began to form in her mind that perhaps she could serve as my grandfather's listening post, and that her understanding of the problems that faced the great masses could help to educate the president in his legislative and policy initiatives. She hoped Franklin could alleviate the nation's difficulties with the right decisions, decisions she could help him make working together, once more and as always, like a team.

A Role Model for Women

It would be nearly impossible to chronicle in these few pages all of the close women friends and colleagues with whom Grandmère shared and learned so much. For many years she surrounded herself with and enjoyed the company of many of the world's brightest and most fascinating women, some well known, others less so. But even as they gave to her, she had tremendous impact on their lives as well.

When Eleanor wrote *It's Up to the Women,* she could never have imagined the implications the book would have. Hastily compiled just weeks after she and FDR took up residence in the White House for his first term, this short volume became a rallying point, a call to action for women of all classes. Throughout its pages women are urged to be the reforming force for change, to assume leadership roles in the movement for social, political, and labor justice. It set into words Eleanor's own priorities for peace, women's rights, civil rights for all, and equal opportunity—social and economic—for every man, woman, and child. It helped provide definition for the course she had set for the rest of her life's work, a course from which she never deviated. It is impossible, I think, to merely extricate Grandmère's work on women's issues from those others so closely related. She was not, as I have said before, strictly a women's activist, for her concerns crossed all boundaries, all rights, and all inequities.

One of Grandmère's friends from FDR's administration was Helen Gahagan Douglas, wife of screen actor Melvyn Douglas and a stage and screen star in her own right. The Douglases originally came to the attention of my grandfather and grandmother as a result of their activism on behalf of California migrant workers. Eventually, at FDR's urging, Helen Gahagan Douglas forsook her stage and screen successes to enter the world of politics, first as a national committeewoman and vice-chair of the California Democratic Party, and eventually to be elected to the U.S. Congress as representative from California. Subsequently, Helen and Grandmère worked closely for many years on issues relating to women's rights. When questioned in later years about Eleanor's impact on a woman's role in politics, Helen responded, "In the White House years she was one of the main pillars in building a strong women's division [in the national party]. It was her leadership that inspired other women all over the country...all over the world. Her courage in taking a stand, expressing herself in a very simple way...she was able to communicate to women... And she did that just by being herself and being courageous and taking stands...never being ugly and abrasive...It was the purity of that motivation that won so many people to her, Republicans as well as Democrats."

Grandmère was continuously chided for not being more outspoken about women's rights, particularly in the early days of the original Equal Rights Amendment, when she declared her opposition to it. The original ERA was drafted as early as 1923 by the women's activist Alice Paul. However, it increased in strength and influence by 1940 when men were sent to war and women took most of the office and factory jobs in the land. In proving their productivity and value to the country, women were able to demand and obtain more changes for the ERA. It wasn't that Grandmère opposed equal rights for women; she was more concerned that

In 1940 Grandmère, Melvyn, and Helen Gahagan Douglas toured a camp of California migratory workers.

Again with Helen and Warren Austin in 1946, at a meeting of the US delegation to the United Nations.

passage of the amendment would threaten certain advances already in place to protect women in the labor force. As Helen Gahagan Douglas explained, "She was against ERA. So was I, so was every leading woman in the Labor Department. That was because the protections that had been set up through the Labor Department for women in industry or in work jobs of any kind were very new, and we were afraid that if we supported the ERA we would lose those protections…[but] had Mrs. Roosevelt lived I am sure that she'd be for the ERA today. It was so difficult [at that time] to put through the reforms that would protect women that we were just fearful that ERA would be an excuse

to do away with them. But she supported everything else that had to do with women's rights, even before she went to the White House."9

Grandmère said in her autobiography, "I became much more of a feminist than I ever thought possible," and she was also an avowed social reformer, whose pragmatism compelled her to view the broader implications of the proposed amendment, implications that could have greater detrimental effect on the *working* woman than it could on women of privilege. It was a difficult position for her to assume, particularly since it meant opposing her own political party.

Grandmère also believed that someday a

Harry Hopkins during a rare moment of relaxation, at Hyde Park.

ER, FDR, and my father, after casting their votes for the "next president of the United States."

woman would be elected president of the United States, but again she did not actively advocate her belief during or after her years in the White House. Interestingly, I think Louis Howe also shared the view that a woman would and could be elected to the highest office in the land, and at one point, perhaps partly in jest, he suggested to Grandmère, "Eleanor, if you want to be President in 1940, tell me now so I can start getting things ready!" Grandmère at the time doubted that the attitude of the country would allow a woman to be elected; "I do not think it would be impossible to find a woman who could be President, but I hope it does not happen in the near future..." she would say, continuing, "I hope it will not be while we speak of a 'woman's vote'...I hope it only becomes a reality when she is elected as an individual, because of

her capacity and the trust which a majority of the people have in her integrity and ability as a person."

Above all, Grandmère saw women as the humanizing strength and motivation of politics, and throughout her life she believed that women possessed a strength of consciousness and conviction that was wanting in most men in politics; that women would drive the reformation of injustice. When it came to women in the role of political partisanship, Eleanor could not have cared less. Although a Democrat and long a stalwart of women in the party structure, it was the individual qualities that defined the person, not party affiliation. To Grandmère, the most important thing was to strive for accomplishments of one's beliefs and principles, and if it meant joining with an otherwise unlikely ally on an issue from time to time, so be it. She shocked some of the leadership in her own party when in 1932, as related by Joe Lash, she urged women to be prepared to reject the party and its candidates "when the need arises." When FDR was elected in 1932, Eleanor worked tirelessly to ensure that qualified women, regardless of party affiliation, were participants in the New Deal administration. One of the first New Deal programs, the Civil Works Administration (CWA), was just a singular example of Grandmère's influence in the admin-

istration. When the original plan for the CWA was unveiled it did not mention the role of women specifically. At the urging of Harry Hopkins, one of FDR's key advisors and a "soul mate" in ER's impassioned reform philosophy, Eleanor called for a White House conference to hammer out a program keyed toward unemployed women. The conference, attended by leaders from across the nation in the field of social welfare, presented a proposal that within one year had secured jobs for more than a hundred thousand women in the CWA.

In sum, Grandmère's belief in the ability of women to be the force of change is best stated in

Left: *Leaving Albany for Washington in 1932 on the Roosevelt Special.*
Right: *FDR reading the results of his landslide gubernatorial success in 1930, to be followed again by his ascendancy to the presidency.*

It's Up to the Women, when she says that her greatest admiration was for those women throughout time "whose hearts were somehow touched by the misery of human beings [so] that they wanted to give their lives in some way to alleviate it." But above all else, women would have to earn their rightful place in politics, as in life, by "putting aside their womanly personalities [and] standing on their own ability, their own character as persons."

A reluctant yet elegant First Lady, posing for her first official photograph at the White House in 1933.

First Lady

I knew what traditionally would lie before me, and I cannot say I was very pleased with the prospect. The turmoil in my heart and my mind was rather great that night.

—Eleanor Roosevelt,
the night of FDR's election
as president

THE WHITE HOUSE LOOMED AHEAD AS A place Grandmère would never be able to call home, but where she would serve as First Lady of a country ravaged by the deep incisions of the Great Depression. The sense of foreboding she felt the night news of Franklin's impending presidency was announced would be etched into deep uncertainty from the beginning. It was as if she were standing at the rim of her hard-won vantage point to regard her new role with foreboding and fading hope rather than with a sense of triumph.

With persistence and tenacity Grandmère had by then managed to combine all the difficult strands of her life into a satisfactory whole: her partnership with Franklin, the friendships with powerful and stimulating women, her children, politics, her homes, teaching, writing, and public speaking. She was now thrust into the role of First Lady of the nation in a society that still wrote its history in the male gender and was staked out for women by norms, prohibitions, and controls. Too much individuality set her in conflict with the rest of society,

As beautiful as the White House may have been that first winter,
inside the administration was dealing with the effects of the Great Depression.

and this was never more apparent than within the traditional context of the presidency. For many women at the time, conflict was still at the center of their vision; change could only be attained through agitation, rebellion, and transgression. Eleanor Roosevelt would reveal herself as unique for choosing to change the reality of her role through information, action, and understanding, not through conflict.

What we know of our lives and what we see in the mirror when we look at ourselves depends on what we know of the world, what we believe to be possible, and whether our private loyalties are to the past, present, or future. Grandmère set her vision to the future, opening a door that would allow women graceful entry into the world

of politics and social change. This would invite all subsequent First Ladies to take up the challenge of their position for the betterment of American society and the strengthening of the country's ties to the rest of the world. Eleanor chose to listen to her yearnings rather than be governed by old ways of thinking, both in her private world and in the public forum. Deeply attuned to new ways of solving conflict and merging social forces, she saw that politics and economics were powerless in the face of the obstinacy of entrenched shortsightedness. She found a new way, changed negative perspectives of the unattainable, and made growth possible for all who desired it. She was a stimulant the White House had never seen before, and perhaps has not seen since to such an extent.

Grandmère entering the official Inaugural Ball.

The Roosevelt Way

Those first few months of transition to the role of First Lady were not easy for Grandmère. Initially she abhorred the limelight, but the Roosevelts settled into the White House and, in their unique way, went about transforming its staid rituals into those more of a small hotel with all of its comings and goings. Friends and visitors came to spend the night and sometimes ended up staying for days, weeks, or in some instances much longer. Members of both Roosevelts' retinues would even occasionally invite their own guests who, feeling completely at home, mingled easily with the children and staff. Grandmère would cook scrambled eggs in a chafing dish every Sunday evening, and everyone gathered together for this informal and intimate supper, mixing talk of politics with gossip and banter, jokes and intimate chats. Years later, remembering her time at the White House, Grandmère admitted that the "Roosevelt way" might have seemed perhaps too strong a breeze of fresh air to a staff accustomed to a different order of things:

> *Judging by the articles our head butler has written lately, I gather my informal ways of doing things were a shock. And I am afraid my husband must have been rather a shock too! He did not like to dress for dinner when we were alone, and we used the small dining room almost entirely and never used the big state dining room except for formal parties. I did not realize at first that I was not supposed to run the elevator but I was gently told that it was not the custom for the First Lady to run an elevator. I was obstinate enough, however, to say that I couldn't be bothered waiting for anyone, and I imagine this will be the feeling of any young woman going into the White House, particularly if she is trying to be a mother to young children, a wife to her husband and at the same time trying to run the White House and meet her social requirements.*[1]

She composed an article for *Redbook* in 1960 in which she gave advice to future First Ladies about life in the White House in her inimitably elegant, feminine, quirky, and perceptive way:

> *I think the mistress of the White House does well to make a tour of the whole house now and then to make sure that she knows every individual and gives them a chance to say a word to her. No matter how good the housekeeping is this is a safeguard. I found on one occasion great friction, which could have been ironed out more quickly if I had been in the habit of giving employees a chance to speak with me now and then when I went on the rounds...Some things you will find amusing, some of them irritating. I remember my consternation when I was told I was very neglectful because something was happening to the coats of the White House squirrels. I had not noticed that anything was happening, but today I have a series of cartoons that came out when it was discovered that the kind of nuts the guards and the public were feeding the squirrels were not the proper diet! I had to have the squirrels caught by the curator at the zoo and after careful examination the squirrels were supplied with the proper diet. Mrs. Hoover told me she was criticized because there was a darn in one of the white curtains in one of the big windows over the staircase. It was still there while I was there and remained for some time because curtains and hangings are very expensive for the big White House windows. Once I was severely criticized for being away too much by a lady who had soiled her white gloves on the railing of the stairs leading up from the basement of the East Room. She said that if I stayed at home I would have time to see to it that the railing was properly dusted. I wrote the lady that it was wiped once every half hour during the day but it seemed impossible to keep it clean all the time.*
>
> *...There is really nothing a woman can do to prevent personal gossip, and constant criticism of herself and of the President and the children, so I think it is as well to remain ignorant as far as possible in this particular and rather inevitable situation. Any woman must live her own personal life as best as she can. It is difficult to have a personal life. It must be had in snatches and this is not an ideal situation. It is difficult for the children because to have a father who is constantly interested in affairs of state that must engross him, means that at times a father is not*

there to share their difficulties. A man in public life makes great sacrifices and the rest of us should help in every way we can to make it easier for his wife and children.

As far as keeping up old friends is concerned, that is possible. Any White House wife must observe protocol and it is impossible for the President's wife to call on diplomatic people, even though they have been old friends, more than a very limited number of times. The moment it is noticed that one group or even one individual has an advantage over another, there is jealousy and possibly really serious international repercussions. So you learn to have your old friends stay with you, to go off when you can with them out of Washington if possible, but to content yourself with your formal duties and your personal life in the White House as far as possible.

I think it is as well to have friendly relations with the press. They can make life difficult for you or they can make it easy. It is wise never to forget that whether you know it or not somebody is always watching you. I remember one day falling off my horse very early in the morning in the park. She had slipped in the mud and I had slid off her back, but I was on again in a minute and rode with Elinor Morgenthau and I think Missy LeHand to the waiting cars. I went home, had my bath as usual, and half an hour later I was sitting in the West Hall having breakfast when Steve Early, my husband's press secretary, came in and exclaimed: "There, I knew it was not so. I told the A. P. it could not have happened that you fell off your horse without my knowing about it." I had to say in a very small voice: "But it did happen, Steve. I just didn't know there was anyone around to let the A. P. know."

Whoever goes into the White House will have

interesting years as the President's wife—trying in some ways, deeply interesting in others. She deserves the help and the loyalty of every woman in the US for life will never be easy for the First Lady of this land.[2]

Oppressive may be an apt word for describing the feeling Grandmère had for those first few months as First Lady. Not only did she have to be far more circumspect in her activities, but she also had restricted access to her friends, her engagements. All the elements she had carefully cultivated in her life were gradually eroding.

Franklin had Missy LeHand, who was by his side all hours of the day, as factotum and devoted confidant. Missy even fulfilled some of those duties expected of but despised by Eleanor, like mixing drinks at cocktail hour, chatting and making small talk, and keeping up with the continuous flow of guests. Because of Eleanor's primordial fear of the effect alcohol had on people—after all, it ruined both her father and her uncles—she withdrew from many of Franklin's cocktail hour gatherings, and Missy took over. But Grandmère's greatest fear was that the White House routine would destroy her working partnership with Franklin, that the Cabinet would compromise her role as a first-line advisor and counselor. She could not bear the thought of being merely a superficial feminine symbol for the nation.

My zest in life is rather gone for the time being…If anyone looks at me, I want to weep…I get like this sometimes. It makes me feel like a dead weight & my mind goes round and round like a squirrel in a cage. I want to run, & I can't, & I despise myself. I can't get away from thinking about myself. Even though I know I'm a fool, I can't help it.[3]

Perhaps for the first time we see the vestiges of depression settling in. Grandmère had successfully overcome depression before by taking up tasks, making herself useful, and following a code of self-discipline. By directing her focus to what was required of her, she was able to not think of things she found painful or depressing. Many of Grandmère's writings throughout her life give hints of periods of depression, and toward the end she admitted that she had suffered for years.

Despite the feelings that threatened to drown her happiness yet again, Eleanor would in moments of crisis renew her faith and gather strength from the emotional and spiritual resilience she had cultivated since childhood. It is always difficult to surmise another person's religious beliefs and the faith they derive from them, but I think Grandmère always professed a strong underpinning of religious belief. The age in which she was raised was one of loyalty to both family and the institutions of life, such as the church, not to say that hers was one of blind acceptance. For Grandmère there was significance to the ritual of the Episcopal Church in whose tenets she was reared (although the early Roosevelt family were followers of the Dutch Reformed movement), and she gained strength from its teachings. She believed that religion could and should be intellectually interpreted as one wished. Perhaps her faith can best be summarized by one of her favorite sacred passages, the *Prayer for a Better World,* which she almost always carried with her:

Dear Lord keep us from being complacent and self-satisfied, make us understand our shortcomings and work for a better understanding of others in order that we may learn to live in peace and harmony with

our brothers throughout the world. Let us learn that seeking for good and giving love are more important than finding evil and developing hate. Give us the courage to go forward in spite of discouragement and when we ask Thy blessing, grant us a sense of Thy peace and Thy strength.

I think most would agree that Grandmère was a moralist, and her intellectual embrace of religious faith was an important part of her morality. However, as she once explained to Edward R. Murrow, the noted columnist of the day, "I don't know whether I believe in a future life. I believe that all you go through [in this life] must have some value, therefore there must be some *reason.* And there must be some 'going on'...there is a future—that I'm sure of. But how, that I don't know."

The President's grandchildren and Miss Hopkins on the White House balcony.

153

I see a nation ill clad, ill housed, ill educated, and ill nourished.

—Franklin Delano Roosevelt

A Remarkable First Lady

In retrospect, the initial loss of moorings in those early White House days were but a blink of an eye in the chronicle of who Eleanor Roosevelt became as First Lady and what she attained during FDR's long presidency. Within a few months she had already started to carve a new identity, coming back to life with a vengeance, forging a path previously unimagined for someone in her position. Soon she would be more firmly established in the public mind than she had ever allowed herself to conceive: She offered a moral standard, an acutely sensitive conscience, a sharply defined personality, and an intellectually forceful mind; in short, an ideal of femininity. But more than possessing a conscience and setting a moral standard, Grandmère became an activist within and without the White House. She recognized that she had gained influence not only in national Democratic Party circles, but with many of FDR's own advisors. She had the power to influence and was not reticent to use it in attempting to shape policy decisions within the Administration. Often she circumvented her husband's advisors, going directly to the President to forcefully lobby her views on matters she considered of crucial importance. It was not unusual for her to invite leaders of the labor movement, civil rights, or other causes to meet with FDR at the White House, and seldom was she denied this privileged access. She not only served as a resource for the presidency, but more importantly for those whose voices could

Clockwise from left: A bread line in New York City; unemployed men at a Volunteers of America soup kitchen; and squatters' shacks filled practically every vacant lot in New York City. Few escaped the ravages of the Depression.

have no audience. And her imprint on many of the early programs of the Roosevelt presidency are indelible, such as the National Youth Administration, the Federal One programs (which included the Federal Writers Project, Federal Theatre Project, Federal Arts Project, etc.).

Her initial unhappiness mirrored the mood of the nation. No decline in American economy would carve such shockingly deep lacunae in industry and in the very fabric of society. Buoyant and sparkling America became a country where breadlines and soup kitchens formed in every city, and families everywhere were evicted from their homes, to stand shivering on pavements and by railway tracks that led only to more poverty and less opportunity. In the eleven-year Depression, industry would grind to an almost complete halt, leaving 10 million Americans, almost 17 percent of the workforce, jobless. More than one-third of the 35 million homes lacked running water; 32 percent had no hygienic facilities; 39 percent lacked a bathtub or shower; and 58 percent had no heat. Of 74 million Americans twenty-five years or older, only two in five had gone beyond eighth grade and one in twenty to college.

The Roosevelts presided over a nation that was "ill clad, ill housed, ill educated, and ill nourished," as FDR so appropriately intoned. Above all, America had lost its faith. Eleanor wrote that the nation was gripped by "...fear of an uncertain future, fear of not being able to meet our problems. Fear of not being equipped to deal with life as we live it today."[4] She recognized that people needed to have something "outside of one's self and greater than one's self to depend on...We need some of the

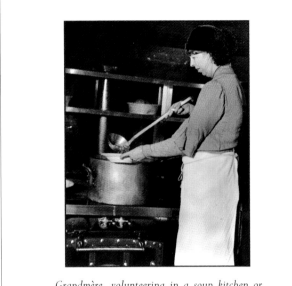

Grandmère, volunteering in a soup kitchen or other places, was not an uncommon sight, but many thought it "unbecoming" of the First Lady.

old religious spirit which said 'I myself am weak but Thou art strong oh Lord!'"[5] Franklin, too, saw that renewing the bond with God would be "...the means of bringing us out of the depths of despair into which so many have apparently fallen."[6] During his first inaugural speech, confident of the nation's ability to renew its faith in its own power, he would encourage everyone to forge ahead with confidence with the famous line "...the only thing we have to fear is fear itself," adding that "This nation asks for action, and action now." And action was what the nation got from them both.

Eleanor's recovery was the first step in the nation's recovery: with inexhaustible energy, high spirits, and deep faith, she went about setting an example for everyone, talking to people about what

really mattered to them. She saw the main cause of malnutrition, for instance, as being not lack of food but a lack of knowledge of menus that were both inexpensive and used simple but nourishing ingredients. She gave a lecture and served "a 7 cents luncheon" at the White House: hot stuffed eggs with tomato sauce, mashed potatoes, prune pudding, bread, and coffee. This event was so successful that soon American women started preparing "Eleanor Roosevelt meals" for their families. While Franklin tried to bolster industry and the economy, Eleanor worked to uplift morale: "At the president's press conference, all the world's a stage; at Mrs. Roosevelt's, all the world's a school,"[7] Bess Furman, an Associated Press reporter, remarked. She also wrote that Grandmère enchanted the press, captivated the public, and became America's greatest champion. In her elegant, direct, unaffected way she talked to everyone about everything, and in order to do so she traveled constantly and visited every area of the United States, descending down mineshafts, crossing muddy fields, flying fledgling airlines when weather conditions were treacherous, and driving with friends and aides to as many places as she could. Eleanor Roosevelt was *everywhere*.

Eleanor was so efficient that she achieved a great deal every day, beginning at 7:30 A.M. with exercise (a habit from Allenswood that she never abandoned) or a ride in the nearby Rock Creek Park on her mare, Dot, often with Missy LeHand or her best Washington friend, Elinor Morgenthau. After breakfast she would see in turn the head usher, the social secretary, and the housekeeper. Raymond Muir, the head usher, oversaw the comings and goings of everyone who came into the White House to see the Roosevelts, including family, guests, and

people with appointments. Edith Helm, Eleanor's social secretary, was tall, elegant, and very correct. Together, Edith and Grandmère went over formal arrangements for suppers, gatherings, invitations, and table seatings. Henrietta Nesbitt, the house-keeper, did all the buying, prepared the menus, and oversaw the household staff. (Grandfather found Mrs. Nesbitt's menus so bland and unappealing that even Grandmère's simple dinners of scrambled eggs were more palatable. He had a palate for exotic foods like wild game and fresh fish, and although Mrs. Nesbitt had nothing to do with the actual cooking, only menu planning, she would ultimately bear the brunt of FDR's displeasure and was often the subject of his many complaining memorandums to Grandmère. One reason he sought a fourth term, he joked with Anna, was so he could "fire Mrs.

Nesbitt." He was reelected, but Mrs. Nesbitt remained faithfully in place.)

Finally, Eleanor would retire to her office with her longtime confidant and assistant Malvina Thompson ("Tommy") to attend to the avalanche of mail that flooded into the White House every day. Letters and letters and letters filled wire baskets all around Eleanor's office, and she and Tommy would even take unanswered correspondence back to Val-Kill, Campobello, or Springwood and continue to write replies on weekends, vacations, and late at

Left: *Another common sight was Grandmère taking her rides through Rock Creek Park in Washington.* Right: *The annual Easter Egg Roll for children on the White House lawn was always a welcome event; here with my aunt Anna, her daughter "Sistie," and head White House usher Ike Hoover.*

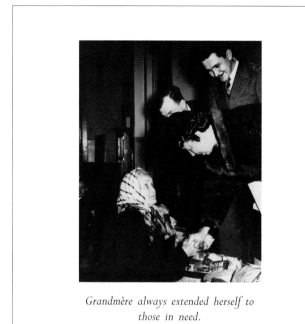

Grandmère always extended herself to those in need.

night. As was her regimen until her death, *all* correspondence deserved an answer; if someone took the time to write, she would find the time to answer. This was Eleanor's way of keeping in touch with ordinary people everywhere who truly felt she was a friend in touch with their needs, requests, and feelings.

When Grandmère wasn't writing letters, she was writing articles, in another successful attempt to be in touch with the people. Louis Howe acted as her literary agent and engineered a contract with the North American Newspaper Alliance to do a monthly 750-word piece for $500 an article. She was asked to write "as one woman to another, of your problems as the woman of the household." Later she wrote a monthly column for the *Woman's*

Home Companion, a magazine that also employed Aunt Anna to help answer the correspondence that came flooding in from American women.

Eleanor remained tireless in her efforts to uplift hearts and revive the spirit of the nation, and within the first few months she had already broken the mold that formed all previous First Ladies. Many were critical of her active involvement and would have preferred her to behave in a more traditionally feminine role, grinning and bearing the burden of anonymity behind an all-powerful husband. But Eleanor was sharply aware that women had a crucial role to play in the rebuilding of a nation gripped by the devastation of the Great Depression. It was, as she had always believed, up to the women to help the nation.

It was Lorena Hickok, who had been assigned by the A.P. to cover Grandmère during the 1932 campaign, who suggested that Eleanor hold press conferences restricted to women reporters, a revolutionary idea at the White House. The conferences proved a great success: They not only gave women reporters the opportunity for "exclusive" coverage of the First Lady, but they also accomplished the higher mission of galvanizing women across the United States to work together with the First Lady to help the country crawl out of the Depression. Hickok also suggested that the "diary" portion of Grandmère's daily letters to her be published. These contained details of Grandmère's workday activities that Lorena felt would interest the whole nation. They would eventually be published as the popular "My Day" column and syndicated to scores of newspapers across the nation.

"Hick," as Grandmère and all of us would come to call Lorena, became a close friend and

One of the first First Ladies to hold her own press conferences, Grandmère insisted that they be limited to women reporters only (here in the Monroe Room of the White House, in 1933).

companion to my grandmother soon after she was assigned to the White House. When they first met, Hick was one of the most highly respected female journalists in the nation and a trophy for the Associated Press. Many considered her brilliant. She had prestige, her writing had earned many awards, her articles were "front page," she was perhaps the best-paid woman journalist of her time, and, of utmost importance, she had friends and sources at the highest echelons of government. These were the qualities that first attracted my grandmother to this exceptional woman. Hick was equally impressed by Grandmère, whose activities never made for dull copy and whose intellect attracted her like a magnet.

Like FDR, Grandmère demanded absolute loyalty from the people she considered her friends. If you were part of her inner circle, you were expected to be trustworthy and totally devoted to her. Within two years of their meeting, Hick had become Grandmère's closest friend: They wrote to each other every day, went on trips, and spent much of their free time, such as it was, together.

Left: In March 1933 FDR gave his first "Fireside Chat," from his Oval Office desk.
Right: Grandmère's first portrait as First Lady in early 1933.

Friends and even White House staff began wondering about the true nature of the relationship, and speculation arose that they were having an affair. Of these speculations, some made on the basis of endearing correspondence between them, I can draw no conclusions. I do believe, however, that my uncles, my aunt, and my father placed little stock in the rumors. Aunt Anna, in her interviews with Joe Lash, reckoned that the friendship damaged Hick's career as a journalist, a fact Grandmère felt terribly guilty about:

I think Mother ruined Hick as a newspaper woman by taking her in too close. I knew her on the campaign train in 1932...But it was not too long after this that Hick would be sleeping in Mother's sitting room and the other reporters came to regard her as a

sort of privileged character. That was not good for her professional status...Mother did not realize that...Hick was truly devoted to Mother but on too emotional a basis.[8]

Whatever the truth, Lorena Hickok remained a close and trusted friend the remainder of Grandmère's life.

Mary R. Beard, a historian and feminist, echoed the admiration of millions when she reviewed *It's Up to the Women* in the *New York Herald Tribune* in 1933: Through her articles, press conferences, and speeches, Eleanor Roosevelt was giving "inspiration to the married, solace to the lovelorn, assistance to the homemaker, menus to the cook, help to the educator, direction to the employer, caution to the warrior, and deeper awareness of its primordial force to the 'weaker sex.'" If the country was used to "the Great White Father in the White House" instructing people in right conduct, now the nation had a "Great White Mother [who] emerges as a personality in her own right and starts an independent course of instruction on her own account."9

Never before had the presidency been conducted in such partnership, with Franklin being the politician and Eleanor his wisest and most active ambassador for domestic affairs. She would constantly bring to his attention issues that he would not otherwise have seen, and their Sunday suppers of scrambled eggs in the chafing dish became a time when Grandmère would invite different people to speak informally of what mattered to them. She would also send her friends on fact-finding missions, such as the time when she sent Lorena Hickock to investigate the Federal Emergency Relief Administration programs and report back to the President and his aids of their shortcomings. In this way FDR was able to form policy based on the living realities of Americans, and his great success as president was founded on never losing touch and the constant and enduring connection between the White House and ordinary households everywhere.

The Roosevelt genius of using informality to preside over a nation was a great gift to a country plunged in hopelessness. It was this informality, this sense of being in touch with the people, that made FDR's famous "fireside chats" so effective at galvanizing a weakened nation. Together Eleanor and Franklin reached out, and in return millions of Americans responded with a renewed confidence and trust.

On the more formal occasions Grandmère excelled as hostess: "The White House had an aura of power and impressiveness about it, but they were themselves," remarked Mrs. Ames, a frequent guest. "They acted as if they had always been there. It was like visiting friends in a very large country house. One was put instantly at one's ease. She was the fantastically most thoughtful hostess I have ever met in my life."10

And so it was that during the first hundred days of his presidency, Franklin had engineered the greatest reformation in law ever passed through Congress; changes that would help sustain and relieve the country from its economic doldrums. And throughout these hectic whirlwind days, Grandmère stood by his side and allied herself completely to his vision. The star of Eleanor Roosevelt was now shining brightly over America.

From March to the end of 1933, that first year of FDR's administration and her first at the forefront of the rapidly changing landscape, Grandmère began her outreach to the nation by simply stating "I want you to write to me," and as a result she received more than three hundred thousand pieces of personal mail—an unprecedented amount for any First Lady. Of course, much of this correspondence was making requests, some of which were quite humorous and unrealistic. One letter, for example, came from a woman who wrote asking Grandmère to find a baby the woman could adopt. Before Grandmère could respond, the lady wrote again saying that if Eleanor was successful in finding the baby, the woman would need a cow, and if she had both baby and cow she would need a new icebox to keep the milk in!

Grandmère and Louis Howe enjoying a bit of relaxation at Campobello,
Louis' last trip before his death in 1934.

Dark Forebodings

In the autumn of 1934 Louis Howe fell gravely ill, and through the months of winter Franklin and Eleanor's faithful advisor grew progressively weaker. After bronchial collapse in January 1935, he was taken from the Lincoln Bedroom at the White House to the hospital, where Grandmère would visit him daily. Grandfather, despite being extremely busy with the reelection campaign, allowed Louis' direct line to him to continue to be switched on from 10:00 A.M. till 4:00 P.M. daily to maintain the appearance that Louis was fully involved in the campaign, as he had been in all political moves of both Roosevelts, and to keep open the link with his old friend, whom he could not often visit in hospital.

On April 18, 1935, Louis finally slipped away quietly while asleep and the president ordered the White House flag to be half-mast in his honor. No one would ever replace Louis in Grandmère's heart, for he had been the Pygmalion who had helped her transform into a wise and shrewd politician and a motivating factor in Franklin's own stellar political career.

Left: *Louis shared my grandfather's love of ship models, and it was said that he himself was an accomplished "modeler."* Above: *Mentor and advisor to both Grandmère and FDR for so many years, Louis Howe passed away in April 1935.*

If the president and his First Lady had captured America's imagination, many Republicans were completely hostile to his politics and desperately wanted him ousted in the 1936 election. During his campaign in 1935 Franklin once more gave women an increased budget and larger space at headquarters, for he viewed their involvement as crucial to his political strategy. At the 1936 Democratic convention, in Philadelphia, he exhilarated and motivated people by outlining the challenges his administration had conquered and encouraging them to follow him in facing new difficulties and new problems, the continued work needed to climb out of the darkness of the Depression. One of his best remembered sentences, "This generation of Americans has a rendezvous with destiny," made the crowds nearly crazy. He masterfully used Republican hatred to his advantage:

Never before in all our history have these forces been so united against one candidate as they stand today. They are unanimous in their hatred for me—and I welcome their hatred.

I should like to have it said of my first administration that in it the forces of selfishness and of lust

*Always at Springwood for his election night results, this for his second term
in 1936, with, from left to right, Anna and her husband, Sara,
FDR on my uncle Jim's arm, and Grandmère.*

*for power met their match. I should like to have it
said of my second administration that in it these
forces met their master.*[11]

When they heard the news of Franklin's victory,
Eleanor was awed by the feeling the country
expressed in the election returns and the messages
that flooded into Springwood, where the family had
gone to await the returns. This was a powerful
demonstration of the pact the president had forged
with the people during his first term of the presidency. This pact was sealed even more deeply as a
second term of new challenges loomed ahead.

In the next four years Grandmère would
gain even greater strength as First Lady; her determination would sharpen, her efforts increase, and
her influence over those closest to the president
become a force to be reckoned with. She would act
as a filter for him, offering clarity and cutting
through the obfuscations of the sycophants. Under
her tutelage civic organizations thrived, and she was
a relentless supporter of dozens of associations that

promised to better the condition of minorities, women, children, and society. Her "back door" route to the president often caused insecurity among his advisors, who feared she had the more powerful influence over him. At times she was regarded as misguided about issues. But Grandmère never abused her prerogative, and the back door remained opened to her, for Franklin not only welcomed her influence but needed her to help formulate his own political opinions.

Despite Franklin's reliance on her as a "pulse" of the public's perception of the administration, he too could become frustrated by her constant entreaties. Their White House was in many respects divided into two households, Franklin's and Eleanor's, and both demanded absolute loyalty from their friends and associates. Harry Hopkins, for instance, was someone Eleanor had cultivated for years, but when he "defected" to become Franklin's most trusted advisor and closest friend, Grandmère felt secretly betrayed by him. It was Grandmère who had originally brought him into the fold of the White House. She had met him through her friendship with his first wife, Barbara, and had worked diligently to arrange for Harry to get to know her friends by inviting them to Hyde Park, Val-Kill. At the White House, whenever she knew FDR would be available, she would take pains to have Harry in evidence. Grandfather himself found Hopkins to be "most congenial company" and in time a brilliant tactician, impressions shared by his two closest personal advisors, Louis Howe and Missy LeHand. In fact, it was shortly following the 1936 election that Grandmère, assuming that this would be FDR's final term in office, began positioning Harry as a possible successor to the presidency, a prospect Grandfather did

Harry Hopkins, long an acquaintance of Grandmère and introduced to FDR by her, became a close advisor to both. He was a supporter within the administration of many, but not all, of Grandmère's causes.

not find altogether remote. In 1938 he named Harry his Secretary of Commerce, an appointment designed to groom him into a viable candidate and transform him from merely a "warm-hearted social worker into a hard-headed business-statesman." Following Barbara's death in 1937 Grandmère became even closer to Harry, and in 1938 she worried over his health, a concern chronicled in a memorandum Harry left for his daughter, Diana:

Just before Christmas in 1938 Mrs. Roosevelt came out to our house in Georgetown to see me.

At that time I was feeling none too well...she told me she thought I seemed to be disturbed about

My grandfather had a marvelous sense of humor. In this never-before published photograph (left), FDR is depicted as the "Imperial President" at an annual Gridiron Club dinner of news correspondents. Right: The President is surrounded by his "Vestal Virgins," including Nancy Cook, Missy LeHand, et al. at a White House birthday celebration.

something and wondered if it was a feeling that something might happen to me and that there was no proper provision for you. She told me that she had been thinking about it a good deal and wanted me to know that she would like for me to provide in my will that she, Mrs. Roosevelt, be made your guardian.[12]

Harry's health declined until 1940. During a White House dinner party he became so ill that FDR insisted that he "stay the night." From that night on Harry Hopkins remained a resident of the Lincoln Bedroom, the same room that had only recently been home of another beloved advisor, Louis Howe. Even before becoming a resident, Harry had successfully filled the void left by Louis' death, and he soon became ingratiated with FDR. And although always a loving devotee of Grandmère, Harry transferred his loyalty completely to the president.

Perhaps because of their intimate and yet in some ways remote personal relationship, Grandmère felt at times a greater sense of insecurity as a result of the influence people like Harry Hopkins and Missy LeHand had on her husband. She feared the overly relaxed atmosphere at his cocktail hour and shied away from the kind of gossip Grandfather enjoyed. Unable to let herself go she was threatened when her husband was overly intimate and cozy with his friends. Perturbed, she would retreat to her own set of rooms or leave the White House altogether and seek refuge at her apartment in Manhattan or at

Val-Kill; sometimes she would simply bury herself in yet another new enterprise.

Her absences created an opportunity for other women to move in and get close to FDR. He was an immensely attractive man to whom women had always been drawn, and now that he was seen as the most powerful person in the world his allure was even stronger. My father, Elliott, was the first to publicly suggest that there might have been a possible affair with Missy LeHand, his faithful, tireless, and completely loyal assistant for over twenty years, and others suspected that Franklin might also have been involved with Crown Princess Martha of Norway, the beautiful and young wife of King Olav.

My grandfather's relationship with Missy developed over the years into one of complete faith and trust, and most probably they shared a deep feeling for each other...perhaps love. She was a tall, handsome woman with large blue eyes and distinctive prematurely gray hair. Many of the staff at the White House considered Missy almost a second wife to the president and took her orders very seriously, for they knew Franklin would always back her up. The fact that Missy never married would seem to indicate more than a superficial devotion to my grandfather, and quite often she would serve as an unofficial hostess at both formal and informal affairs. Missy, in failing health, retired from her duties in 1940 and returned to her native Massachusetts. In 1941 she suffered a debilitating stroke and remained an invalid for the remainder of her life. The extent to which FDR cared for her is demonstrated by a provision in his own last will and testament, in which he provided that all of Missy's medical expenses be paid out of the estate's income, up to 50 percent, with only the remainder going to support Grandmère.

Grandmère with Crown Prince Olav and Princess Martha of Norway in 1941. It was believed that Princess Martha reciprocated FDR's attentions and affection.

Princess Martha, on the other hand, was beautiful, young, and impressionable—and obviously enthralled by the attentions of my much older but still handsome grandfather. Martha's father was a Swedish prince, her mother a Danish princess, and she an only child when she met her first cousin and future husband Prince Olav, the son of King Haakon VII of Norway, whose younger sister was Martha's mother. Their marriage produced three beautiful children: princesses Ragnhild and Astrid and prince Harald, the present king of Norway. My grandfather had met both Olav and Martha in the spring of 1939 when the royal couple traveled to the United States to dedicate the Norwegian exhibit at the World's Fair. From the moment he laid eyes upon her, Franklin was enthralled by her beauty and sparkling personality. Olav and Martha accepted an invitation from Grandfather to spend a weekend at Springwood, to the utter delight of Sara, where they attended a picnic, a concert, and a large country dinner. Even today that visit is commemorated by a photograph standing among those of other royal visitors in the "Dresden Room" at Springwood.

The Nazi invasion of Norway in April 1940 gravely endangered the royal family, and Martha and the children accepted my grandfather's offer of asylum. Martha arrived at Springwood with her children, her lady-in-waiting (who sported a tattoo on her arm), the court chamberlain, and a retinue of servants.

Princess Martha and her children later moved to a mansion in Washington, D.C., where she and FDR continued to see each other for "tea." Diana Hopkins Halstead, Harry Hopkins' daughter, who moved into the White House with him, recounts how her stepmother Louise, Harry's second wife, was frequently asked to fill the uncomfortable role of chaperone:

> She worked as a nurse's aid at the Columbia Hospital, and she'd go off in the morning and come back in the afternoon. The president began to rely on her as his chaperone to go and visit Princess Martha. Mummy would get home from the hospital, and there would be a message that "the president wants you to go to tea with Princess Martha—now." No time to get out of the uniform, nothing—and zap, off to Princess Martha's house. Then they'd get there, and Princess Martha would say, "Louise, why don't you go and see the children." And so Louise would go and see the children, and the president and Princess Martha would have tea, and this was one hell of a tough situation for Mummy to get into. But she did it with as much grace as she had.[13]

A hopeless flirt, FDR once observed, "Nothing is more pleasing to the eye than a good-looking lady, nothing more refreshing to the spirit than the company of one, nothing more flattering to the ego than the affection of one." However, it is doubtful that after his affliction with polio there was much chance that he was capable of any significant physical intimacy. I am told that, although not certainly, his paralysis probably caused impotence as well.

Grandfather's continuous flirting must have been trying for Grandmère. Such flirtatious behavior was so totally foreign to her that she could never make peace with this side of his nature. She often felt rejected and usually simply withdrew from it all.

The War Years

The clouds of uncertainty and anxiety have been hanging over us for a long time.
Now we know where we are.

—Eleanor Roosevelt

WHILE THE NATIONS OF THE WORLD were waging savage war against each other in 1940, the United States, still maintaining its isolationist stance, was preparing for another presidential election. Third terms for presidents had never been the custom of the country. From the early preparations of the Democratic campaign until almost the last minute Franklin kept his plans veiled from everyone, including his wife and children. He played with time and innuendo to fuel speculations as to whether he would submit his name in candidacy for another four years of presidency.

Grandmère had her own strong views on the issue; she felt sure that once they left the White House she would find plenty of interesting work that would be uniquely hers. She also looked forward to being able to live her life more freely, developing in ways that were impossible while she remained First Lady. When Bess Furman, the Associated Press reporter, asked her to sum up the last thirty years as the wife of an officeholder, Grandmère replied tellingly, "It's hell." She could also be humorous about the requirements expected from the wife of a public man:

Always be on time. Never try to make personal arrangements. Do as little talking as humanly possible. Never be disturbed by anything. Always do what you're told to do as quickly as possible. Remember to lean back in a parade, so that people can see your husband. Don't get too fat to ride three on a seat. Get out of the way as quickly as you're not needed.[1]

Even though she proved herself incredibly skilled at combining the social duties of First Lady with her own interesting and varied life, her position would have tested the patience of a saint: In 1939 Tommy reckoned Grandmère had 4,729 people for meals; 323 houseguests; 9,211 tea guests; and received (meaning received but didn't feed) 14,056 people, totaling 28,319 White House attendances in all![2]

The threat of war hung heavily upon America: Hitler's armies and air force struck westward, invading the Low Countries, penetrating into France, seizing Paris, and outflanking the Maginot

Line. Mussolini had entered the war, and desperate European leaders were deluging the White House with pleas for help. Staunch pacifists such as Archibald MacLeish, Walter Millis, and Harold Ickes were reluctantly admitting that the time was close when Congress would seriously have to consider joining the war. The pressure on Franklin mounted quickly, as it was felt that only he could successfully navigate the country to the safe shore of the New Deal, and that he was possibly the only Democratic leader Americans would trust in the event of the nation joining the Allied Forces. In June it became apparent to Eleanor that Franklin had made up his mind to submit his name for the Democratic nomination, and she promptly departed for her cottage at Val-Kill, away from the political chaos. The week of the Democratic convention, Grandmère was at her beloved cottage swimming, riding, playing tennis, and relaxing with Tommy. Then she received an urgent call from Chicago to come to the convention. Franklin had decided that he would personally not attend the convention, leaving the political machinations to his trusted advisors…except that perhaps his single most valuable counselor was absent from the convention floor.

> I got a call from the convention begging me to come out. I called Franklin, and he said, "Well, would you like to go?" and I said, "No, I wouldn't like to go. I'm very busy, and you told me I didn't have to go." He said, "Well, perhaps they seem to think it might be well if you came out." And I said, "But do you really want me to go?" and he said, "Well, perhaps it would be a good idea." So that meant, I suppose, that I had to go.[3]

Franklin had chosen the controversial Secretary of Agriculture Henry Wallace as his running mate, and the news had been greeted with boos and catcalls in the convention hall. The delegates threatened to revolt, and from the White House the president retaliated by threatening not to run. This was fuel for the fire for Republicans, who accused FDR of seeking a third term with the express wish to destroy the United States by leading it into war. In their view, he was attempting to establish himself in an "Imperial Presidency." (Fortunately they never saw a jesting photograph of FDR taken at a news correspondents' roast of the president, depicting him in exactly that pose!) The convention was spinning out of control. Eleanor, dressed in a simple blue silk coat and dress, arrived and performed what many would regard as a miracle:

> Pandemonium had broken loose in the convention hall. You couldn't hear yourself speak. The noise was something terrible. I went forward and stood and, to my surprise and everyone else's, I imagine, there was silence in a very short time.[4]

"Delegates to the convention," she began. "This is no ordinary time. You cannot treat it as you would treat an ordinary nomination in an ordinary time." Whoever became president, she told the hushed audience, faced:

> …a heavier responsibility, perhaps, than any man has ever faced before in this country. This is no ordinary time… So each and every one of you who give him this responsibility, in giving it to him assume for yourselves a very grave responsibility because you will make the campaign. You will have to rise above considerations which are narrow and partisan. This is a time when it is the United States we fight for.[5]

She talked briefly, directly, and without notes, even

As the United States came closer to joining the war, Grandmère concentrated on her work with the Office of Civilian Defense, and is photographed here at a rally of OCD volunteers.

though she had prepared her speech carefully. In her quiet, understated way, Grandmère was electric. She brought everyone up to face the extreme difficulties that would unfold before the country, and yet promised to renew her and her husband's bond to Americans, pulling everyone together in a joint effort toward peace and safety. She concluded her speech by sealing the ancient promise of the Roosevelts to the people:

> *No man who is candidate or who is President can carry this situation alone. This is only carried by a united people who love their country.*[6]

The hall erupted in tumultuous applause. They agreed on Franklin's choice of running mate and approved of a third term of his presidency. As she finished her speech the hall became absolutely still, petty rancor and political rivalries melted away by her prophetic words.

Months later, in November, the Roosevelt family met at Springwood to listen to the results of the election, clustering around radios in the Big House. Grandmère, as usual, made everyone feel comfortable, served scrambled eggs—by now an expected if not altogether welcomed family tradition—and considered quietly what another four years at the White House would do to her, to Franklin, and to their children. Could she face it? As news of his victory poured in, Franklin, Harry Hopkins, and others went out on the front lawn to be cheered by the crowds of reporters and neighbors who had gathered in the night. Franklin gave a little speech, went back indoors, and then headed out again for more rejoicing. My uncle Franklin Jr. went to retrieve Grandmère and told her, "Mother, they want you. There are seven hundred people still standing there in the dark, asking for you. You'll have to go to them." For the citizens of the country, Eleanor now counted as much as if not more than her husband.

Joining the Allied Forces

At the inauguration of the third term, Grandmère's heart was laden with unanswerable questions. "I looked at my children, at the President's mother, and then at the President himself," she later wrote in her journal, "and wondered what each one was feeling down in his heart of hearts." Eleanor knew only too well the process of searching deep in times of crisis to find the resilience one needs to pull through. However, this was a time of crisis for everyone, not just for her: Her three boys would most probably be conscripted, and Franklin would need all his strength and courage to guide the country through the war while simultaneously working to repair the deep cuts of the Depression. These were trying times.

Until then Grandmère had been patron of innumerable causes, but now, with England beset daily by Hitler's Luftwaffe and the whole world locked in the inferno of war, she concentrated on two causes: enabling in every way she could the State Department to issue visas to the United States to the thousands of refugees from Europe, and helping New York City's mayor Fiorello LaGuardia to manage the Office of Civilian Defense (OCD).

Albert Einstein had remarked to Eleanor that the State Department seemed to have built a "wall of bureaucratic measures" between victims of fascist cruelty in Europe and safety in the United States. Grandmère, outraged because she knew that even a few weeks could mean the difference between life and death for many of the refugees, used her influence to impose a degree of urgency on the department so that as many people as possible would be able to reach safety in the States. The

My father interviewing Albert Einstein, who often expressed strong views on the immigration policies of the United States that limited access of victims of fascism.

OCD would function as a hub between government departments and agencies to join forces and establish an ambitious national program of civil defense. This would be the equivalent of the British Home Front, fondly nicknamed "Dad's Army," which became a crucial part of the war effort and in which everyone's participation—women, the elderly, and even children—was needed. The OCD would educate American citizens on the basics of civil defense in a national effort for preparedness, and Eleanor was inspired by the example set by Britain, where even young princess Elizabeth was photographed in mechanics' overalls, changing a truck's tires.

On September 7, 1941, Sara Delano Roosevelt passed away, and with her an era during which families like the Roosevelts could live peacefully in their large country estates, protected from the chaos of the

Grandmère and "Granny" (Sara) at Campobello awaiting FDR's arrival on the yacht "Sewanna."

ER, Frederic Delano, and Sara at FDR's "Message to Congress," January 1939.

Four generations: Sara and FDR, with FDR, Jr. and baby FDR III, 1940.

world. Now, her son the president and his whole family were directly involved with the biggest conflict the world had ever known. Grandmère described Sara's last hours in a letter to her friend Maude Gray:

> *She had been somewhat of an invalid all summer but was home from Campo, enjoyed Franklin's day at home tho' she had a slight temperature. About Sat. midnight a clot in the lung caused a circulatory collapse & she became unconscious & remained so until her breathing stopped at noon last Sunday. I think Franklin will forget all the irritations & remember only pleasant things which is just as well. The endless details, clothes to go through, check books, paper. I began on Sat.*[7]

Grandmère had struggled in the relationship with Sara for thirty-six years and so felt perhaps no great

sense of loss. But Franklin was grieving deeply, and despite previous promises to the contrary, he told his family that Springwood would not be changed at all and that he planned to leave the house exactly as his mother had had it. This painfully confirmed once more to Grandmère that Springwood had been and would always be Sara and Franklin's home, not hers. No sooner had she begun sorting through Sara's belongings than she was called to the Walter Reed Hospital in Washington, where her brother Hall Roosevelt was struggling in his last few days. After the death of his son Danny, Hall had lapsed back into alcoholism and unhappiness, and his liver had not been able to bear the burden. As Grandmère wrote,

> *My idea of hell, if I believed in it, would be to sit or stand & watch someone breathing hard, struggling for words when a gleam of consciousness returns &*

Left: *With Fiorello LaGuardia at the Office of Civilian Defense in 1941. Much to the chagrin of her detractors, Grandmère played an important initial role in this wartime agency.* Right: *This photo was taken on a visit to California just prior to my uncle Jim joining the US Marine Corps.*

thinking "this was once the little boy I played with & scolded, he could have been so much & this is what he is." It is a bitter thing & in spite of everything I've loved Hall, perhaps somewhat remissibly of late, but he is part of me. I do have a quieting effect on him & so I stood by his bed & held his hand & stroked his forehead & Zena (Hall's wife) *stood by me for hours. She won't give up hope of his recovery & keeps asking me if I don't think he's strong enough to pull through till I could weep.*

That September had been emotionally grueling for Grandmère, but two days later she was back at work at the headquarters of OCD, lending the country all her support.

Grandmère spent the afternoon and early evening of December 6, 1941, in her sitting room with Judge Justine Polier and Paul Kellogg working on OCD business, then took her two guests to bid the president good night. Franklin greeted them with the announcement that he had just sent the emperor of Japan a last plea of peace between their two countries. The next day Eleanor was expecting Franklin to attend a large lunch at the White House, but when he didn't turn up and she went to check on him she was faced by the most devastating news:

All of ER's sons immediately joined the war effort. Here my father with my mother, sister, and brother at just about the time he shipped overseas with the Army Air Corps.

negatively on the president, decided with LaGuardia that the OCD needed new leadership in these critical times, and so both resigned their positions. LaGuardia was replaced with James W. Landis, who proved a far more efficient administrator in time of crisis.

Uncle James went to the West Coast to train with the Marine Raiders Battalion, while my father was about to join a bomber squadron in the Army Air Corps. Grandmère knew her sons would have to set the example for all the sons of the nation, but the thought did not prevent her from sobbing every time she recalled how hard it had been to say good-bye. She carried a prayer in her purse, a reassurance perhaps that this was one of those times when war was necessary and as such we all had to make ourselves worthy of the sacrifice of those who died for our cause:

> Dear Lord,
> Lest I continue
> My complacent way,
> Help me to remember,
> Somehow out there
> A man died for me today.
> As long as there be war,
> I then must
> Ask and answer
> Am I worth dying for?

The Japanese had bombed Pearl Harbor, sealing America's fate with the Allied Forces. Overnight, America was in tumult and Washington a changed city. She found her sons James and Elliott already in uniform, and her heart ached when James announced that he wanted to serve active duty with the Marines.

Now more than ever the OCD would have to perform with absolute efficiency. A number of criticisms had been hurled at Fiorello LaGuardia and Eleanor for the shortcomings of an organization that was attempting to mobilize an entire country. Eleanor, feeling that anything she was personally involved with and that came under critical fire would reflect

Grandmère and Tommy replied to every letter that was sent to them by all the young men and women working at the OCD or being sent away to war: These were not formal replies, but personal and individual letters encouraging each to stand strong in these grave times; it was as though she were writing to her own children.

Shortly after US troops had been deployed to Britain Grandmère made an important trip to strengthen our nation's commitment. Here she was visiting the British Royal Family at Buckingham Palace.

By September of the following year, 1942, King George VI and Queen Elizabeth extended an invitation for Grandmère to visit Britain and to stay at Buckingham Palace. Franklin encouraged closer relationships both with the British monarchs and with the new Prime Minister Winston Churchill and his wife, Clementine. Eleanor would also have an opportunity to see my father, who was stationed seventy miles outside of London, and to lend support to the homesick American troops.

Eleanor was to travel in extreme secrecy, accompanied only by Tommy. When they arrived at Buckingham Palace, they were given a set of rooms so large that my father, who joined them at the royal residence, calculated that his room alone was the equivalent of the long corridor at the White House. She had tea with the king and queen, and met princesses Elizabeth and Margaret. She then spent days traipsing up and down the country talking to the Americans stationed there to help in the war effort. She journeyed to Chequers, the PM's country residence, and spent time with the brilliant but somewhat irascible Winston Churchill (whose famous words before his afternoon nap were always "Bugger them all"). Her visit was extremely well reported in the American and British presses, and she did truly help boost the morale of both countries. In between the inspections and official lunches, she met the king of Greece, the president of Poland, Belgian Premier Pierlot, Mary the Queen Mother, the king of Norway and Crown Prince Olav, and gave a speech at the BBC that was listened to by 51 percent of the British population, one of the highest ratings ever awarded.

Winston Churchill had likewise been captivated by Grandmère's grace, presence, and work; shortly before she left he sent her a handwritten note saying, "You certainly have left golden footprints behind you." And Chalmers Roberts, head of the War Information Office in London, reported to FDR, "Mrs. Roosevelt has done more to bring a real understanding of the spirit of the United States to the people of Britain than any other single American who has ever visited these islands." From then on and for the remainder of the war, Winston Churchill established a close relationship with FDR, sometimes moving with his butler into a set of rooms in the White House for weeks at a time.

On this same trip, Grandmère met with my father and homesick US troops at their posting in England.

Churchill, a frequent wartime visitor in Washington, shown with FDR during a period of relaxation, fishing at the presidential retreat "Shangri-La" (now Camp David).

What would happen after the war was the question on everyone's minds. Churchill pressed for a world order based on Anglo-American supremacy that would reflect the glory of the foundations he and FDR would set. Eleanor, however, voiced her support for a postwar organization that should include all people who believed in democracy. Military monopoly in the hands of Britain and the United States, she felt, would only be the cause for further eruptions after the war. Her view included all people and all races, for she saw that continuing to submit supinely to the same doctrine was a grave mistake. The related protests Americans were raising on the inclusion of black soldiers in the war effort also angered her, especially when some Southerners insisted that she and the president were stirring up the black population on purpose:

What you do not seem to realize is that no one is "stirring up" the colored people in this country. The whole world is faced with the same situation, the domination of the white race is being challenged. We have ten percent of our population, in large majority, denied their rights as citizens. In other countries you have seen the results of white domination, Burma, Singapore, et cetera. You have seen the intelligent handling in the Philippines.

She felt strongly that she should help people understand that the effort to diminish human suffering could only be successful if people would transcend color and race barriers. She tirelessly confronted men and women in power to face up to their moral obligations and work through issues in the most enlightened, progressive way. Eleanor Roosevelt's views

177

Grandmère became a close friend and an admirer of the young, beautiful, and tireless Madame Chiang Kai-shek.

were never just theoretical, and she sought to put her principles in practice whenever she could.

Throughout the war years Grandmère's concern with domestic issues never wavered. While many in the Administration were preoccupied with international affairs, she increased her outspokenness and possibly became even more controversial in her domestic advocacy. She would, for instance, plant the seed for the eventual integration and equality of African Americans in the armed services. She also pushed for more rights and services for women who were now so critical to America's wartime economy. Grandmère's role as guardian on all domestic issues had never been more essential, and at the same time her activities on the international front continued.

On February 17, 1943, Mme. Chiang Kai-shek arrived at the White House for a two-week stay. Eleanor immediately felt a great rapport with this most unusual First Lady, whose character resembled that of a dragon disguised as a butterfly. Mme. Chiang had come to appeal to the president and to Americans to regard Japan as equal an enemy as Germany and to heed the pleas of her country. Grandmère was deeply impressed by this petite woman with porcelain skin and dark eyes that flashed fire and ice, wrapped in the most exquisite silks. Mme. Chiang repeatedly extended an invitation to Eleanor to visit her in China, urging her to persuade Franklin to let her go, but the president always thought that a state visit by the First Lady to China would be too controversial at this delicate juncture in the war effort, and never gave his consent. Mme. Chiang captivated Eleanor thoroughly, though some people at the White House, such as Tommy and Harry Hopkins, considered her imperious, spoiled, and ruthless in her quest to have China's interests adhered to in the great discussions for the next world order.

Unable to go and be with Mme. Chiang, Grandmère prepared to visit the GIs in the South Pacific. From Honolulu her first stop was Christmas Island, a coral atoll where the commanding officer assured her there were no snakes, something that terrified her. She was horrified, however, when she found the floor of her bedroom that night crawling with tropical bugs. "I might have screamed if I had not been the only woman on the Island and I knew

Top: *Entertaining troops on the White House grounds, Grandmère felt it her duty to become a "surrogate mother and grandmother" to the boys who were giving so much for their country.* Bottom: *On one of her many inspection tours, this to visit injured soldiers on Christmas Island in the South Pacific war zone.*

a feminine scream would have attracted a great deal of attention," she quipped. On her next stop, the Cook Islands, she was astonished to find just how

Generalissimo Chiang Kai-shek, FDR, Churchill, and Madame Chiang at the November 25, 1943 Cairo Conference. A decline in FDR's health was then becoming more apparent.

much bigotry pervaded the attitudes of some soldiers and commanders in their relationships with each other and women of the Maori race:

> *The Colonel, regular army, Mass. Republican, and snobby was not pleased to see me. I'm sure he would sleep with a Maori woman but he told me he does not believe in mixed marriages, and he would like some Army nurses because some of his younger officers want to marry some of the native girls. He has both white and colored troops and he is much worried since he has some white Southerners and he is afraid some day a white boy will find his native girl that he went out with last night is off with a colored boy the next night and then there would be a shooting and a feud would start between white and colored troops. He thinks we should have all colored and all white on an island, but he owns that the colored have done very good work so he prays hell won't break loose.[8]*

Many army officers viewed Grandmère as nothing more than a meddlesome "do-gooder" and dreaded her arrival, but inevitably she won everyone over with her positive spirit, friendly almost motherly touch, and her incredible energy. Admiral William "Bull" Halsey, who became a great admirer, described her day at his base in New Zealand:

Four days later, a tired FDR mediated a meeting of Churchill and Stalin at the Tehran Conference.

Here is what she did in twelve hours: she inspected two Navy hospitals, took a boat to an officer's rest home and had lunch there, returned and inspected an Army hospital, reviewed the 2nd Marine Raider Battalion (her son Jimmy had been its executive officer), made a speech at a service club, attended a reception, and was guest of honor at a dinner given by General Harmon.

When I say she inspected those hospitals, I don't mean that she shook hands with the chief medical officer, glanced into a sun parlor, and left. I mean she went into every ward, stopped at every bed, and spoke to every patient: What was his name? How did

he feel? Was there anything he needed? Could she take a message home for him? I marveled at her hardihood, both physical and mental, she walked for miles, and she saw patients who were grievously and gruesomely wounded. But I marveled most at their expressions as she leaned over them. It was a sight I will never forget.[9]

When she arrived in Australia the authorities had expected the cold and stiff state visits typical of the royal family and were astounded by Eleanor's approachability and ease. She resented too much protocol and fuss around her, preferring instead to visit the GIs and talk to them at length about their condition. They were far more important than presidential pomp. In Guadalcanal she recounted a wonderful and funny story: a sad Marine whose unit was due to leave the South Pacific felt he couldn't leave until he had shot a Japanese. So his officer advised him to stand up on the ridge and shout 'To hell with Hirohito,' and a Japanese would certainly appear and then he could bag him. Next day the officer came upon the still depressed Marine. "What happened?" asked the officer. "I did as you said, Sir, and a Japanese did climb out of his foxhole, but he yelled 'To hell with Roosevelt' and how could I shoot a fellow Republican?"

In her visit to the South Pacific she toured seventeen islands, New Zealand, and Australia, and saw four hundred thousand men in camps and hospitals. She was exhausted emotionally and physically, but, as Admiral Halsey remarked, "She alone had accomplished more than any other person, or any group of civilians, who had passed through my area." She explained in a radio broadcast the feelings her trip had elicited:

> I wonder if I can transmit to you the feeling which I have so strongly. In a nation such as ours every man who fights for us in some way, is our man. His parents may be of any race or religion, but if that man dies, he dies side by side with all of his buddies, and if your heart is with any man, in some way it must be with all.[10]

Upon her return from the South Pacific, FDR announced that a conference between him, Stalin, and Chiang Kai-shek was at last to take place in Cairo. He would then go on to Tehran to help mediate talks between Churchill and Stalin, but he did not want Grandmère to go with him. As the war wore on, Franklin had become more resolutely obstinate in his views, as if he had less energy to accommodate the needs of anyone around him.

At the conference the leaders discussed the breakup of the German Reich and plans for a postwar peacekeeping organization. When he returned the family celebrated Christmas at Hyde Park with Aunt Anna, Uncle Franklin Jr., John, and many of the grandchildren. As magical as the time in the Big House was for everyone, FDR returned to Washington ill with a strong bout of the flu and returned after only two weeks to Springwood to recover. In 1944 he would face yet another campaign, this time for his fourth term as president, and though his commitment to the position was now stronger than it had ever been, the stresses and strains were taking a toll on his body and mind. The issues of the New Deal were lying half-forgotten in the tumult and devastation of war. Eleanor remembered their promise to Americans daily and claimed that she had not laid the New Deal "away in lavender." Keeping that promise was as important to her as winning the war, and she pressed Franklin on the concerns that still needed resolution in order to successfully conclude their pact with the people of the land.

The "Last August President"

In March 1944 Grandmère went on a Caribbean tour to lift the spirits of the troops; she returned to Washington to find a husband who did not seem able to recover his physical strength. She felt his illness was simply more than physical: "The nervous tension as well as the long burden of responsibility has a share in the physical condition I am sure." The results of medical tests showed a moderate degree of arteriosclerosis, cloudiness in the sinuses, and bronchial irritation, which could be cured by less smoking. A young heart specialist, Dr. Howard G. Bruenn, diagnosed hypertension, hypersensitive heart disease, cardiac failure in the left ventricular chamber, and acute bronchitis.

It would seem strange that neither Eleanor, Anna, nor anyone else was made aware of FDR's condition, quite possibly at his insistence. The doctors recommended a period of rest after lunch and evenings dedicated to relaxation. Grandmère had always had a Spartan view of physical ailments, and with her high degree of energy she seemed to soldier on no matter what and recover easily from illness, even flu. Thus it was perhaps difficult for her to fully recognize the seriousness of Franklin's rapidly waning strength. Nevertheless, knowing the restorative powers Springwood had for him, she made the Big House nice for him that June so that he could come to rest, surrounded by children, grandchildren, and the ever-flirtatious Princess Martha of Norway who had also joined the party.

Aunt Anna, after talking the arrangements through with her mother, agreed to move into Springwood and take care of her father full-time. He loved having her around, and she was perhaps a less demanding presence than Grandmère, who was constantly pressing him with urgent affairs of state. Anna had found a new closeness with her father and so moved into the White House as well, taking over many of Grandmère's responsibilities. In fact, Franklin used her to shield himself from those who brought too many burdens before him, and occasionally that even included his wife, and Anna became an almost constant companion and confidant.

During this time Anna would play a somewhat equivocal role in the relationship between my grandparents: she knew that Lucy Mercer, now Rutherford, visited Franklin at the White House while her mother was away, sometimes even presiding as hostess at various functions. Never informing Grandmère of these visits, Anna would often serve as "chaperone," most likely as the elusive chaperone. Without question, Anna was placed in an almost untenable position by her father, that of being privy to secrets that would obviously hurt her mother. No one knows for certain when the contact between FDR and Lucy resumed, or if it ever really ceased in the first place, or when her White House visits began. We do know, however, that there was at least one other occasion when they met socially; a time that may have rekindled the old attraction of their prior affair.

The invasion of Europe was impending in late spring 1944 and Grandfather was busier than ever and more focused on his work, closeting himself away from everyone. His health fluctuated wildly, and he had become querulous and weary. The impending campaign didn't help. He had chosen Senator Harry Truman as his running mate, and Eleanor, although only too aware of what the presidency was doing to him, felt that the country could not be handed over to anyone else until the war had been won. He remained aloof, indifferent, and withdrawn from the campaign. Did he care to win? Perhaps he had stepped into the shadow of the responsibilities that faced him and could not give energy to yet another race.

He did, however, win an unprecedented fourth term. On the night of the election he was so tired he allowed himself to be wheeled out on the

*Greeting election night well-wishers for the last time at Springwood,
Grandmère was now very concerned about FDR's failing health and was privately opposed to a fourth term.*

lawn of Springwood to greet the well-wishers. "There was a great deal of excitement all through the evening among many people about us," Eleanor wrote, "but I can't say that I felt half as excited as I will feel the day the war is over." They were both in for it for another four years, a prospect that would have been anything but appealing seeing as how the world was rocking on its foundations under the threat of the Germans using the atomic bomb to wipe out what they hadn't yet destroyed.

Two days after the inauguration the president left for the Yalta Conference, taking Anna with him. Grandmère was by now deeply worried about his irri-

tability, his impatience, and his acquiescence. She prodded him constantly, unable to admit what everyone else could readily see but was unwilling to acknowledge. On February 11 Roosevelt, Churchill, and Stalin announced the results of the historic conference in a joint statement. When Grandfather addressed Congress on the results of the conference, he asked the indulgence of his audience as he spoke from a sitting position, explaining for the first time in his public career that he was wearing ten pounds of braces on his legs. Gore Vidal calls my grandfather the "last august president of the United States," perhaps because of his incredible stateliness in leading the

*Just two days after his inauguration in 1945, FDR insisted on attending
the famous Yalta Conference with Churchill and Stalin, this time taking my aunt Anna as his assistant.*

nation from the darkness of the Depression and war to the light of understanding, compassion, and a new world order. By March the president was at Warm Springs, Georgia, recuperating the strength that eluded him. He looked terribly thin, worn, and gray, and his hands shook uncontrollably. Grandmère many years later wrote in hindsight:

> I knew when he consented to "address Congress" sitting down that he had accepted a certain degree of invalidism...I was pleased when he decided to go to Warm Springs where...he always gained in health and strength. He invited his cousins, Laura Delano and Margaret Suckley, to go down with him. I knew that they would not bother him as I should have by discussing questions of state...[11]

In April Eleanor wrote him a chatty letter telling him about the goings on of their children and sending news from the White House—it was to be the last communication between them.

The afternoon of April 12, Grandmère was in her sitting room in a meeting when Tommy signaled her urgently to take the phone. She learned that Franklin had fainted and had been carried to his bed. Concluding the meeting quickly but giving no clue as to her agitation, Eleanor then received

Anna's "complicity" in the ongoing friendship between FDR and Lucy made the relationship between mother and daughter difficult for a time. However, both before and eventually later, Grandmère and Anna had a very close and loving relationship.

another call suggesting that she fly down to Warm Springs. She knew in her heart that Franklin had died but was unable to formulate the thought into words. She was completely composed when she arrived just before midnight and went into the bedroom where her husband lay, closing the door behind her.

According to Bernard Asbell, who helped Aunt Anna collate the voluminous correspondence between her and Grandmère in a book entitled *Mother & Daughter,* it was then that Grandmère sat

down on a sofa and asked Miss Suckley and Miss Delano, Grandfather's cousins, to tell her exactly what had happened. According to Asbell it was Laura Delano who broke the terrible news to Grandmère:

> When the turn came to Laura Delano, an aristocratic eccentric occasionally given to dying her hair purple, Mrs. Roosevelt got more of "exactly what happened" than anyone expected. For reasons that her companions were not able to explain, except that Miss Delano was a sayer of blunt truths, she chose to include in her detail of exactly what happened that the portrait of the President, for which he was sitting at the moment of his collapse, was being done by Elizabeth Shoumatoff, a friend of Lucy Mercer Rutherford; that, in fact, the portrait had been commissioned by Mrs. Rutherford; and that, verily, Mrs. Rutherford, at the moment of the collapse, had been sitting in that window alcove right there, and had been Franklin's visitor, inhabiting the guest cottage, for the past three days.[12]

My stunned grandmother then asked other questions of cousin Laura and received truthful answers: Yes, Franklin had seen Lucy on other occasions and, most shocking of all, Anna had served as hostess. Uncle James later wrote about Anna's awkward position in my grandparents' marriage:

> Mother was angry with Anna for participating in the deception of the final years. But what was Anna to do? Should she have refused Father what he wanted? She was not in a position to do so even had she wanted to. Accepting the confidence of Father, should she have betrayed him by running to report to Mother on every move he made? A child caught between two parents can only pursue as honorable a course as possible. Anna could no more serve as Mother's spy on Father than she could as Father's spy on Mother.

The death of FDR was a source of grief felt worldwide, but Grandmère was seemingly completely removed emotionally.

Anna suffered some private anguish, but she was as true as she could be to both our parents and she was blameless in this matter.[13]

When Grandmère was sorting through Grandfather's belongings at Hyde Park, she found the small watercolor that Lucy's friend Madame Shoumatoff had painted of him while at Warm Springs during his last days. She instructed her secretary to send it to Lucy, who in turn wrote Grandmère the following:

Thank you so much, you must know that it will be treasured always. I have wanted to write you for a long time to tell you that I had seen Franklin and of his great kindness about my husband when he was desperately ill in Washington, and of how helpful he was too, to his boys—and that I hoped very much that I might see you again...I think of your sorrow—you— whom I have always felt to be the most blessed and privileged of women must now feel immeasurable grief and pain and they must be almost unbearable.

As always, affectionately,
Lucy Rutherford[14]

It was on the long train from Warm Springs back to Washington that my grandmother
had to deal with her husband's final deception and, she hoped then, her complete return to anonymity.

In *Mother & Daughter* my aunt Anna remembered once when she was in the room with both Lucy and her father, and Lucy saying, "You know, your father drove me in his little Ford up to (what's the name of that mountain where he loved to go on picnics?) Dowdell's Knob. You know, I had the most fascinating hour I've ever had. He just sat there and told me some of what he regarded as the real problems facing the world now. I just couldn't get over thinking of what I was listening to, and then he would stop and say, 'You see that knoll over there? That's where I did this or that,' or 'You see that bunch of trees?' Or

whatever it was. He would interrupt himself, you know. And we just sat there and looked." It was then that Anna says she realized that the one thing FDR needed most, someone to just listen to him talk, was the one thing Grandmère was not capable of being. Perhaps that is the main reason his relationship with Lucy endured for so many years. In June 1945, following the death of FDR, Lucy burned all letters she had received from him. Three years later she was diagnosed with leukemia, and she died in July 1948 at the age of fifty-seven. She was buried next to her husband at Tranquility Farms in Allamuchy, New Jersey.

*Grandmère, with Anna to the left and my father in uniform
on the right, at FDR's final resting in the Rose Garden at Springwood.*

Grandmère and Anna, after an initial period of coolness caused by Anna's role in the rekindling of the affair, became closer than ever. But on the day of my grandfather's death and for months thereafter, those feelings of betrayal must have felt as sharp as shards of glass to Grandmère. No one will ever know how intensely she suffered this disloyalty, nor for how long it lingered, as she never spoke about it to anyone. She did, however, write:

I lay in my berth all night with the window shade up, looking out at the countryside he had loved and watching the people at stations, and even at the crossroads, who came to pay their last tribute all through the night.

The only recollection I clearly have is thinking about The Lonesome Train, *the musical poem about Lincoln's death. I had always liked it so well—and now this was so much like it.*[15]

As the funeral train moved to Washington, she accompanied the president on his last journey.
For Grandmère an era had ended. She faced an uncertain future, but one that she surely thought would be simpler, quieter, and less demanding. Little could she imagine what lay ahead.

PART FIVE

Strength, Courage, Confidence

You gain strength, courage, and confidence by every experience in which you really look fear in the face...You must do the thing you think you cannot do.

—Eleanor Roosevelt

THERE WAS A COMMON THREAD RUNNING throughout Grandmère's life, work, and accomplishments: her ever-present inquisitiveness, which questioned the bounds of society's status quo and challenged what was thought to be sacrosanct. Why were the laws and traditions that reinforced social injustice and economic imbalance perpetuated? In asking such questions and demanding answers, she would challenge other leaders about society's accepted norms. She sought to strip those institutions and laws of the elements that separated people. There was a purity, some would say naïveté, in her vision and course. She held the single belief that all people *are* equal, and that no law or institution can place conditions on equality. Her inquiry was always direct and unmediated, seldom mitigated. These attributes lent all the more power to her positions, for she would not hesitate to ask questions that others should ask but wouldn't. That the conditions of some people within the family of humankind were intolerable not by their own fault but by societal strictures was an unacceptable condition of the status quo, and Grandmère was completely undeterred in her determination to make changes. She believed that one person could influence change if only they had courage and determination.

I have always seen life personally...Any interest or sympathy or indignation is not caused by an abstract cause but by the plight of a single person whom I have seen with my own eyes. It was the sight of a child dying of hunger that made the tragedy of hunger become of such overriding importance to me. Out of my response to an individual develops an awareness of a problem to the community, then to the country, and finally to the world.

America's Spiritual Crisis

When she arrived in the White House, Grandmère had no real plan, no specific philosophy that would guide her work, merely a strong belief that the Great Depression was America's "spiritual crisis" that could eventually lead to a new social order, a redefinition of democracy.

The prevailing belief was that poverty was caused by the personal failure of individuals. However, the view that she had come to adopt over the years was that poverty was in fact a social ill caused by inequality and the imbalanced distribution of both social and economic resources. While the Great Depression served to solidify these beliefs for Eleanor, its greater impact was to enforce her own evolution from sporadic involvement to a strong personal commitment; from a passive observer she became a strong advocate and activist for legislative reform.

She served as the president's eyes and ears, and the majority of Americans suddenly discovered that they had a voice in the White House, someone who truly listened to them and understood. Soon members of the administration began to recognize the important role that Grandmère was playing, and quickly gained such respect for her contributions that her advice was sought on important policy and program issues.

Her imprint and influence became apparent in many of the New Deal program designs. One of the first initiatives of FDR's new administration was the Federal Emergency Relief Administration, established under the direction of his trusted advisor Harry Hopkins. Of the more than two million people put to work within the proposed relief administration structure, initially more than one hundred thousand women would be included, and all at pay equal to that of the men.

She was also pivotal in the creation of the National Youth Administration (NYA), a combination of both relief *and* reform established under the far-reaching umbrella of the Works Progress Administration (WPA). The program's purpose was to provide meaningful employment opportunities for youth, combining federal planning with local community rebuilding efforts and all the while enabling the young people involved to continue their education. NYA services, at Grandmère's insistence, had to be equally available to all youth who needed them—blacks, other minorities, and the homeless in particular. In fact, expressing a view in 1935 so prophetic for her day, she would say, "I have periods of real terror, when I think that we may be losing this generation. We have got to bring these young people into the active life of the community and make them feel that they are necessary."[1] Her support and concern for the provision of opportunities for young people would be an abiding concern throughout her life.

Above: Grandmère with Mary McLeod Bethune, director of the National Youth Administration, addressing the 1939 National Negro Youth Conference. Opposite: Traveling extensively, in 1934 Grandmère spoke to a large assembly in St. Croix, the Virgin Islands.

We Are a Mixed Nation of Many People and Many Religions

It was largely through her early work with the preeminent black educator Mary McLeod Bethune that Grandmère's commitment to civil rights became a primary focus for the rest of her life. And perhaps no other issue created a greater philosophical division between her and her husband.

Grandfather was an ever-pragmatic politician, often hesitating to take any proactive stance regarding the question of blacks for fear that doing so would compromise his relationship with the Southern members of Congress, members whose support was vital to his New Deal experiment and later with the nation's entry into World War II. Eleanor, on the other hand, refused all attempts at compromise made by FDR and was vocally intolerant of his pragmatism. It was not at all unusual for

her to circumvent her husband on many civil rights matters, going directly to other influential administration leaders upon whom she knew she could depend for support, or who might one day need her support on some other issue.

Grandmère was herself realistic when dealing with the issue. Her approach before white audiences was noticeably different than that used with predominantly black audiences. With whites she would distinguish between legal and political inequality on the one hand, and moral inequality on the other, reaffirming that all discrimination was a moral issue that would certainly undermine the very foundation of American democracy. Social acceptance of equality, she reasoned, would be slow in coming, since no government could dictate tolerance. On the other hand, government could and should remove all legal barriers to equality—in employment, the judicial system, rights of equal representation, and so on. With black audiences, however, she would say repeatedly, "...but great changes come slowly. I think they are coming, however, and sometimes it is better to fight hard with conciliatory methods," stressing that blacks must assume more than a nominal measure of responsibility for their own fate. She would rally them to the notion that they had to work within the existing framework of society and government to develop their skills and abilities, urging compromise as the most practical path toward achieving equality. In practice, however, she was never so compromising. When the minimum wage was first introduced in 1938, many employers felt that if they were forced to pay a minimum wage to anyone it would be to white employees, not blacks. Grandmère's reaction was immediate and uncompromising: "This is a question of the right to work, and the right to work should know no color lines."

The Marian Anderson Affair

Perhaps the event most demonstrative of Eleanor's intolerance of bigotry and discrimination was the Marian Anderson affair. Marian Anderson was an imposing, majestic African-American contralto whose voice, even in normal speech, so enthralled her listeners that she became one of the most highly regarded performers of her time. My grandmother and Marian Anderson's lives interlocked when the president of the Daughters of the American Revolution refused to grant permission for use of Constitution Hall for a fund-raising concert benefiting Howard University in Washington on the grounds that no "Negro artist"

would ever be permitted to perform in the hall. The public outrage was immediate, but what made a local display of bigotry a worldwide cause célèbre was Grandmère's decision to publicly resign from the Daughters of the American Revolution. Her resignation received broad approval and was widely acknowledged for awakening white consciousness among conservative as well as moderate citizens.

Immediately a plan evolved for a free open-air concert to be given at the base of the Lincoln Memorial. At Grandmère's persistent urging, Harold Ickes, Secretary of the Interior, gained the tacit approval of FDR, and the concert was held on a Sunday afternoon to an estimated crowd of more than seventy-five thousand. As Ickes later wrote in his diary, "The whole setting was unique, majestic, and impressive." What he could not have known was the tremendous political implications this single occasion would have on the future of civil rights in the nation. For more than thirty years Grandmère would maintain her staunch and ardent stand for the cause of civil rights.

As World War II loomed large on America's horizon in 1940, just at the time of FDR's third presidential campaign, one of the most troubling social issues for the Roosevelt Administration was the outright discrimination against African-Americans in the armed forces. With only a few exceptions, throughout all branches of the services blacks were relegated to performing menial jobs, and in some cases those thought to be too dangerous for white servicemen. One of the concerns within the black leadership community was that the discriminatory practices would ultimately lead to the creation of "labor battalions" made up solely of blacks. Grandmère's involvement in the matter of civil rights, particularly as it applied to discrimination in the armed forces, was noted in the diary of Henry L. Stimson, FDR's Secretary of War, as "Mrs. Roosevelt's intrusive and impulsive folly."[2] He further recalled that she had previously and often "stirred up trouble" on the race question. Nevertheless, it was only after her constant badgering of her husband and his colleagues that blacks were eventually allowed to receive equal training, serve in all-black fighting units, and experience a significant increase in the number of black officers. Through her efforts the tide began to turn, though full desegregation of the United States Armed Services did not occur until the administration of President Harry S. Truman.

Harold Ickes, one of Grandmère's closest allies within the Administration and instrumental in arranging Marian Anderson's famous Lincoln Memorial concert, photographed here in his private library.
Opposite: With Walter Walker, consul general of Liberia, Grandmère honors Marian Anderson with the Order of African Redemption in 1943.

I have to believe that of all of my grandmother's work for social and civil rights, especially up to FDR's death in 1945, her primary focus and most effective work was that performed on behalf of the African-American population. Roy Wilkins, former Executive Director of the NAACP, would say that Franklin Roosevelt was:

A friend of Negroes only insofar as he refused to exclude the Negro from his general policies that applied to the whole country, whereas Mrs. Roosevelt was the Negro's true friend. The personal touches and the personal fight against discrimination were Mrs. Roosevelt's. That attached to Roosevelt also—he couldn't get away from it—and he reaped the political benefit from it.[3]

A year to the day following FDR's death, Grandmère is joined at a memorial dinner, from left to right, by Henry Morgenthau, Jr., Justice Hugo Black, Henry Wallace, Frank Walker, Frances Perkins, and Robert Wagner.

Leaving the White House

Within but a few days of the death of my grandfather in April 1945, Grandmère left the White House and Washington, D.C., for her Washington Square apartment in New York. It was expected that Grandmère would drift off into obscurity, only to surface for those periodic ceremonial duties expected of former First Ladies. Indeed, even Grandmère may have thought at first

that such *would* be her future, for when asked what would happen to her now by a reporter just days after leaving Washington, she replied simply, "The story is over."

The old insecurity—the sense that she had not accomplished anything; it was all her husband's doing—was resurfacing. As she wrote to New Zealand's Finance Minister, Walter Nash, "I shall hope to continue to do what I can to be useful, although without my husband's advice and guidance

I feel very inadequate." Perhaps in those immediate days after FDR's death she too felt the void that grasped the nation—and the world. A friend of Eleanor's wrote, "I am frightened, who will take care of us now?" In the House of Representatives a young congressman, Lyndon B. Johnson, with tears in his eyes exclaimed, "God, God how he could take it for us all!"[4]

But the story was far from over. For Grandmère it was merely the beginning of a new, perhaps even more productive phase of her life. She did not realize, could not have realized, that she would survive the shadow cast by her husband, the experiences of her early childhood years, and the dominance of her mother-in-law. Perhaps without even recognizing it herself, she would emerge an emancipated woman. She was poised to move forward with a strength, energy, and renewed passion she herself had not come to realize; to stand alone; to speak not for Franklin Roosevelt but for herself on the issues that mattered most to her. She was poised, as Joe Lash would say, to "leave her mark on time."

A friend of mine, Porter McKeever, who worked first as press officer for the Human Rights Commission at the United Nations and at the American Association for the United Nations (AAUN), precursor to today's United Nations Association and the UNA/USA, and eventually as president of the United Nations Association, once observed that it was during these first few months following FDR's death that Grandmère gladly relinquished her role as First Lady of the United States, only to assume the much more important role of "First Lady of the World." Thirteen years of strenuous and tumultuous times had been a training ground for what would become seventeen more productive

years of carrying the banner for world peace and equality for all humankind. Little did she realize that her day was not over; it was, in fact, just beginning.

Lying awake in her compartment on the train cortege carrying the body of the fallen president from Warm Springs to Washington and then on to Springwood, Grandmère's future would begin to take form. "I did not want to run an elaborate household again," she would recall thinking. "I did not want to cease trying to be useful in some way. I did not want to feel old."

Nevertheless, she was faced with beginning her life anew as widow of a president, with tremendous uncertainty and not a little bitterness. Thus, whenever asked of her feelings about that time, her answer would be one of almost impersonal detachment. His death was "a terrible blow" but not a "personal sorrow." It was more a sadness felt by "all those to whom this man who now lay dead, and who happened to be my husband, had been a symbol of strength and fortitude."

As she led the family behind the coffin at FDR's funeral service, she wore but one piece of jewelry at her throat, a small golden fleur-de-lys given to her as a wedding gift by Franklin some forty years before. She had told a close friend that she had not loved Franklin since discovering the Lucy Mercer affair, but that she had given him "a service of love because of her respect for his leadership and faith in his goals."[5] Perhaps this is what she believed, but I would question such absolute loyalty to merely an ideal. It may be that even she could not recognize the lingering but repressed love she held for the man who years before had been able to give such purpose to her life. Perhaps it was a repressed realization that an attachment to FDR and his work provided leverage for the success of her own pursuits. But whatever the reason and despite the anxieties she felt at this time, her life from now on would change dramatically. She was about to achieve her own international celebrity: no longer would she be simply a "citizen" of this nation, but of all nations worldwide.

Just days following FDR's internment in the Rose Garden at Springwood, twelve years of life's accumulated belongings had been hastily removed from the White House. Eleanor's most immediate concern was what to do with the estate at Hyde Park. Although FDR provided in his will that she and the children could live there throughout their lives, at which time it would be deeded over to the government, Grandmère decided that she would not return there. It had never been home to her, and held only an unhappy memory of a marriage so thoroughly dominated by Sara.

Life Was Meant to Be Lived

Exactly one year to the day after Franklin's death, at a ceremony attended primarily by family, President Truman, and local residents of Hyde Park, Springwood and the Franklin Delano Roosevelt Library were formally transferred to the people of the United States. In making the gift, Grandmère would say, "It is with pleasure that our children and I see this house dedicated to the people and opened to them. It was the people, all of the people of this country and the world, whom my husband loved and kept constantly in his heart and mind. He would want them to enjoy themselves in these surroundings, and to draw from them rest and peace and strength, as he did all the days of his life."[6]

And so, as was perhaps her intent all along, Grandmère would return to live at her beloved Val-Kill Cottage, not to recede into genteel retirement but to write her "My Day" column, give speeches, and continue her advocacy for social, economic, and political reforms. She quickly found that not only had the interest in her views *not* diminished; they had intensified once the restrictions of being a president's wife were lifted. Grandmère's freedom now provided her with an even more forceful voice on those issues of concern.

Although many of her friends and associates would encourage her to enter politics, many believing that a seat in the U.S. Senate was hers for the asking, they would be rebuffed at every turn. Politics itself held little interest for her, although what she had learned of the political process, her adeptness at "playing the game," and the scores of important contacts made during her years at the core of state and national politics would serve her well in the days to come. Indeed, although I doubt she would ever have admitted to such, Grandmère had learned at the hands of two political masters—FDR and Louis Howe—how to be as clever and effective as the next at political manipulation. She would continue her activism in Democratic reform politics, both at the state and national levels, and she would continue to champion New Deal ideals.

When FDR chose the senator from Missouri as his vice presidential running mate in 1944, Eleanor joined several other members in FDR's circle of advisors in questioning Mr. Truman's ability to assume the office of president, should it become necessary, at such a critical time in national and international affairs. She was well aware that FDR's health was declining rapidly, but she also knew of his determination to end the war in Europe and the Pacific and hoped that he would live to witness the culmination of his last twelve years of work. His tireless pace, however, would hasten the inevitable. Although she had doubts and in fact would not offer her endorsement until very late, Grandmère eventually recognized in Mr. Truman a dormant potential that would awaken immediately upon his assumption of the presidency. His ability to grasp the complex intricacies of the fall of the Nazi terrorist reign in Europe, his capacity to alone make the troubling decision to use the nation's atomic arsenal to quickly bring the Japanese empire into submission in the Pacific, and his delicate maneuvering on the broad and diverse diplomatic front to begin rebuilding a peaceful world would quickly gain her admiration and respect.

When asked about President Truman's convictions prior to being thrown into the presidency in a 1957 television interview with TV commentator Mike Wallace, she said, "No, I would not have [said he had great convictions]. Again, I did not know him very well before. I would say of Mr. Truman that he rose to the responsibilities thrust upon him in a manner that was very remarkable really, and that his big decisions very likely are going to mean he will go down in history as one of our *very* good presidents."[7]

During his first difficult yet triumphant year in office President Truman would often seek the advice and counsel of Grandmère, for no other reason than he feared her stature among black and women voters. In fact, she continued to be the "friend of the people" and seemed always to be as in tune with the nation's sentiment as anyone possibly

With President Truman in the Oval Office in 1947, likely conferring about the United Nations and her appointment to the first US delegation.

could be. She had been an early and vocal advocate of a world body that could foster a peaceful world and embody the coexistence of all people through understanding, love, and social, political, and economic equality. Grandmère still supported the original concept of the League of Nations, a concept that would evolve into the United Nations, and so in 1946, at the outset of this bold experiment in world peace, President Truman would again thrust Eleanor Roosevelt onto center stage by appointing her to the American delegation to the United Nations, much to the chagrin of her detractors and against the advice of some of his own advisors. Although there were often tense relations between them, I believe he recognized Grandmère's unfailing dedication to the cause, along with a depth of compassion and understanding that would be vital to the future of a world of peace and equality.

Shown at the first convening of the UN in 1946, Grandmère's participation was not universally popular, especially among her colleagues in the delegation.

A Legacy in Her Own Right

As for accomplishments, I just did what I had to do as things came along. I got the most satisfaction from my work in the UN. There I was part of the second great experiment to bring countries together and to get them to work for a peaceful atmosphere in the world...

WHEN PRESIDENT TRUMAN CALLED Grandmère to tell her of his intentions to appoint her to the first delegation to the United Nations,

she voiced skepticism as to her knowledge of international affairs and of parliamentary protocol. At the urging of her family and friends, in whom she confided she reluctantly agreed, and feeling that she had a duty to serve if asked by the president, she wrote:

> Some things I can take to the first meeting: A sincere desire to understand the problems of the rest of the world and our relationship to them; a real goodwill for people throughout the world; a hope that I shall be able to build a sense of personal trust and friendship with my co-workers, for without that understanding our work will be doubly difficult.

As the Scripps-Howard columnist Thomas L. Stokes would comment, "She has convictions and does not hesitate to fight for them. The New Deal era was richer for her influence in it. That influence was far greater than appeared publicly."[1] Stokes would go on to say, "She, perhaps better than any other person, can represent the little people of this country, indeed of the world." But Westbrook Pegler, the noted conservative columnist who throughout her tenure in Washington had been her harshest critic, even to the point of mudslinging, personal attacks, and outright vulgarity, criticized her appointment as a complete waste of money for an undeserving representative. Although the appointment was generally lauded throughout the United States and the rest of the free world, there were skeptics of her ability to be tough enough to "stand up to the Russians" and questions about her lack of diplomatic experience.

The U.S. delegation consisted of some of the most prestigious names in American diplomacy: Secretary of State James F. Byrnes; U.S. representative on the Security Council Edward Stettinius Jr.;

*In January 1946 the delegation arrived at Southampton, England. Grandmère with
delegation members, from left to right, Arthur Vandenberg, Edward Stettinius, and Tom Connally.*

Senator Tom Connally, chairman of the Foreign Relations Committee; Senator Arthur Vandenberg, ranking member of the Foreign Relations Committee; and Eleanor. Alternate members included the chairman of the House Foreign Affairs Committee, Representative Sol Bloom; the committee's ranking Republican member, Charles A. Eaton; the former chairmen of both the Democratic and Republican Parties, Frank Walker (also a former postmaster general) and John G. Townsend; and, finally, John Foster Dulles.

Even among her colleagues in the delegation there was considerable skepticism about her appointment, not to mention jealousy over the attention accorded her upon their arrival in London for that first General Assembly meeting. The opening of the first session was presided over by the assembly's newly elected president, Paul Henri Spaak, the Socialist foreign minister of Belgium. In accepting his election as the first president, Spaak solemnly took special note of those present "who have done much more for peace than I have." He then followed:

*Among them there is one delegate to whom I wish to
extend particular sympathy and tribute. I refer to her*

who bears the most illustrious and respected of all names. I do not think it would be possible to begin at this Assembly without mentioning her and the name of the late President Roosevelt and expressing our conviction that his disappearance was a great grief to us all and an irreparable loss.

Her time in London was extremely busy, possibly busier than any of the other delegates since she was invited to attend countless social engagements, make unending speeches, have visits with the Churchills and other old friends, and visit the royal family. In fact, there were so many speeches that at one point she completely lost her voice for several days.

Committee III

Grandmère was assigned to Committee III, dealing primarily with immigrant and refugee issues; an assignment considered to be of little consequence by the other members. As it turned out, however, this committee quickly became contentious, a real hotbed of East-West conflict. To put it simply, the Russian and Communist position was that the refugee question, which addressed the fates of more than one million men, women, and children, was not the business of the international community but something to be dealt with as each individual country saw fit—regardless of the brutality involved. The debate raged for weeks, with Grandmère confronting Andrei Vishinsky, head of the Russian delegation and a seasoned, wily, and most formidable debater. Vishinsky was outraged that he would have to debate Eleanor Roosevelt, as not only was this a woman known throughout the world for her humanitarian views and sympathies; this was the wife of one of the world's most revered men...even in his own Russia. Always spoken without prepared text or the scantest of notes, Grandmère's arguments, which blended historical and factual examples of refugee brutality with common sense and a smattering of emotionalism, proved quite persuasive, so much so, in fact, that her staunchest critics on the U.S. delegation, John Foster Dulles in particular, were soon singing her praises as "one of the most solid members of the delegation." They were all amazed at her rhetorical abilities, her calm under fire, and above all her excellent judgment. Respect for her soared to new heights. Originally written off as a "rattle-brained" woman by some of her colleagues, Grandmère left

Originally one of her most vocal detractors, John Foster Dulles, above with ER and Adlai Stevenson, soon became one of her strongest supporters.
Opposite: Great Britain expressed its gratitude for FDR's support during World War II with a most remarkable memorial, dedicated by Grandmère in 1948.

London at the conclusion of that first General Assembly with a feeling of pride of accomplishment, as did her colleagues. It was a difficult time, that first assembly of the new world body, but it proved to be a preamble to what lay ahead.

One of Grandmère's more persuasive arguments during her frequent "discussions" with Mr. Vishinsky was when she referenced the guarantees of fundamental human rights as written into the original

At the December 1948 Paris press conference announcing the
Universal Declaration of Human Rights, considered Grandmère's most important lifetime accomplishment.

UN charter. It was, in her opinion, significant that the charter provided for the establishment of a commission for the promotion of human rights, and it was the aim of the United States to see a Declaration of Rights annexed to the charter. Since no one coming out of the London meeting better personified the cause for human rights than she, was it any wonder that the Economic and Social Council of the United Nations would ask her to serve on the start-up (or "nuclear") Human Rights Commission? It was none other than her colleague and early nemesis Senator Arthur Vandenberg who vociferously acclaimed her appointment. It should be remembered that following FDR's death, Senator Vandenberg voiced the strongest opposition, at times in most unflattering ways, to the announcement of ER's appointment to the London delegation. Now he would say, at almost every opportunity, "I want to say that I take back everything I ever said about her, and believe me it's been plenty!"[2] At the first meeting of the new Human Rights Commission Eleanor was elected chairwoman by acclamation. Throughout 1946 the debate over repatriation of refugees raged, with Grandmère again locking horns with the Russian delegate Mr. Vishinsky. And again Grandmère vanquished the venerable Russian.

Grandmère, at almost six feet in height, seemed to tower above her most formidable opponent in the human rights debate, Russia's delegate Andrei Vishinski (to the left of ER).

Madame Chairwoman

In 1947 President Truman, more convinced than ever of Eleanor Roosevelt's diplomatic skills and capabilities, appointed her to a four-year term as the U.S. representative on the eighteen-nation Human Rights Commission. And once again she was elected chairwoman by unanimous vote. Serving with her were the commission's vice-chairman, Dr. Peng-Chung Chang of China, and Dr. Charles H. Malik of Lebanon as secretary (*rapporteur*). The plenary session of the commission was marked primarily by long discussions of philosophical interpretation, as in defining the role and responsibilities of the individual to a society, or society to the individual; in other words, what comes first, the needs of the individual or the needs of the society?

A drafting committee was established to develop a working document for debate by the members of the commission. Meeting after meeting was devoted to new drafts, with long hours spent quibbling over minute phraseology or even single words. Eventually the original drafting committee of three was expanded. Under the direction of Chairwoman Roosevelt the committee began preparing a bill, a bill that stood some chance of being acceptable to the full body of the fifty-five member nations of the United Nations. Although specificity of the wording was a concern, a more troubling consideration was the character of the rights that were to be included. Smaller nations wanted something more than a mere "moral manifesto"; they wanted states to assume a "treaty obligation to grant, protect, and enforce the rights enumerated in the Declaration."[3] Grandmère, in an effort to assuage both sides, suggested that two documents be prepared—one a Declaration of Principles that would enumerate a "common standard of achievement" and the other a more precise Convention that would become a treaty obligation and part of the laws of those nations ratifying it.

To further complicate matters, there was a changing tide of sentiment in the United States toward the United Nations, and specifically around the rising belligerence of the Russians. The end of World War II did not bring world peace as expected, the aggressiveness of the Soviet Union and its allies was of increasing concern, and the return to a robust postwar economy had not yet occurred. Suddenly there was considerable doubt that the United States would ratify a Convention, even one that was principally authored by its own delegation, and perhaps not even a Declaration. It was clear that Grandmère had her work cut out; not only would she and her drafting team have to develop documents that were acceptable to the majority of the members of the Human Rights Commission, and eventually to the United Nations membership as a whole, but she would likewise have to convince her own government of the importance of accepting the final product.

Throughout the remainder of 1947 and the first six months of 1948 the drafting process proceeded at an excruciating pace. The skills required to resolve the wording for a final Declaration of Human Rights was absolutely incredible. In an "almost final" draft the opening of the first article, patterned after the United States' Declaration of Independence, began, "All men are created equal..." This would never do, said some of the women delegates, many of whom served in very senior positions within their own countries. They feared that within their countries such wording would be interpreted literally, making the declaration applicable to men only. In the final version the opening was changed to "all human beings," and subsequent articles began "everyone" or "no one." Then the "are created" became a contentious point, particularly with delegates from Communist nations, who said it implied a Divine Creator, and so "are created" was changed to "are born." Finally, the week before Christmas 1947, the commission delegates approved a final Declaration version by a vote of 13-4. Grandmère had proved a relentless taskmaster, driving her colleagues to near exhaustion, but the endless hours and constant deliberations had finally brought reward. There would have to be some fine-tuning before submitting the Declaration to the General Assembly (primarily to put it into words even the common man could understand), but a finished product appeared close at hand, much to the relief of Grandmère.

After eighty-five grueling, tedious sessions, the Declaration was finally approved by Committee III and referred to the General Assembly.

At 3:00 A.M., December 10, 1948, the Universal Declaration of Human Rights was passed by the General Assembly of the United Nations. The vote: 48 for, 8 Soviet bloc abstentions, 2 absent, 0

Here with a Spanish translation of the
Universal Declaration, I think Grandmère's tremendous satisfaction is apparent.

opposed. In a rare display of emotion and personal tribute, the entire assembly of delegates rose in unison to accord Grandmère a standing ovation. As she would write, "Long job finished." Accolades poured in from around the world, but perhaps none was more poignant than that of Helen Keller, who wrote after reading the Declaration in Braille, "my soul stood erect, exultant, envisioning a new world where the light of justice for every individual will be unclouded."

When people think of Grandmère today, of all of her work over the years and in so many different areas of human concern, the single greatest accomplishment most would accord to her life was passage of the Universal Declaration of Human Rights. She was proposed for the Nobel Peace Prize in 1948 and nominated by President Kennedy in 1961. Although she never received the Nobel, the first United Nations Human Rights prize was awarded to her posthumously, an award I suspect she would have found even more gratifying than the Nobel Peace Prize, since it was recognition accorded by those colleagues to whom she felt closest.

Eleanor Roosevelt would conclude her appointment as a member of the U.S. delegation to the United Nations in 1953. Other tasks and challenges lay ahead, and again, to the dismay of many, she accepted each and every one with a renewed vigor and undying commitment and determination.

UNIVERSAL DECLARATION OF HUMAN RIGHTS

PREAMBLE

WHEREAS recognition of the inherent dignity and of the equal and inalienable rights of all members of the human family is the foundation of freedom, justice and peace in the world.

WHEREAS disregard and contempt for human rights have resulted in barbarous acts which have outraged the conscience of mankind, and the advent of a world in which human beings shall enjoy freedom of speech and belief and freedom from fear and want has been proclaimed as the highest aspiration of the common people.

WHREAS it is essential, if man is not to be compelled to have recourse, as a last resort, to rebellion against tyranny and oppression, that human rights should be protected by the rule of law.

WHEREAS it is essential to promote the development of friendly relations between nations.

WHEREAS the people of the United Nations have in the Charter reaffirmed their faith in fundamental human rights, in the dignity and worth of the human person and in the equal rights of men and women and have determined to promote social progress and better standards of life in larger freedom.

WHEREAS Member States have pledged themselves to achieve, in co-operation with the United Nations, the promotion and universal respect for and observance of human rights and fundamental freedoms.

WHEREAS a common understanding of these rights and freedoms is of the greatest importance for the full realization of this pledge.

Now, Therefore,
The General Assembly
Proclaims

THIS UNIVERSAL DECLARATION OF HUMAN rights as a common standard of achievement for all peoples and all nations, to the end that every individual and every organ of society, keeping this Declaration constantly in mind, shall strive by teaching and education to promote respect for these rights and freedoms and by progressive measures, national and international, to secure their universal and effective recognition and observance, both among the peoples of Member States themselves and among the peoples of territories under their jurisdiction.

ARTICLE 1. All human beings are born free and equal in dignity and rights. They are endowed with reason and conscience and should act towards one another in a spirit of brotherhood.

ARTICLE 2. Everyone is entitled to all the rights and freedoms set forth in this Declaration, without distinction of any kind, such as race, color, sex, language, religion, political or other opinion, national or social origin, property, birth or other status.

Furthermore, no distinction shall be made on the basis of the political, jurisdictional or international status of the country or territory to which a person belongs, whether it be independent, trust, non-self-governing or under any other limitation of sovereignty.

ARTICLE 3. Everyone has the right to life, liberty and security of person.

ARTICLE 4. No one shall be held in slavery or servitude; slavery and the slave trade shall be prohibited in all their forms.

ARTICLE 5. No one shall be subjected to torture or to cruel, inhuman or degrading treatment or punishment.

ARTICLE 6. Everyone has the right to recognition everywhere as a person before the law.

ARTICLE 7. All are equal before the law and are entitled without any discrimination to equal protection of the law. All are entitled to equal protection against any discrimination in violation of this Declaration and against any incitement to such discrimination.

ARTICLE 8. Everyone has the right to an effective remedy by the competent national tribunals for acts violating the fundamental rights granted him by the constitution or by law.

ARTICLE 9. No one shall be subjected to arbitrary arrest, detention or exile.

ARTICLE 10. Everyone is entitled in full equality to a fair and public hearing by an independent and impartial tribunal, in the determination of his rights and obligations and of any criminal charge against him.

ARTICLE 11. (1) Everyone charged with a penal offense has the right to be presumed innocent until proven guilty according to law in a public trial at which he has had all the guarantees necessary for his defense.

(2) No one shall be held guilty of any penal offense or of any act or omission which did not constitute a penal offense, under national or international law, at the time when it was committed. Nor shall a heavier penalty be imposed than the one that was applicable at the time the penal offense was committed.

ARTICLE 12. No one shall be subject to arbitrary interference with his privacy, family, home or correspondence, nor to attacks upon his honor and reputation. Everyone has the right to the protection of the law against such interference or attacks.

ARTICLE 13. (1) Everyone has the right to freedom of movement and residence within the borders of each state.

(2) Everyone has the right to leave any country, including his own, and to return to his country.

ARTICLE 14. (1) Everyone has the right to leave any country to seek and to enjoy in other countries asylum from prosecution.

(2) This right may not be invoked in the case of prosecutions genuinely arising from non-political crimes or from acts contrary to the purposes and principles of the United Nations.

ARTICLE 15. (1) Everyone has the right to a nationality.

(2) No one shall be arbitrarily deprived of his nationality nor denied the right to change his nationality.

ARTICLE 16.(1) Men and women of full age, without any limitation due to race, nationality or religion, have the right to marry and to found a family. They are entitled to equal rights as to marriage, during marriage, and at its dissolution.

(2) Marriage shall be entered into only with the free and full consent of the intending spouses.

(3) The family is the natural and fundamental group unit of society and is entitled to protection by society and the State.

ARTICLE 17. (1) Everyone has the right to own property alone as well as in association with others.

(2) No one shall be arbitrarily deprived of his property.

ARTICLE 18. Everyone has the right to freedom of thought, conscience and religion; this right includes freedom to change his religion or belief, and freedom, either alone or in community with others and in public or private, to manifest his religion or belief in teaching, practice, worship and observance.

ARTICLE 19. Everyone has the right to freedom of opinion and expression; this right includes freedom to hold opinions without interference and to seek, receive and impart information and ideas through any media and regardless of frontiers.

ARTICLE 20. (1) Everyone has the right to freedom of peaceful assembly and association.

(2) No one may be compelled to belong to an association.

ARTICLE 21. (1) Everyone has the right to take part in the government of his country, directly or through freely chosen representatives.

(2) Everyone has the right of equal access to public service in his country.

(3) The will of the people shall be the basis of the authority of government; this shall be expressed in periodic and genuine elections which shall be by universal and equal suffrage and shall be held by secret vote or by equal free voting procedures.

ARTICLE 22. Everyone, as a member of society, has the right to social security and is entitled to realization, through national effort and international co-operation and in accordance with the organization and resources of each State, of the economic, social and cultural rights indispensable for his dignity and the free development of his personality.

ARTICLE 23. (1) Everyone has the right to work, to free choice of employment, to just and favorable conditions of work and to protection against unemployment.

(2) Everyone, without any discrimination, has the right to equal pay for equal work.

(3) Everyone who works has the right to just and favorable remuneration ensuring for himself and his family an existence worthy of human dignity, and supplemented, if necessary, by other means of social protection.

(4) Everyone has the right to form and to join trade unions for protection of his interests.

ARTICLE 24. Everyone has the right to rest and leisure, including reasonable limitation of working hours and periodic holidays with pay.

ARTICLE 25. (1) Everyone has the right to a standard of living adequate for the health and well-being of himself and his family, including food, clothing, housing and medical care and necessary social services, and the right to security in the event of unemployment, sickness, disability, widowhood, old age or other lack of livelihood in circumstances beyond his control.

(2) Motherhood and childhood are entitled to special care and assistance. All children, whether born in or out of wedlock, shall enjoy the same social protection.

ARTICLE 26. (1) Everyone has the right to education. Education shall be free, at least in the elementary and fundamental states. Elementary education shall be compulsory. Technical and professional education shall be equally accessible to all on the basis of merit.

(2) Education shall be directed to the full development of the human personality and to the strengthening of respect for human rights and fundamental freedoms. It shall promote understanding, tolerance and friendship among all nations, racial or religious groups, and shall further the activities of the United Nations for the maintenance of peace.

(3) Parents shall have a prior right to choose the kind of education that shall be given to their children.

ARTICLE 27. (1) Everyone has the right to freely participate in the cultural life of the community, to enjoy the arts and to share in scientific advancement and its benefits.

(2) Everyone has the right to the protection of the moral and material interests resulting from any scientific, literary or artistic production of which he is the author.

ARTICLE 28. Everyone is entitled to a social and international order in which the rights and freedoms set forth in this Declaration can be fully realized.

ARTICLE 29. (1) Everyone has duties to the community in which alone the free and full development of his personality is possible.

(2) In the exercise of his rights and freedoms, everyone shall be subject only to such limitations as are determined by law solely for the purpose of securing due recognition and respect for the rights and freedoms of others and of meeting the just requirements of morality, public order and the general welfare in a democratic society.

(3) These rights and freedoms may in no case be exercised contrary to the purposes and principles of the United Nations.

ARTICLE 30. Nothing in this Declaration may be interpreted as implying for any State, group or person any right to engage in any activity or to perform any act aimed at the destruction of any of the rights and freedoms set forth herein.

After completing her work with the UN, Grandmère knew
that, in her own words, there still remained "So many things to do!"

So Many Things to Do!

You are the people who are preparing the next gen-
eration for leadership. And, believe me, it can't be
done with fear. Men can never lead if they are afraid,
for the leader who is afraid will never be followed.
—Eleanor Roosevelt

FOLLOWING PASSAGE OF THE DECLARATION of Human Rights many of Grandmère's friends and family thought she would and should begin to slow down, to reduce her activities and enter into a period of at least semiretirement. But as she remarked to a *New York Times* interviewer in 1948, "I sometimes think of quickly finishing up all the things I have to do, and then just not doing any more, but there always seems to be so many things to do!"[1]

She not only continued her United Nations duties but launched into even more new endeavors. She resumed writing her columns and articles for various magazines and newspapers; began a radio talk show with Anna; and undertook a television show produced by my father. She joined or rejoined the

*Val-Kill remained always her favorite place to work
and entertain; here she is with Fala and members of a UNESCO delegation.*

boards of several organizations, including Brandeis University and the Americans for Democratic Action, and began spending hours and hours working with the organization she helped to found, the American Association for the United Nations (AAUN). She also began an extensive lecture tour and was often a spokesperson for the United Jewish Appeal, the National Association for the Advancement of Colored People, and the Citizens Committee for Children, among others. As Joe Lash would note, "These were her regular jobs; but in between the fixed points that they constituted in her schedule, a swarm of invitations, requests for her aid, for her opinion, for interviews managed to proliferate."[2]

Anyone who thought Eleanor Roosevelt would go quietly into the night of retirement certainly underestimated my grandmother! After all, she was only sixty-four, and by her own reckoning there was too much to be done to slow down.

On the family front things were changing as well. My father, Elliott, had entered into partnership with Grandmère to farm the eleven hundred acres bought from the government when the entire 1,365-acre Springwood estate was turned over as a

*King Gustav of Sweden in 1950,
obviously making a humorous point!*

historical site. Both Franklin Jr. and James had entered politics, Franklin as a U.S. congressman from New York and Jimmy, who had been chairman of the California Democratic Party, considering a race for governor against Earl Warren. Grandmère tried to temper her sons' political ambitions, but her advice more often than not took second place to their sometimes impetuous, sometimes grandiose ambitions, as would be the case throughout their lives.

My dad was often called "the most lovable" of the boys. He was, like his grandfather Elliott before him, restless, and possessed personality traits that most assuredly reminded Grandmère of her own father. He was also perhaps the most impetuous of all the Roosevelt children. Even before the war he had entered a succession of business enterprises, from ranching to radio, and now was venturing into the fledgling world of television and

writing. He too would consider the political arena, at different times contemplating runs for Congress, governor of Texas, governor of Colorado, and the U.S. Senate. In the end he was elected mayor of Miami Beach, Florida. Only my uncle John remained out of an active political life, preferring instead a peripheral role in the Republican Party.

Of all the changes now taking place, the one that was of immediate concern for Grandmère was the fact that her friend, confidant, advisor, and most able assistant, Tommy, was rapidly fading in health. Tommy was in many ways closer to her than any of her children. As she wrote just prior to leaving for the 1948 Paris General Assembly meeting, "Tommy is exhausted. I think this is the last time I can uproot Tommy, so I pray she will keep well..." By 1950 Tommy could no longer carry on, and it was then that Grandmère began training her successor, Maureen Corr. I must revel at Grandmère's good fortune—Tommy had joined Grandmère in 1928 as her personal secretary and remained a loyal and dedicated friend for over twenty-two years, and now Maureen joined her as Tommy's replacement, a most competent replacement I might add. Maureen too became a dedicated friend and assistant until the time of Grandmère's death, and even now she remains a close, loyal, and understanding family friend.

By the early 1950s Grandmère was spending more time with family and friends, all of whom would congregate at Val-Kill at every possible opportunity. Along with her five children would come no fewer than nine wives and ex-wives, twenty-two grandchildren, two great-grandchildren, assorted close and distant cousins, nieces and nephews, and a constant processional of friends, colleagues, politicos, statesmen, and neighbors.

Grandmère would frequently find herself serving as referee and mediator in the periodic tumult of relations between her children and their spouses and former spouses. Throughout their lives, the relationships between her children would often run hot and cold, as though they could never outgrow their sibling rivalries. It must have been difficult for them to have, from a very young age and throughout their lives, even their most personal actions subject to almost constant public scrutiny. Ordinarily, if one person was subject to derogatory press, other members of the family would be objective if not supportive. But the almost continuous feuds and squabbles among themselves would inevitably draw Grandmère into the middle, often requiring the use of her honed skills of diplomacy to settle the dispute. There were times, for example, when my father and one or another of his brothers might not be speaking due to some real or perceived disagreement or slight. Refusing to enter into the feud on either side but constantly trying to persuade the two to "see each other's point of view," one of Grandmère's favorite tactics would be to invite all of the family to Val-Kill for some festive occasion (Christmas or Thanksgiving, for example) thus bringing about an almost forced truce. Seldom would anyone dare decline one of Grandmère's invitations for a family gathering, where it was tacitly understood that no discussion of the internal strife would be accepted. It was really quite amazing how this tactic could diffuse even the most volatile of feuds. Toward the end of my father's life he and his brother Jim had a prolonged period of silence. When I asked my dad what the issue was, he laughed and said, "You know, it's been so long I can't remember." I suspect that happened more than once over the years.

America's Conscience

Democratic politics remained one of Grandmère's principal interests, and in 1952 she became one of Adlai Stevenson's most ardent supporters, considering him the standard-bearer of FDR's New Deal principles. With reluctance she accepted an invitation to address the 1952 Democratic convention. With a clear if not direct statement of what she believed to be the Stevenson mantra, she used the words of a speech written by FDR to be delivered after his death: "If civilization is to survive, we must cultivate the science of human relationships, the ability of all people of all kinds, to live together." Her speech brought down the house, and Stevenson was the guaranteed nominee of the party. But no matter how hard Grandmère worked to promote his candidacy, he was defeated in the election by General Dwight D. Eisenhower. Thereafter, she resigned her seat on the Human Rights Commission, and Eisenhower replaced her as a member of the U.S. delegation to the United Nations in 1953.

Although a private citizen once more, she quickly and unabashedly became one of the McCarthy era's most outspoken antagonists, defending those being purged by the smear tactics of Senator McCarthy and his Communist-hunting colleagues. Grandmère was one of the few influential public persons to have the courage to face down the feared McCarthy and his House Committee on Un-American Activities. To her, Joseph McCarthy and his "Red-hunting" colleagues were more dangerous in their ideology and tactics (which essentially ignored the rights of citizens guaranteed to all Americans) than the threat posed by the so-called Communists they sought to purge. "We must preserve our right to think and differ…That must be part of the freedom of the American people." She exposed the often ridiculous McCarthy tactics when recounting that one day she was visited by agents of the Federal Bureau of Investigation who were investigating the loyalty of Secretary of State John Foster Dulles, one of the most ardent "Cold Warriors" of the Eisenhower administration. No matter how outspoken she was, no matter how often she challenged them, the senator from Wisconsin and his colleagues could never muster the courage to call her to testify before the committee. They must have realized what a terrible mistake that would have been!

In the campaign of 1956 Grandmère again played an active and pivotal role in Adlai Stevenson's campaign, but this time, as never before, she herself came under attack by the liberal wing of the Democratic Party and others with whom she'd been aligned throughout her political life. In 1954 the U.S. Supreme Court had outlawed segregation in schools. Grandmère maintained the stance of *gradual* social integration, a stance she had adopted throughout the years in many other similar issues. Her position, which was Stevenson's as well, caused an outrage with the NAACP and a break with the Americans for Democratic Action. In her mind, rights belonged not to any single group or organization but to individuals. Although her forcefulness may have influenced acceptance of a more moderate plank in the Democratic platform and mollified the still powerful Southern bloc of voters, Stevenson was again unsuccessful in his bid for the presidency. Grandmère hoped to help her friend gain office in his third and last attempt at the presidency in 1960, but this time it was a young senator from Massachusetts, John Fitzgerald Kennedy, who proved Stevenson's undoing. Her initial lack of enthusiasm for Kennedy, influenced not only by her loyalty to Stevenson but also by her dislike for Kennedy's father, Joseph Kennedy, FDR's one-time ambassador to Great Britain, was eventually replaced with a respect for the younger man's intelligence and ideals. In 1961 Grandmère returned once again to the United Nations, where she served with her dear friend Adlai Stevenson, whom Kennedy had appointed ambassador to the United Nations. Grandmère also assumed chairmanship of the Kennedy administration's Commission on the Status of Women and held a seat on the Advisory Board of his innovative Peace Corps.

In 1961, just one year before her death, Grandmère was still a frequent and welcomed visitor on the floor of the UN, here with her close friend Adlai Stevenson, the US Ambassador to the United Nations.

In all that Eleanor Roosevelt accomplished, in all of the trials and disappointments of her own life, she never once lost faith in the innate goodness of humankind, and she could never relinquish the belief that it was her duty to help all people enjoy the fulfillment of a life well lived. Shortly after her seventy-fifth birthday she summed up her entire life: "On that seventy-fifth birthday I knew that I had long since become aware of my overall objective in

life. It stemmed from those early impressions I had gathered when I saw war-torn Europe after World War I. I wanted, with all my heart, a peaceful world. And I knew it could never be achieved on a lasting basis without greater understanding between peoples. It is to these ends that I have, in the main, devoted the past years."

At age seventy-seven, the active nature of Grandmère's life had not diminished in the least, but many of her friends were noticing an evident change. She pushed herself unmercifully, giving speeches and making personal appearances, writing, and taking in the steady stream of visitors who sought her advice and counsel about so many matters. Perhaps the never-ending demands prevented Grandmère from retiring, but I think she simply refused to give up what she viewed as her duty to her countrymen...the world over. Accolades for her poured in from all corners of the world, but perhaps none were more poignant than Malvina "Tommy" Thompson's when she said to Lorena Hickok, the newspaper reporter with whom Grandmère had built such a close and lasting friendship for almost thirty years: "[Working with Mrs. Roosevelt] gave me a reason for living. My boss is a very big person, just about the biggest person in the world. Anything I can do to help her—no matter what—justifies my existence."[3] On another occasion, when one of my young cousins asked Tommy, "Who is Grandmère?" she replied, "Why, your grandmother." "I know that," came the retort, "but who is she? Daddy listens to what she says. You do what she tells you to do. Everybody stands up when she comes in. [So] who *is* Grandmère?" Perhaps Tommy might have answered: Your grandmother is America's conscience.

Welshpool, the principal village on Campobello as it appeared in c. 1920s, was the center of one of the most important places in my grandparents' lives, and some of their most intimate and profound years together.

Campobello

I know a place where resonant tranquility reigns, for if useless thoughts are stifled there, the echo of others returns again until I can hear it. A place for choosing, where choices are made. A retreat, a defense against excess, against too much speed, and the crowds that confuse the game of life.

—Anonymous, translated from the original French

ONE OF THE MOST EXTRAORDINARY things about Grandmère's life was the extent to which she traveled the world. She was one of the best traveled women in history, from those trips in early childhood touring Europe with her parents to her times with Mademoiselle Souvestre and the almost endless crisscrossing of this nation while serving as her husband's eyes and ears. And in the later part of her life there were visits to the far reaches of the world to further the cause of human rights and peace. She experienced grand palaces and sumptuous luxuries. She witnessed firsthand the ravages of war and the horrors of abject poverty. But always, no matter how exotic the itinerary of her most recent trip, Grandmère longed for home.

As a Roosevelt, Grandmère visited and lived in some of the grandest and most notable estates of the country: Algonac and Tivoli, ancestral homes of the Hudson Valley, as well as the homes of her parents in New York and Meadowbrook on Long Island. Grandmère remembered Sagamore Hill, her uncle Ted's beautiful estate overlooking Long Island Sound, which rang with raucous laughter and good cheer, as one of the most joyous "homes" of her childhood. Once married, she spent weekends, summers, and holidays at Springwood, Franklin's pastoral lifelong home and the place dominated so thoroughly by his mother, Sara. And who could forget the four-story brownstone in Manhattan, Eleanor and Franklin's first home as a young married couple, joined as if by umbilical cords at every floor to Sara's own brownstone? Finally, of course, there was the White House, the one place she never wanted to call home.

There were many places in Grandmère's life, each with its own memories. Some separated public life from her private moments, and all played a role in her being, but only two would she ever truly consider *home*. Val-Kill is the place most commonly associated with Grandmère; that small farm gave her sanctuary from her busy life, particularly after the White House days. But another, less publicized place that was an integral part of the annual summer rituals of her life was the "cottage" at Campobello. "There [were] good and bad memories

there," Grandmère would say about Campo, "but the bad get the better of me when I'm there alone." To her, Campobello was perhaps an enigma, the only place where she and Franklin shared life, alone as a family with their children, the one place she felt she could be wife, mother, and mistress of the household without the ever-present interference of Sara. But as she said, there were also bad times and difficult associations with Campobello.

Campobello Island, a small Canadian isle just off the coastal Maine town of Lubec, is the largest and southernmost of a chain of small islands plunked in the Passamaquoddy Bay, which itself feeds into the Bay of Fundy. The waters are icy-cold, seldom reaching above 50 degrees even in the summer months, and are known for having the most dramatic tidal changes anywhere in the world—ranging from 17 to 20 feet or more. Just nine miles in length and three miles at its widest, its craggy cliffs and rugged beaches emerge from the sea. It boasts pristine, bucolic meadows and gentle dark pine forests with vistas embracing, as Senator Edmund Muskie once said, "the solidity of the coast and the exuberance of the open water."

This is an island of stark contrasts. The western side enjoys no natural harbors, and the cliffs rise high above the almost inaccessible beach to heavily wooded forests. The northernmost part is said to resemble Scotland, with its thin topsoil and open, gently rolling meadows. The southern portion of the island, however, is often shrouded in fog and is almost tropical and primordial in the abundance and luxuriance of its vegetation. It is here, at Liberty Point, that Grandmère loved to walk with grandchildren in the eerily dark, gray-green lichen-hung forest called Fog Forest. On almost every day of my holidays on the island, I recall walking there with Grandmère, surrounded by fireflies even during the late afternoon, and being assured by her that I had nothing to fear, as these were only little elves who were there to help guide our way through the forest.

It is on the eastern side of Campobello that most of its inhabitants live, for this is the side that provides the most hospitable harbors. The earliest settlers of this incredible little island came in the early 1700s, if not before...no one seems really certain. It was in 1770 that the first "Principal Proprietor of the Great Outer Island of Passamoquoddy," Captain William Owen, arrived with a royal grant from King George III in hand, granting him almost kingly powers. Indeed, for several generations, until the late 1800s, these Principal Proprietors were the lords of the island (one even adopted the self-proclaimed title "Prince of Campobello"), and the people were merely their tenants. In 1881 Mrs. Cornelia Robinson-Owen, the last descendant of the Owen family, sold her interest in Campobello to a group of American businessmen, whose intent was to turn the island into a summer resort for wealthy Americans. Over the next three years, no less than three luxury hotels were built: the Owen, built upon the original homestead of the Owen family, the Tyn-y-Coed, and the Tyn-y-Maes. Built during the "Gilded Age" of American prosperity and indulgence, the hotels of the Campobello Company thrived and prospered until about 1910. The hotel brochures would proclaim the virtues of the resort as "provided with all the comforts of a refined home, a quiet and retired life, made wholesome by the soft yet bracing air, never too hot and seldom too cold...here is the

sanitarium, the corrective. Baths of fog are as needful to the senses and the skin as the sun." The varied pastimes available to guests attracted many of America's most prominent aristocracy, among them the Roosevelts of Hyde Park, New York.

Arriving first in 1883 to stay at the Tyn-y-Coed Hotel with their one-year-old son, Franklin, James and Sara Delano Roosevelt immediately fell in love with the island. Before summer's end they had bought ten acres of land on the high point overlooking Friar's Bay, and promptly began construction of their fifteen-room summer "cottage," which was not completed until 1885. Soon after their decision to purchase and build, several other prominent Victorian families followed: the Wells, Porters, Sturgis, the Cochranes of Philadelphia, and the Kuhns of Boston; there was even a family from St. Louis. As the resort thrived, the "regulars" were provided with a vast array of social activities. There was the Campobello Dramatic Club and the Grand Annual Ball; the Campobello Debating Society, begun by John Calder and George Byron (who, as legend would have it, refused membership to a young FDR because he was not eloquent enough—they considered his wife, Eleanor, the more accomplished speaker!).

The residents of this island have been seafaring people from the beginning, and it is the residents—perhaps twelve hundred strong year-round and not much more during the "tourist season"—who provide the island with its real history, not the Roosevelts nor the other aristocratic Americans who became summer dwellers, nor even the early landed Principal Proprietors, who ruled the land almost as their own feudal fiefdom. And it was the people of this island, primarily fishermen and a few small farmers, who were so loved and respected by both

My grandparents with Anna, Franklin Jr., John, Miss Sherwood, and "Chief."

Eleanor and Franklin. Folklore has it that most all of the islanders descend from perhaps ten families going back to the earliest days, and even today everyone knows everyone's business. They are a gentle and supremely kind people, always quick to assist a stranger but slow to accept outsiders into their fold. Over the years, however, these genteel yet ordinary people reciprocated the warmth that Eleanor and Franklin held for them by accepting our family, and perhaps all that came with us, into their lives. Well, perhaps "accept" is not the proper word, but they were always gracious and patient with our intrusions into the tranquility of their lives.

I think everyone who has ever visited the family compound on this idyllic island has to be, in one way or another, deeply impressed, not by the house or the expected trappings of luxury, for there really were few, but simply by the place. Campobello is one of those magical places, a romantic vision drawn from a great painting or a classic tale, a place of the imagination suddenly appearing in reality, the kind of place to which your soul clings. My own memories of my visits as a young boy have left deep feelings within me. Every time I return the floodgates of memory open wide and fill me with many joyous recollections, some perhaps imagined, as happens with childhood memories. For me, Val-Kill will always embody the "essence" of Grandmère, the complexities of the woman she was and the life she lived. But Campobello will be the one association I have with Grandmère that is strictly of her as my "grandmother." This was a mystical, magical place—it still is for me, and perhaps for my siblings and cousins

221

*At the helm during a "stiff Bay of Fundy breeze,"
FDR's love of the water began early in life
(Campobello c. 1888).*

too. This was the "other home," where she would break away from the sequential and all-too-busy daily routine and regain her sense of well-being and oneness. It was here, as perhaps nowhere else, that she could be comfortable and secure in having her children and grandchildren at the center of her universe—at least for a few precious moments in time.

My memories of Campo are indelible. It's an island that looks fantastically eerie on a full-moon night and stunningly beautiful at sunset. Island days shrouded in fog assume that quiet, peaceful rhythm so perfectly conducive to dreaming. There was always an atmosphere of great excitement when preparing for an expedition to Campobello. I would arrive at the little Maine town of Lubec in a carload of excited and tired siblings, cousins, and accumulated others after a long drive, usually from Hyde Park. The arrival time had to be well planned, for as I recall the only way to transport this entourage and their baggage was by a small car ferry. Actually, it was merely a small scow tied to and powered by an even smaller outboard motorboat. It was so rickety that I was certain we would never reach our destination, a feeling reinforced for me by tales of prior disasters related by an older brother, sister, or cousin. The strength of the tides in the narrows was such that the boat operator had to aim for a landing point high above the actual target, but somehow they always made the desired point. Of course, what seemed to me an endless expanse of water, with the island itself usually obscured by fog, was in fact a mere several hundred yards. In days gone by and before the advent of telephones, the residents of Campobello used to literally shout their grocery and supply orders across the waters, to be filled by local merchants and later transported across by ferry.

This fearsome arrival was soon forgotten as my senses filled with the joy that was Campobello: the lush green of the landscape, the crisp air, the constant breeze, and the silence, disturbed only by the wondrous sounds of birds and gently lapping water. To me, a little boy from Texas, my every arrival on Campobello can only be described as one of the greatest adventures of my young life. I couldn't imagine that another place like this existed anywhere else in the entire world. It was entirely foreign to all that I had known—a dreamland, a place so quiet and pure, a place that somehow I knew was special...not just to me but to my grandmother. I could almost sense that Campobello had uplifted any burden she might have been carrying and filled her with peace and tranquility.

My grandfather's lifelong love affair with the

With neighboring friends, sailing was an almost constant summer pastime (c. 1890).

sea was born here, during his childhood. It was Captain Eddie Lank and Shep Mitchel who taught FDR how to handle a boat with confidence and adroitness to navigate the tricky, sometimes treacherous tidewaters of Passamaquoddy Bay and the Bay of Fundy. Captain Lank was sufficiently impressed by his abilities at age ten to pronounce, "You'll do now. You're a full-fledged seaman, sardine-sized." Indeed, by his teen years Franklin had already become an expert seaman and wanted nothing more than to

223

FDR on a sailing trip with James and Elliott.

spend his days on the water. For his entire life, through good and bad times, it was to his beloved island that FDR was always drawn. And it was to Campobello that he turned to replenish his heart and soul, even after the place had "stolen from him," or so said Sara, his physical strength and mobility.

The stories of FDR's yachting and sailing adventures at Campobello are both abundant and fascinating. There were long cruises at summer's end with many male companions (no wives) on the family yacht, *Half Moon*, and many day trips with children and assorted guests on the twenty-four-foot sailing sloop *Vireo*. While Assistant Secretary of the

Navy he occasionally visited the island on the battleship USS *North Dakota*. On one such trip FDR assumed the battleship's helm in a bad fog from its young commander, Lieutenant William Halsey Jr. (later Admiral "Bull" Halsey, Commander-in-Chief of the Third Pacific Fleet), who would recall years later how a "white-flannelled yachtsman" who "really knew his business" had taken his ship through that menacing and dangerous channel. And of course, there were the multitude of family excursions to picnics and visits to friends on the village of St. Andrews and at Welshpool. No place drew my grandfather like Campobello did, until he contracted

The "Half Moon," a frequent sight in the waters off Campobello
when the Roosevelts were "in residence."

his disability there and dedicated his life to the almost all-consuming business of politics. In later years FDR would visit Campo less frequently, partly due to the demands of his responsibilities but also because of his physical limitations. My uncle Franklin Jr., who was born on the island in August 1914, would say that his father would not return as a disabled person to the place where he had so often walked and run, whose cliffs and forests he had explored, or where he had often gone horseback riding. It was perhaps too painful to relive those days of wistful freedom.

As important as this enchanting island was to

FDR, it seems to me that Grandmère's love for it may well have surpassed even that of her husband. She first visited the Roosevelt cottage in the summer of 1904 as a young bride-to-be, wanting to ingratiate herself with her future mother-in-law, who as we know had already made her displeasure of the blossoming love between the two quite clear. Taken as she was with Franklin and with the daunting task ahead of winning Sara's tacit approval, I doubt that Grandmère realized how attached she would become to this island retreat and its inhabitants. The significance of Campobello would reveal itself only in later years. Every summer for the next four years Eleanor

and Franklin would return, staying in the cottage with Sara, to bask in the welcome climate and leisurely times enjoyed by the summer residents.

During those early days at Campo, Grandmère would participate in most all of the usual activities—golfing, tennis, bike riding—but seeing as how she was not an accomplished athlete, these were pastimes that did not give her a real sense of enjoyment. She much preferred taking long walks around the island, through the lush green meadows, along the shoreline, and penetrating deep into the woods and forests, particularly Fog Forest with its ferns growing in the darkest shade to head height. It was the solitude of such walks, and of the

days nurturing her young children, Anna and James, that brought her so much joy during those first four years. In Campobello she also had enough time to indulge her passion for books, and would spend hours consuming classical literature and the popular books of the day. It was also during these days that she finally began to overcome her long-held fear of the water, at least to the extent that she could accompany FDR and friends on short sailing trips aboard the family yacht or by motor launch across to St. Andrews Island. On one such trip FDR would report to his mother, "...though slightly rough in Passamaquoddy Bay, for a few minutes, Eleanor did not show the least paleness of cheek or edge toward the rail."Grandmère even learned to fish, although this is not a pastime I recall her finding particularly pleasant. It was the custom in those days that ladies would not accompany their husbands on the longer sailing trips, so after provisioning the *Half-Moon* for FDR's late summer cruise to Nova Scotia or along the coast of Maine, Grandmère would bid farewell from the pier and enjoy the next two weeks or so in relative solitude.

Those years, however, were just an introduction to the greater joy she would soon experience, for in 1909 she and Franklin would have their very own cottage next door to—yet adequately separated from—Sara's. Originally built by Mrs. Hartman Kuhn of Boston, this would become the very first home that Eleanor and Franklin could truly share alone. Mrs. Kuhn had specified in her will that upon her death, which occurred in late 1908, Sara could purchase the house for $5,000, but only on the condition that it would be immediately given to Eleanor and Franklin. It is obvious that Mrs. Hartman Kuhn had great affection for Grandmère, and quite perceptively had seen the need for the young couple to escape from the dominance of the ever-imperious Sara. The Kuhn house, which stands even today, would become the center of all activity for the growing Roosevelt clan for many years to come. I can only imagine the memories my aunt and uncles shared of summers spent at Campobello, for most certainly they counted among the happiest of their lives. The stories passed along by my father and uncle Franklin were of many adventures. There were sailing trips and walks along the cliffs with their father, picnics and hayrides with their mother, tennis and golf; a multitude of friends and activities—always something to keep them

Grandmère and her Aunt Maude
"testing the waters" of the chilly Bay of Fundy.

busy, but not necessarily out of mischief, according to my uncle, who describes the Roosevelt brood as "a bunch of wild Indians." In recalling the days of the wood-burning stove and old-fashioned icebox, uncle Franklin would say almost wistfully, "You forget how good the living was..." Above all, it was a time when the children could demand, and receive, the attentions of both father and mother, something that was difficult to achieve during the normal routine of their everyday lives. I too can remember the days of almost constant adventure. The daily ritual of walking among the cliffs and shoreline, picking

wild blueberries and black raspberries that were later to be made into the evening's fresh dessert. I remember the berry picking as being a truly dangerous task for a six- or seven-year-old; trudging through the rocks, being attacked by thorns or bumblebees, but worst of all was the fear that if I didn't fill my berry pail there wouldn't be enough pie for me that night! These were days of simple fulfillment that would forever define Grandmère's life with her husband and children.

Grandmère's times at Campobello were, however, not always good. The summer of 1921—the summer in which Grandfather contracted the disease that would render his legs completely worth-

less for the rest of his life—would prove to be a time of unparalleled change in the lives of my grandparents. The trauma of those August weeks, with Grandmère's constant vigil and continuous nursing followed by the realization of the finality of his disability, would add a new dimension to the meaning of Campobello for Grandmère. When asked about FDR's affliction with polio and the effect it had on her personally, she said, "…I do not think I ever stopped to analyze my feelings. There was so much to do to manage the household and children and to try to keep things running smoothly that I never had time to think of my own reactions. I simply lived from day to day and got through the best I could."

A typical beach picnic, in full and appropriate attire.

Grandmère with my uncle John, Dad, and Anna.

It is interesting to note that in later years Grandmère would credit FDR's illness of that summer as a significant source of future strength: It gave him the ability to relate to the individual suffering experienced by the people he would eventually lead through the Great Depression and World War II. It was "…a blessing in disguise, for it gave him strength and courage he had not had before. He had to think out the fundamentals of living and learn the greatest of all lessons—infinite patience and never ending persistence." In many ways, her words were as applicable to herself as to Franklin; from this trying time she too would find a strength and courage not experienced before.

Grandmère's love for Campobello never diminished over the years following FDR's death in 1945, although in her later years her own schedule prevented her from spending more than a scant few days a year in this place of idyllic solitude. But even for those short respites she would often surround herself with her closest, most intimate friends and advisors, never quite relinquishing completely the work and responsibilities that so consumed her life. Throughout the late 1940s and 1950s she would manage to have as many of the grandchildren and other family members as possible arrive for parts of the summer, and some of my uncles and cousins would stay for several weeks, but generally

A favorite pastime, Sara Delano reading aloud as ER relaxes on a warm summer afternoon.

Grandmère's time was limited by her many other obligations. Nevertheless, her escapes to the island restored her soul.

Following the sale of the Campobello house in 1960 to the Hammer brothers, Armand (chairman of Occidental Petroleum), Harry, and Victor, Grandmère's visits became even more infrequent. In frail and fleeting health, just three months before her death in 1962 and just released from a lengthy hospital stay, Grandmère returned for one last visit to her island of tranquility. Staying for five days at the cottage she had loved so much, she spent her time visiting old and dear friends, taking brief walks along old familiar paths, and, I would have to guess, reliving in her heart and soul those fifty-eight years of pleasure given her by Campobello Island and all that it was. Upon leaving she stopped along the way to pay her last visits to Bishop and Leah Scarlett and her friend from years of women's politics, Molly Dewson, and lastly with Esther Lape, one of her oldest and dearest friends. Upon returning to Val-Kill she wrote the Hammers a note in which she said, "I am leaving much stronger than I came and attribute the renewal of my strength to the peace and quiet I found here."[1]

The end of her life was close; an end for which she was both prepared and accepting. Of the long drive back to Boston from Campobello Trude

Lash would recall that "On the long drive to Boston …she hardly spoke, and when she did it was so faint we could hardly understand her…but after Labor Day the fevers and the chills and the blood transfusions and endless injections took over and the lonely descent began."[2]

Just days after Grandmère's last visit to Campo, the Roosevelt International Bridge linking the island with Lubec, Maine, was dedicated by my uncle James. A year later President John F. Kennedy proposed a further strengthening of the ties between Canada and the United States by establishment of the first ever international park to be jointly administered by the two nations. Officially opened in January 1964, the Roosevelt International Park today preserves and shares the history of the Roosevelts at Campobello for all to enjoy, and indeed thousands do so each year.

After Grandmère's death, many members of the family would continue to return periodically to that mystical island. On my last trip, in 1984, my daughter, Chandler, who was but nine years old at the time, accompanied me. We spent hours exploring this wonderland, playing and reminiscing with my uncle Franklin and numerous cousins. We took a daylong motor yacht cruise through the thick, almost impenetrable fog to St. Andrews for a waterside picnic of fresh lobster and other assorted

goodies at the home of some close family friends. We ate wild strawberries and blueberries, as I had with Grandmère, and I tried to remember stories of how it was when I first went there. When I asked Chandler her recollections of that trip, what meaning it had for her, she spoke of the chilling fog followed by brilliant sun in a crystal blue sky, of the never-ending blankets of wildflowers and the gentle rippling of emerald green meadows, of the warmth of the cottages, and of the locals. And then, after a brief pause, she said, "Dad, it was as though I could feel Grandmère. I never knew her before that trip, but I do now. She was there, I could feel it."

I know. She was there, and a part of her will always be there, at Campobello.

In August 1962, three months before her death, Grandmère and Maureen Corr made her last return to her beloved island. Although ill and in pain, it is obvious the serenity she felt there.

Epilogue

I think it is a necessity to be doing something which you feel is helpful in order to grow old gracefully and contentedly.

—Eleanor Roosevelt

N THE LATE 1950s THERE WERE ALMOST constant suggestions of retirement by her friends, colleagues, and family members, or at the very least a slowing down of activities. But despite even her own belief that it was perhaps time that she begin to yield on some of the demands made of her and quietly retire to Val-Kill, this choice was contrary to her nature. Aunt Anna remembered that because Grandmère had achieved so much in her later life, she felt an obligation to continue working:

Most people at 61 begin to slow down. I had a feeling on this whole UN thing that really and truly Mother developed more personal satisfaction from this...It was during this period that she developed her real political acumen. People said to me, "Don't let anyone ever say your Mother is not a smart politician."[1]

The demanding routine of her life continued. Although by 1960 she was no longer involved at the United Nations in an official capacity, her interest in the work yet to be done there never waned. She would be in her office at the AAUN as often as her schedule would allow, often until late in the evening. In an effort to cut back, what was formerly a daily column now appeared only three times a week, but it was syndicated in more than forty newspapers nationwide. The demands for her on the lecture tour provided the primary source of her income, which in the later years amounted to more than $100,000 annually—much of which she gave to family, friends, and a long list of charities she had assisted for many years.

At age seventy-five she even undertook a new career as a visiting lecturer at Brandeis University, upon whose board she had served for a number of years. She faithfully met her classes once a week, usually traveling by airplane or train, a trip that took several hours if the weather was bad. She loved meeting with her classes, as she felt that the dialogue she had with young students was both stimulating and thought-provoking. Teaching allowed her to stay in touch with the thoughts of young people, just as she had done throughout her busy life. Indeed, she felt she could relate to them on their level and perhaps instill in them the feeling for human justice and equality to which she had devoted so much of her life. She placed great stock in the younger generation, confident that they could lead to a better world.

Grandmère's Legacy

By the late 1950s and early 1960s most of her grandchildren were in their late teens and early twenties. We had grown up spending our summers together at Grandmère's Val-Kill and Campobello or visiting her at her apartment in New York. She had been the "glue," the focal point, of our very extended family, and the person who had given us joy, freedom, and a context as we were growing up.

As is true with most families, the extent of a relationship, the influence of one individual on the lives of other family members, is often not realized until later reflection. Grandmère was first and foremost a powerful figure for us all, and we each embraced the dichotomy between her public profile and her private self. Within the intimacy of that family frame, Grandmère inspired, taught, laughed, and talked with each of us. All the while, and I suspect with no forethought, she was imparting in us

her own legacy, her vision of a better world. And yet, for most of us the extent of her influence on our lives has only come during these years following her death, as we each in our own way come to realize and appreciate the interaction of her life and ours.

The rites of family were extremely important to her: the Christmases and holidays surrounded by family and close friends; summer days at Val-Kill and early morning walks through the woods; traveling with grandchildren; storytelling and simply sharing time and space; and of course the never-ending letter writing. Grandmère kept in touch with most all her daughters-in-law at all times, as a way of

maintaining the connection with her grandchildren as well as, and equally important, to maintaining a relationship formed in other circumstances and other times. Her correspondence with my mother, long after the divorce of my parents, bears witness to Grandmère's continuing friendship and love with most all who were or had once been an integral part of her extended family. In those unique moments of privacy we each shared with her, Grandmère revealed herself to be as fascinating and

individualistic as the world perceived, except that on those occasions she was a real and accessible presence for those of us who loved her most.

She indelibly touched the lives of the Roosevelt clan. If her public life was a journey on a grand scale encompassing the larger questions of society, politics, and the human condition, it can only be said that her private domain was intimate, connected, and inspiring. She continued to extend her presence in each of our lives in small but consistent ways, a remarkable feat given how busy she remained until the end of her days. In her own childhood she had struggled to breach the isolation that had characterized it, but in later years, when she became grandmother to twenty-two of us, she always sought to bind, showing us again and again the special gift she had for friendship and understanding. Despite the seriousness of her worldly quest, she had for us a deep vein of amusement and good humor. Her conversation was witty and erudite, but even for the youngest of us she had a wonderful way of drawing us out so that she might know us better. Times with the family restored her equilibrium, and these calmer moments with her children and their wives and husbands and children brought her a constant sense of joy and serenity.

The legacy she gave us was as diverse and multifaceted as was her extraordinary life. There was her emphasis on education and the arts. She enjoyed going to the theater, listening to Gregorian chants late at night while writing her correspondence, and reading good literature. She exposed us to those same wondrous pastimes, as it was a way for her to share her interests with us and perhaps to teach us something of our heritage. I can remember her joy at taking me to see the Broadway production of *Peter Pan,* and afterward taking me backstage to meet the production's star, Mary Martin. Naturally, I was excited to meet "Peter Pan" in person, but the even greater recollection was Ms. Martin's reaction to meeting my grandmother; she seemed as excited about meeting Grandmère as I was at meeting her. (I must admit that I was equally impressed to learn that "Peter Pan" actually came from a Texas town neighboring my own home!)

Of course, there was the social aspect of being a Roosevelt. Born into one of the more notable families in the United States, Grandmère continually broke with tradition, not only that of her social class but also of the stereotypical woman of the time. She was above all an individualist, both in public and in private, and she taught us to be individuals too.

One of the most remarkable qualities I remember was her ability to listen, to draw others out and extend an invitation for them to talk about things that really mattered to them. She did this with everyone, from heads of state to friends, family members, and most certainly her grandchildren. We were all made to feel important—no concern was too trivial; no point of view too childish or insignificant. Despite the extraordinarily busy schedule she kept until nearly the end, she always wanted to have her grandchildren around her at Val-Kill, in her apartment in New York City, or even on some of her official and nonofficial visits abroad. Watching us grow and spending time with us was one of the nourishing springs of her life, and with twenty-two of us she was possibly the busiest grandmother in the world!

One of the many roles Grandmère fulfilled for the nation and for the world at large was as a teacher. She taught women to take action and participate in politics and social change. She taught Americans self-confidence during the years of the Great Depression. She taught Franklin that the circumstance and the individual were as important in the game of world politics as the grand and far-reaching. With her family and grandchildren she taught by example, eliciting in us a thirst for knowledge and a desire to learn about others as well as ourselves.

Grandmère's life was a dramatic statement of self-transformation. From insecure beginnings she grew into one of the most famous women in the world. Ever inquisitive and always curious, she never stopped learning from others: about people, events, and life itself. In public as in private, my grandmother was forever a student of life.

Perhaps the greatest quality Grandmère displayed again and again was the ability to be absolutely ordinary, and in that simplicity to be most extraordinary. In my eyes, Grandmère will always be greatly beloved and will exert her continuing influence in our lives and in the lives of our children. This is perhaps the greatest testament to her life.

The End of an Extraordinary Life

The end of my grandmother's life did not come quickly or easily. She was diagnosed with aplastic anemia as early as 1958, but David Gurewitsch, her personal doctor and dear friend, was sworn to secrecy. She was determined to persevere, as she had throughout her seventy-plus years in the face of so many other obstacles, and I think she truly believed that "when you cease to make a contribution, you begin to die." Grandmère was not yet ready to die; she had not finished her work on this earth. But by the end of 1960 the deterioration of her health became more rapid, more visible, and certainly more

pronounced. For Grandmère, life had become exhausting; she felt a guilt that she was now to become a burden for others. Finally, by mid-1962, the end was in sight. She entered the hospital in July, and as her dear friend Trude Lash would recall

> There was only suffering for Mrs. Roosevelt from the first day in July when she was taken to the hospital for the first time. There was no moment of serenity. There was only anger, helpless anger at the doctors and nurses and the world who tried to keep her alive...She was completely alone and felt betrayed and persecuted by all of us...She was not afraid of death at all. She welcomed it. She was so weary and so infinitely exhausted, it seemed as though she had to suffer every human indignity, every weakness, every failure that she had resisted and conquered so daringly during her whole life—as though she was being punished...

She did not want even those closest to her to see her as an invalid, and when Adlai Stevenson tried to visit her toward the early weeks in October he was summarily turned away by Dr. Gurewitsch. "Dearest Eleanor," Adlai would write, "...I *pray* it won't be long before I can come to see you...I love you dearly—and so does the whole world!" At the insistence of family, he finally had the opportunity for that last visit, just days before her death, but it is unlikely that she recognized him. Adlai was devastated by what he saw, unable to believe that his dear friend had reached the end. On October 25 her disease was at last correctly diagnosed as a rare form of bone-marrow tuberculosis, which she had likely contracted initially as far back as 1919. As she would make clear to those around her, Grandmère was ready and determined to die.

This is the last photograph of Grandmère and my father, about five months before she died.

She thought of herself as an ugly duckling, but she walked in beauty in the ghettos of the world...And wherever she walked, beauty was there forever.

Finally, on November 7, 1962, Anna Eleanor Roosevelt died.

Three days later they were all there: President John F. Kennedy and Jacqueline, Vice President Lyndon Johnson and Lady Bird, former presidents Harry Truman and Dwight D. Eisenhower, heads of state, ambassadors, governors, senators and congressmen, family, friends and neighbors, and just plain folk. They were there to pay tribute to the end of an era and to say good-bye to a friend, and I my

Grandmère. All she ever really wanted was to be loved and to give love in return. She succeeded.

And so the story of Eleanor Roosevelt ended; her incredible life concluded. But for me and my family and children—as for so many others whose lives were nurtured by her example—the life of Grandmère continues. She gave so much to so many and asked so little in return. There will come the day, I know, when the word *Grandmère* will pass the lips of my own grandchildren as easily as it does my own, and they will share the legacy of this fascinating human—that part of their heritage, Grandmère—with all others whose lives are encouraged by her example. It is, I think, an endless story.

237

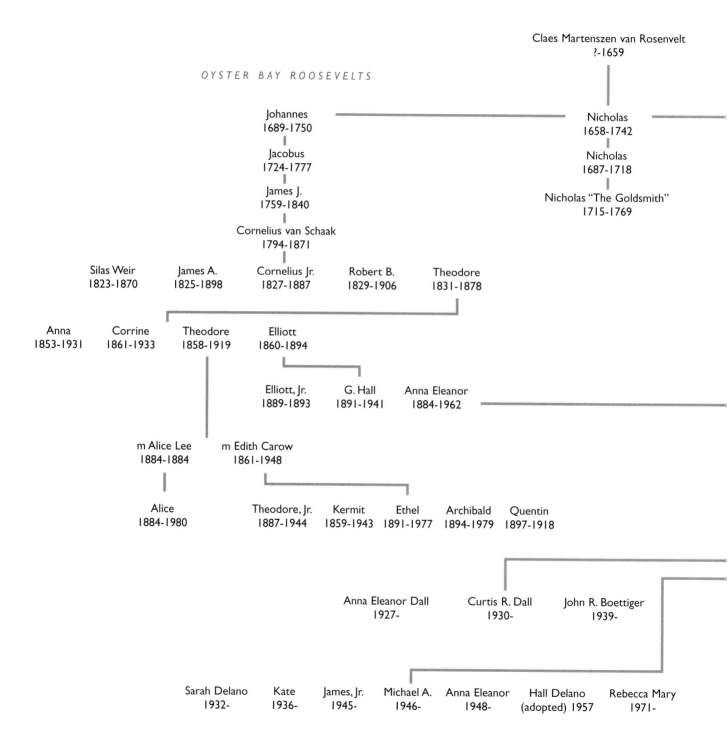

OYSTER BAY ROOSEVELTS

Claes Martenszen van Rosenvelt
?-1659

Johannes
1689-1750

Nicholas
1658-1742

Jacobus
1724-1777

Nicholas
1687-1718

James J.
1759-1840

Nicholas "The Goldsmith"
1715-1769

Cornelius van Schaak
1794-1871

Silas Weir
1823-1870

James A.
1825-1898

Cornelius Jr.
1827-1887

Robert B.
1829-1906

Theodore
1831-1878

Anna
1853-1931

Corrine
1861-1933

Theodore
1858-1919

Elliott
1860-1894

Elliott, Jr.
1889-1893

G. Hall
1891-1941

Anna Eleanor
1884-1962

m Alice Lee
1884-1884

m Edith Carow
1861-1948

Alice
1884-1980

Theodore, Jr.
1887-1944

Kermit
1859-1943

Ethel
1891-1977

Archibald
1894-1979

Quentin
1897-1918

Anna Eleanor Dall
1927-

Curtis R. Dall
1930-

John R. Boettiger
1939-

Sarah Delano
1932-

Kate
1936-

James, Jr.
1945-

Michael A.
1946-

Anna Eleanor
1948-

Hall Delano
(adopted) 1957

Rebecca Mary
1971-

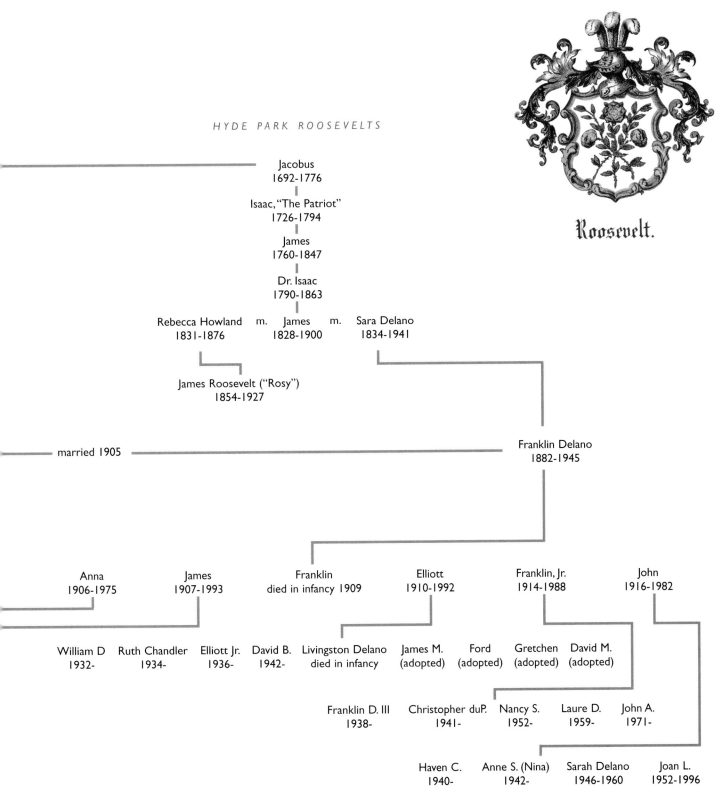

HYDE PARK ROOSEVELTS

Roosevelt.

Jacobus
1692-1776

Isaac, "The Patriot"
1726-1794

James
1760-1847

Dr. Isaac
1790-1863

Rebecca Howland   m.   James   m.   Sara Delano
1831-1876   1828-1900   1834-1941

James Roosevelt ("Rosy")
1854-1927

married 1905   Franklin Delano
1882-1945

Anna   James   Franklin   Elliott   Franklin, Jr.   John
1906-1975   1907-1993   died in infancy 1909   1910-1992   1914-1988   1916-1982

William D   Ruth Chandler   Elliott Jr.   David B.   Livingston Delano   James M.   Ford   Gretchen   David M.
1932-   1934-   1936-   1942-   died in infancy   (adopted)   (adopted)   (adopted)   (adopted)

Franklin D. III   Christopher duP.   Nancy S.   Laure D.   John A.
1938-   1941-   1952-   1959-   1971-

Haven C.   Anne S. (Nina)   Sarah Delano   Joan L.
1940-   1942-   1946-1960   1952-1996

Bibliographical References

PART ONE
Grandmère

[1] Bassanese, Lynn A. and Metreaud, Michelle S., ed. *Her Star Still Shines*. Hyde Park, NY: Franklin D. Roosevelt Library, 1995

[2] Herhan, Stella K. *The Candles She Lit*. Eleanor Roosevelt Study Center, Hyde Park, New York, 2000

[3] *Ibid.*

[4] Bassanese, Lynn A. and Metreaud, Michelle S., ed. *Her Star Still Shines*. Hyde Park, NY: Franklin D. Roosevelt Library, 1955

PART TWO
Born in Another Era

[1] Teague, Michael. *Mrs. L.* New York: Doubleday, 1981, pp. 18-19

[2] Roosevelt, Eleanor. *Strength and Energy*. ER's papers, Franklin D Roosevelt Library, Hyde Park, NY

[3] Roosevelt, Robert. Quoted in Miller, Nathan. *The Roosevelt Chronicles*. Garden City, NY: Doubleday & Co, 1979

[4] Lash, Joseph P. Interviews, Franklin D Roosevelt Library, Hyde Park, NY

[5] Roosevelt, Eleanor. *This is My New York City,* 1959. ER Papers. Franklin D Roosevelt Library, Hyde Park, NY

[6] Roosevelt, Elliott. *Oral Histories.* Franklin D Roosevelt Library, Hyde Park, NY, June 20, 1979

[7] Teague, Michael. *Mrs. L.* New York: Doubleday, 1981, pp. 19-20

[8] *Eleanor Roosevelt's My Day: Her Acclaimed Columns 1936-1945.* Edited by Rochelle Chadakoff with an introduction by Martha Gellhorn. New York: Pharoze Books, 1989. And *Volume II: The Post War Years. Her Acclaimed Columns 1945-1952.* Edited by David Emblidge with an introduction by Pamela C. Harriman, 1990

[9] Lash, Joseph P. *Eleanor and Franklin.* New York: W. W. Norton & Co, 1971, p. 3

[10] Roosevelt Lindsley, Chandler. *Oral Histories.* Franklin D Roosevelt Library, Hyde Park, NY, June 20, 1979

[11] Roosevelt Gibson, Nina. *Oral Histories.* Franklin D Roosevelt Library, Hyde Park, NY, August 13, 1979

[12] Halstead Collection, Franklin D Roosevelt Library, Hyde Park, NY

[13] Wiesen Cook, Blanche. *Eleanor Roosevelt, Volume I: 1884-1933.* New York, London, Sydney, Toronto, and Auckland: Penguin Books, 1992, p. 23

[14] *Ibid.* p. 46

[15] *Eleanor Roosevelt's My Day: Her Acclaimed Columns 1936-1945.* Edited by Rochelle Chadakoff with an introduction by Martha Gellhorn. New York: Pharoze Books, 1989. And *Volume II: The Post War Years. Her Acclaimed Columns 1945-1952.* Edited by David Emblidge with an introduction by Pamela C. Harriman, 1990

[16] Teague, Michael. *Mrs. L.* New York: Doubleday, 1981, p. 151

[17] Teague, Michael. *Mrs. L.* New York: Doubleday, 1981, p. 151

[18] Roosevelt, Eleanor Anna, ed. *Hunting Big Game in the Eighties: The Letters of Elliott Roosevelt, Sportsman.* New York: Charles Scribner's Sons, 1933.

[19] ER Papers, Franklin D Roosevelt Library, Hyde Park, NY

[20] Collier, Peter with David Horowitz. *The Roosevelts: An American Saga.* New York: Simon & Schuster, 1994

[21] *Ibid.* p. 233.

[22] Wiesen Cook, Blanche. *Eleanor Roosevelt, Volume I: 1884-1933.* New York, London, Sydney, Toronto, and Auckland: Penguin Books, 1992, p. 81

[23] *Ibid.* p. 84

[24] Teague, Michael. *Mrs. L.* New York: Doubleday, 1981, p. 154

[25] Letter from Mlle. Souvreste. ER Papers. Franklin D Roosevelt Library, Hyde Park, NY

PART THREE
Franklin

[1] Collier, Peter with David Horowitz. *The Roosevelts: An American Saga.* New York: Simon & Schuster, 1994, p. 121

[2] Lash, Joseph P. Interview with Alice Roosevelt Longworth. Franklin D Roosevelt Library, Hyde Park, NY

[3] Notes for article in *Reader's Digest,* 1957. ER Archives, Franklin D Roosevelt Library, Hyde Park, NY

[4] Miller, Nathan. *The Roosevelt Chronicles.* Garden City, NY: Doubleday & Co, 1979, p. 246

[5] *Ibid.* p. 185

[6] Lash, Joseph P. *Eleanor and Franklin.* New York: W. W. Norton & Co, 1971, p. 117

[7] *Ibid.* p. 117

[8] Roosevelt, Franklin D. "The Roosevelt Family in New York Before the Revolution." Franklin D Roosevelt Library, Hyde Park, NY

[9] Roosevelt, Elliott, ed. *FDR: His Personal Letters.* New York: Duell, Sloan & Pearce, 1948.

A Very Close Partnership

[1] Lash, Joseph P. Interviews with Anna Roosevelt Halstead. Franklin D Roosevelt Library, Hyde Park, NY

[2], [3], [4], [5] *Ibid.*

[6] Roosevelt, Elliott. *Oral Histories.* Franklin D Roosevelt Library, Hyde Park, NY, June 20, 1979

[7] Teague, Michael. *Mrs. L.* New York: Doubleday, 1981

[8] Roosevelt, Elliott. *Oral Histories.* Franklin D Roosevelt Library, Hyde Park, NY, June 20, 1979

[9] Lash, Joseph P. Interviews with Anna Roosevelt Halstead. Franklin D Roosevelt Library, Hyde Park, NY

[10] Roosevelt, Elliott. *Oral Histories.* Franklin D Roosevelt Library, Hyde Park, NY, June 20, 1979

[11] *Ibid.*

[12] Lash, Joseph P. Interviews with Anna Roosevelt Halstead. Franklin D Roosevelt Library, Hyde Park, NY

[13] Lash, Joseph P. Interviews with Anna Roosevelt Halstead. Franklin D Roosevelt Library, Hyde Park, NY

[14] *Poughkeepsie Eagle News,* July 16, 1920

[15] Roosevelt, Franklin Delano III. *Oral Histories.* Franklin D Roosevelt Library, Hyde Park, NY November 1, 1979

[16] Roosevelt, Elliott, Jr. *Oral Histories.* Franklin D Roosevelt Library, Hyde Park, NY, June 20, 1979

PART FOUR
It's Up to the Women

[1] Article on Strength and Energy. ER Papers. Franklin D Roosevelt Library, Hyde Park, NY

[2] Lash, Joseph P. Interviews with Anna Roosevelt Halstead. Franklin D Roosevelt Library, Hyde Park, NY

[3] Lash, Joseph P. *Eleanor and Franklin.* New York: W. W. Norton & Co, 1971, p. 280

[4] *Speeches and Articles.* Eleanor Roosevelt Papers. Franklin D Roosevelt Library, Hyde Park, NY

[5] Lash, Joseph P. Interviews with Anna Roosevelt Halstead. Franklin D Roosevelt Library, Hyde Park, NY

[6] Roosevelt, James with Bill Libby. *My Parents.* Chicago: Playboy Press, 1976

[7] Asbell, Bernard. *Mother & Daughter. The Letters of Eleanor & Anna Roosevelt.* New York: Coward, McCann & Geoghan, 1982

[8] *Ibid.*

[9] Gahan Douglas, Helen. *The Eleanor Roosevelt We Remember.* New York: Hill & Wang, 1963

First Lady

[1] Roosevelt, Eleanor. *Problems of the Next First Lady.* Redbook, 1960. Franklin D Roosevelt Library, Hyde Park, NY

[2] *Ibid.*

[3] Kearns Goodwin, Doris. *No Ordinary Time.* New York: Touchstone Books, 1995

[4] Lash, Joseph P. *Eleanor and Franklin.* New York: W. W. Norton & Co, 1971, p. 359

[5] *Ibid.* p. 359

[6] *Ibid.* p. 359

[7] *Ibid.* p. 363

[8] Lash, Joseph P. Interviews with Anna Roosevelt Halstead. Franklin D Roosevelt Library, Hyde Park, NY

[9] Beard, Mary R. Review of *It's Up to the Women* by Eleanor Roosevelt in *The New York Herald Tribune Books,* November 13, 1933

[10] Interview with Mrs. Amyas Ames in Lash, Joseph P. *Eleanor and Franklin.* New York: W. W. Norton & Co, 1971, p. 377

[11] Rosenmann, pp. 134-135. FD Roosevelt. *Public Papers,* cited 1936, pp. 566-73

[12] Hopkins, Harry. *Memorandum.* January 19, 1945. Franklin D Roosevelt Library, Hyde Park, NY

[13] Hopkins Halstead, Diana. *Oral Histories.* Franklin D Roosevelt Library, Hyde Park, NY, May 15, 1979

The War Years

[1] Eleanor Roosevelt Papers. Franklin D Roosevelt Library, Hyde Park, NY

[2] Letter from Malvina Thompson Scheider to Emma Bugbee, January 10, 1940

[3] PBS Special, *The American Experience: Eleanor Roosevelt*

[4] *Ibid.*

[5] Lash, Joseph P. *Eleanor and Franklin.* New York: W. W. Norton & Co, 1971, p. 623

[6] *Ibid.*

[7] Letter from Eleanor Roosevelt to Maude Gray, September 14, 1941. Franklin D Roosevelt Library, Hyde Park, NY

[8] Letters from Eleanor Roosevelt to Malvina Thompson, August 19, 22, 23, and 25, 1943. Franklin D Roosevelt Library, Hyde Park, NY

[9] Halsey, William F. and J. Bryan. *Admiral Halsey's Story.* New York: McGraw-Hill, 1947

[10] Eleanor Roosevelt's Radio Broadcast for War Bonds, September 27, 1943

[11] Bernard Asbell. *Mother & Daughter. The Letters of Eleanor*

& *Anna Roosevelt.* New York: Coward, McCann & Geoghan, 1982, p. 186

[12] and [13] *Ibid.* p. 186

[14] Kearns Goodwin, Doris. *No Ordinary Time.* New York: Touchstone Books, 1995

[15] Asbell, Bernard. *When F. D. R. Died.* New York: Henry Holt, 1961

PART FIVE

Strength, Courage, Confidence

[1] *New York Times,* May 7, 1934

[2] Lash, Joseph P. *Eleanor and Franklin.* New York: W. W. Norton & Co, 1971, p. 532

[3] *Eleanor Roosevelt: An American Journey.* Edited by Jess Flemion and Colleen O' Connor. San Diego: San Diego State University Press, 1987

[4] Lash, Joseph. *Eleanor: The Years Alone.* New York: W. W. Norton & Co, 1972

[5] Lash, Joseph P. *Eleanor and Franklin.* New York: W. W. Norton & Co, 1971, p. 723

[6] Miller, Nathan. *The Roosevelt Chronicles.* Garden City, NY: Doubleday & Co, 1979, p. 338

[7] Interview with Mike Wallace, 1957

A Legacy in Her Own Right

[1] Lash, Joseph. *Eleanor: The Years Alone.* New York: W. W. Norton & Co, 1972, p. 37

[2] *Ibid.* p. 56

[3] *Ibid.* p. 65

So Many Things To Do!

[1] Lash, Joseph. *Eleanor: The Years Alone.* New York: W. W. Norton & Co, 1972, p. 168

[2] *Ibid.* p. 169

[3] *Ibid.* p. 237

[4] *Eleanor Roosevelt: An American Journey.* Edited by Jess Flemion and Colleen O' Connor. San Diego: San Diego State University Press, 1987

Campobello

[1] Nolan, Allen. *Campobello, The Outer Island.* Toronto and Vancouver: Clark Irwin & Co, 1975, p. 117

[2] *Ibid.* p. 327

Epilogue

[1] Lash, Joseph P. Interviews with Anna Roosevelt Halstead. Franklin D Roosevelt Library, Hyde Park, NY

ACKNOWLEDGMENTS

I AM NOT AT ALL CERTAIN HOW ONE MANAGES TO adequately acknowledge all of those who have been so vital to the preparation of this book. There being no logical beginning, I'll simply start with Melissa Shaw, who performed an almost impossible task in the initial selection of images, culling from thousands of photographs of my grandmother. And while speaking of photographs, my sincere thanks to Mark Renovitch of the FDR Library for his knowledge of the archives, guidance, and above all patience with our project. I would be remiss to forget my friend Dr. David Woolner of the Franklin & Eleanor Roosevelt Institute, who read early manuscript drafts, made critical observations of the relationship between FDR and Grandmère, and provided constant encouragement every step of the way.

No book is possible, of course, without the publisher, and I couldn't possibly say enough about the incredible team at Warner Books who have been so supportive of my efforts: Maureen Egen, who believed in a concept and convinced me that it could be done; my publisher, Jamie Raab, who must surely have wondered if this wasn't a perpetual "work in progress"; the incredible marketing and sales team of Jimmy Franco, Martha Otis, Karen Torres, and Bruce Paonessa, all of whom believed that this was a worthwhile work for others to enjoy, and, finally, the efficiency and proficiency of Jim Spivey who oversaw the production. For a first-time author, I could never have hoped for the talents of not one, but two unbelievably perceptive editors: Jackie Joiner spent over two years providing endless support, hand-holding, giving critical counsel, and guiding me along that sometimes treacherous path toward becoming a writer, but who, just months before a completed manuscript, followed her heart into marriage; and Jessica Papin, who stepped into Jackie's position and never missed a beat, gently guiding, at times pushing, me toward the end. To Jackie and Jessica I owe a never-ending debt of gratitude.

There are those who inevitably pay a price when a project like this begins, and my family most certainly paid that price in my lack of attention at times, periods of frustration, if not downright grumpiness, but they were always there with words of support, understanding, and patience. And when it came to a need for some familial approval of my work, I turned to those I knew I could trust to be honestly critical of what I'd written—my sister Chandler and brother Tony. Thank you all, because without your belief I would not have reached this point.

To my colleagues Mike Wallace and Allida Black, thank you for giving validity to this work in your respective and important contributions. And to Her Royal Highness Princess Margriet, my sincerest gratitude for a most special contribution. My pride lives deep within my Dutch heritage.

As with everything worthwhile, it all starts with an idea, a dream, and *Grandmère* was certainly only that for a very long time. Finally, I spoke about it to a close friend, Kathy Eldon, herself a most talented and perceptive lady. Kathy in turn introduced me to the people who really make something like this happen, Philip Dunn and his entire Book Laboratory team, perhaps some of the most talented people I've ever known. Beginning with our first meeting at Kathy's apartment there

was an obvious connection, and from their introduction of the concept at the Frankfurt Book Fair and throughout the entire process of writing, editing, design, layout...well, absolutely everything, they were there. Lisa Zuniga, our copyeditor, must have wondered throughout whether I could pull two sentences together, but they indeed came together because of her talents. Magda and Malcolm Godwin of MoonRunner Design in England have made the imaginative layout and incorporation of photographs into the text not only an effective extension of the written word, but have given *Grandmère* the impact of artistic expression that I never could have conceived. Thank you Philip, and your entire team, for believing.

And last but certainly not least, my co-author Manuela Dunn Mascetti. If ever there was a single force behind making *Grandmère* a success it is this most talented person. When two people work collaboratively almost every day for three years, they either become close friends or something else altogether. It became apparent from the very initial drafts that I, like most, had difficulty baring my innermost emotions about the one person who had such tremendous impact on my life, and putting those feelings in words for others to share. Gently prodding, delicately directing, scolding on those occasions when necessary (and deserved), but always with understanding, Manuela provided the guiding light so needed to bring *Grandmère* to reality. She has led me on a journey of discovery, that emotions are meant to be shared, as are the memories that heretofore have existed only in my private domain. Above all else, Manuela has been a teacher, the signpost enabling me to express in writing experiences and thoughts I hope will be pleasing to all who read this work. It is said that practically every writer at some stage or another "hits the wall" when putting words on paper. Most certainly I encountered many such walls, but always Manuela was there to lead the way over, or around. Thank you, Manuela. Without you *Grandmère* would still be buried deep within me, a mere dream.

I know there must be others I have forgotten to mention, but to you I offer my deepest appreciation as well.

PHOTO CREDITS

Every effort has been made to trace all present copyright holders of the material used in this book, whether companies or individuals. Any omission is unintentional and we will be pleased to correct any errors in future editions of this book.

I, II, 4, 8, 9, 10/11, 13, 15, 18, 21, 22/3, 24/5, 30/1, 25, 36/7, 39, 42/3, 45, 46/7, 48/9, 50/1, 52, 55, 56/7, 60/1, 62/3, 64/5, 67, 71, 74, 76/7, 78/9, 80/1, 82/3, 84, 87, 88, 90/1, 94/5, 96/7, 99, 100/1, 102/3, 104/5, 106/7, 108/9, 110, 113, 117, 130, 132/3, 134, 138, 140/1, 142/3, 145, 146/7, 149, 153, 154, 158, 160, 162/3, 165, 167, 168, 171, 172/3, 174/5, 177, 179, 180/1, 185, 186/7, 188, 195, 200/1, 202, 204, 207, 214/5, 222/3, 225, 226/7, 228/9, 230/1, 233, 234, 237: FDR Library. 2, 6, 17, 19, 68/9, 72, 75, 84/5, 92/3, 114, 121, 166, 218, 221, 224, 226, 232, 236: David B. Roosevelt. 4, 5, 12: Chandler Roosevelt Lindsley. 11: *New York Post.* 11, 118, 148, 160, 164, 199: Corbis. 27, 145, 150, 157, 189: UPI, courtesy of FDR Library. 14, 16: *Life Magazine.* 28, 29: Martin H. Simon, 1997. 32: Mosse Photo, courtesy of FDR Library. 38, 40, 79: The Piersaull Collection (public domain), courtesy of FDR Library. 39: The Ihlder Collection (public domain), courtesy of FDR Library. 100, 124: Underwood & Underwood. 111: Lyman Cotton, Jr., courtesy of Doubleday & Co, Random House, NY. 136, 146, 156, 157, 173, 178, 192: AP/Wide World Photos. 169: Associated Photo Press. 174: American Airlines. 176: Cecil Beaton, Camera Press, London. 178: Hessler, courtesy of FDR Library. 190: Sylvia Salmi, courtesy of FDR Library. 193: *The News.* 194: Bettman Archives, courtesy of FDR Library. 205: Leo Rosenthal, courtesy of FDR Library. 212: Phillippe Halsman, courtesy of FDR Library. 213: UN photo. 217: *New York Times.*

TEXT ACKNOWLEDGMENTS

GRATEFUL ACKNOWLEDGMENT IS MADE TO ALLIDA M. Black for permission to print her Foreword and to Mike Wallace for permission to reprint part of his interview with Eleanor Roosevelt in the book's Introduction. A most grateful acknowledgment is made for permission to reprint Her Royal Highness Princess Margriet of The Netherlands' special contribution.

Grateful acknowledgment is also made for permission to reprint passages from the Oral Histories, housed at the Franklin D. Roosevelt Library, in Hyde Park, New York, reproduced by kind permission of Chandler Roosevelt Lindsley and Elliott Roosevelt, Jr. Quoted articles and writings by Eleanor Roosevelt, part of the Eleanor Roosevelt Estate, have been reprinted here by kind permission of the Estate's Literary Executor, Nancy Roosevelt Ireland.

Passages from interviews conducted by Joseph P. Lash with Alice Roosevelt Longworth, Franklin D. Roosevelt, Jr., and Anna Roosevelt Halstead, have been reprinted here by kind permission from Trude W. Lash.

Quoted passages from *Mrs. L.*, copyright © 1981 by Michael Teague, are reprinted here by kind permission of Doubleday & Co., New York.

And finally, a special acknowledgment to the staff at the Franklin D. Roosevelt Library, Hyde Park, New York, who have been so unfailingly helpful in guiding us through the thousands of documents in their possession and for their most kind assistance.